Pick of Punch

"This will be the tenth time I've bailed out and it doesn't even look like rain yet!"

Pick of

Pu

nch

Edited by ALAN COREN

HUTCHINSON
London Melbourne
Sydney Auckland
Johannesburg

Hutchinson & Co. (Publishers) Ltd

An imprint of the Hutchinson Publishing Group

17–21 Conway Street, London W1P 6JD

Hutchinson Publishing Group (Australia) Pty Ltd
PO Box 496, 16–22 Church Street, Hawthorne,
Melbourne, Victoria 3122
PO Box 151, Broadway, New South Wales 2007

Hutchinson Group (NZ) Ltd
32–34 View Road, PO Box 40–086, Glenfield, Auckland 10

Hutchinson Group (SA) Pty Ltd
PO Box 337, Bergvlei 2012, South Africa

First published 1984

© Punch Publications 1984

Printed in Great Britain by
Redwood Burn Ltd, Trowbridge, Wiltshire
and bound by Butler & Tanner Ltd,
Frome, Somerset.

"We bought the house off a Sixties pop star."

CONTENTS

"Well, let's get started—you haven't got all day."

"I didn't know the Salvation Army was using mercenaries."

INTRODUCTION

The Editor of Punch would like to thank the
following, without whom this book would not have
been possible:

Adolf Hitler, Jeremy Isaacs, God the Mother, Arthur
Scargill, Nancy Reagan, Gay News, Mark Thatcher,
Mahatma Gandhi, Dennis Skinner, the Prince Andrew
Escort Agency, Konstantin Chernenko, Sir Winston
Churchill, Bambi, Billy Cotton, Elizabeth Taylor,
T. E. Lawrence, Benham & Reeves, Jayne Torvill, the
Ayatollah Khomeini, Eamonn and Julie Andrews,
Tony Benn, Muffin the Mule, Rudolf Hess, Geoffrey
Boycott, Mrs John Timpson, Wan Fu Wines, the
Marquess of Bath, Gary Hart, Ruby Murray, Neil
Kinnock, Luis Buñuel, Kenneth Livingstone, Anna
Ford, Kinworth & District Domino League, IBM, Ian
MacGregor, Sir Ranulph Twistleton-Wickham-Fiennes
y Dorita, Lupin Pooter, Sun Guiying, Rupert Murdoch,
the Royal Gynaecological Novelty Co, Hurricane
Higgins, Sarah Keays, Ian Paisley, Buddha, Peter Jay's
nanny, Buster Mottram, David Owen, the Mayor of
Grantham, Fidel Castro, Rudyard Kipling, GCHQ
Cheltenham, John Glenn, Germaine Greer, Nigella
Lawson, Roland Rowland, Sarah Tisdall, Bob Willis,
Eric Blair, HRH Princess Margaret, Dr Crippen, Lord
Dacre, Henry Kelly, Barbara Cartland, Irving and
Isaiah Berlin, Shergar, Francis Pym, NASA, Britt
Ekland, the London Rubber Company, Clark Kent,
Moskva Dynamos, Russell Harty, T. S. Eliot, Jack
Solomons, British Nuclear Fuels, Sir Keith Joseph,
Dr J. Collis Browne, Teddy Kennedy, St Paul Johnson,
Terry Wogan, Viscount Linley, James and Jan Morris,
BL Cars, Desmond Wilcox, Norman Tebbit, Martina
Navratilova Esq, Magda Yacoub, Lorraine Chase,
Monsignor Bruce Kent, and Yasser Arafat.

Whether they want to thank him remains to be seen.

HANDELSMAN FREAKY FABLES

A CANTERBURY TALE

Arcite and Palamon,

CAPTURED BY THESEUS, WERE SENTENCED TO LIFE IMPRISONMENT IN A HIGH TOWER…

…FROM WHICH, ONE MORNING, PALAMON BEHELD HIS CAPTOR'S WIFE'S SISTER WALKING IN THE GARDEN.

Ye gods (all ninety-four of them, but especially Venus)!

♪ Blink to me only with thine eyes… ♪

SNIP

What is it?

I stongen am unto the herte!

Please, no Chaucerian — the cell is crowded enough without footnotes.

Come and have a look then.

By Mars! I am in love with her!

Traitor! She is mine! I saw her first!

Mine! I saw her last!

♪ …and I will hedge with mine… ♪

SNIP

SEVEN YEARS LATER. ARCITE'S SENTENCE HAD BEEN COMMUTED TO EXILE, BUT HE HAD RETURNED IN DISGUISE AND OBTAINED EMPLOYMENT WITH THESEUS HIMSELF.

Alas! Ah me! How long must I wear this false nose? — Palamon!

Yes, traitor! I busted out of the clink and I am desperate! Lend me a weapon so I can kill you!

ENTER THESEUS.

Hey! Hey! No swordplay in this park between 8 and 11 a.m.! Did you not see the sign?

So what? We are illegal in any case.

UPON LEARNING THE FACTS, THESEUS RELENTED AND ARRANGED FOR A SPLENDID MOCK-BATTLE, THE WINNER TO WED THE FAIR EMELIE.

THE TEMPLE OF VENUS

O Venus! Let me be the bridegroom.

Petition granted — but the name is Aphrodite. Try to remember in future.

THE TEMPLE OF DIANA

O chaste Diana! Am I to marry one of those men?

Yes, and the name is chaste Artemis.

I might add that you ask pretty dumb questions.

THE TEMPLE OF MARS

O Mars! Let me win the mock-battle!

Mock-battles bore me, but OK. Incidentally, the name is Ares.

What shall we do, Saturn? We made contradictory promises!

I didn't.

Leave it to me — and the name is Kronos.

HAVING WON THE BATTLE (AS MARS AGREED), ARCITE FELL OFF HIS HORSE AND DIED (AS SATURN ARRANGED).

The winner is — oh, damn.

CLUNK

This is very sad, but now Emelie has to marry Palamon. We mustn't make liars of the gods.

True.

Given a choice, I do prefer a live husband, at least to begin with.

MORAL: Putting deities in an embarrassing position may be fatal (but not for them, of course).

Alan COREN
HER UPSTAIRS

God is not a male deity and there is a case for addressing God as "Our Mother", according to a report published yesterday by the Church of Scotland.

The Times

Dear Mr Coren:

I am a first-time writer but a long time reader, I hope you will excuse this approaching you out of the blue but I do not know where to turn and I have always understood you to be straight with people, esp. women, you are virile but humane and will not make cheap jokes etc. about God not being able to find Her lipstick, that is not your way. This Church of Scotland announcement could do big things for the Women's Movement, is it true She made the world in six days?

Alice Cole (Ms), Yarmouth

Dear Ms Cole:

Thank you for putting your trust in me, you are absolutely right about my taking this seriously, it is not every day that one wakes up to find that God has changed sex, even in Scotland.

Strictly speaking, no, She did not make the world in six days. Not everything in the Bible is to be taken literally, as I'm sure you know. But, and here's the point, She *got* it done. She knew this absolutely wonderful little firm round the corner, and they did all the basic labouring, dividing the waters which were under the firmament from the waters which were above the firmament, and so on, after She told them where the firmament had to go. She said, *Let there be light*, and lo! they put it in.

She did all the carpets and curtains Herself, though.

Dear Mr Coren:

I have a boutique and a husband and two small children and there always has to be a hot meal on the table, never mind if the Sales are on, even, or we are awaiting deliveries from Belgium or similar. What I want to know is, how did God manage to combine a successful career with raising a family, i.e. Her only begotten Son?

Shirley Roth (Ltd.), Barnes

Dear Limited Shirley:

A good point, and we have to face the fact that She did *not* actually raise Her only begotten Son. She employed a couple. It is probably the only way open for a working Mum.

Of course, being God, She was able to take delegation even further than most working Mums in that She also got the couple to have the only begotten Son *for* Her, thus enabling Her to carry on working right through the pregnancy. It is a neat trick, but not generally available on

the NHS; I understand, however, that Mr Patrick Steptoe is able to offer something along similar lines, at a price, although you would have to select your couple with great care. Pick a middle-class pair, for example, and He might end up as a barrister and that would be the last you saw of Him, you can earn £80,000 a year as a QC, it beats wandering around in sandals and touching lepers for a living.

Dear Mr Coren:

All right, okay, great, big deal, terrif, God was a woman, is that supposed to make everything nice, you condescending eunuch bastard?

Just what kind of a woman *was* She? Why didn't She send an only begotten *Daughter*, tell me that, I would have thought that if you were trying to save the world, I mean do you have any *idea* how men have screwed up this planet, the last thing you'd send is a, a, *yegh!*

Tell me that, you Nazi pig.

Malvolia Greenham, Cockfosters

Dear Malvolia:

While I agree absolutely that women by their very natures are much nicer people and that an only begotten Daughter would have been absolutely ideal in some ways, in others it would have been rather tricky.

In early AD, a woman just could not go around on her own, she would not get served in pubs or be allowed to play golf unescorted, in short she would not have access to those places you had to get into if you wanted to redeem personkind. The only course would have been to arrange for an only begotten Son-in-Law, possibly even only begotten Grandchildren, and not only would the teleological conundra have become virtually insuperable, the only begotten Daughter would have had a terrible time at public meetings, with women asking questions about combining homecare and careers instead of listening to useful homilies.

She would almost certainly have had to appoint an only begotten Chairman to keep order, and half his time would have been spent with nonsense like *We have a question from a Galilean listener who would like to run over that recipe again, is it five loaves and two fishes, or two loaves and . . .*

I trust you take my point, Malvolia. Times were not then as they are now. I'm convinced the Second Coming will be entirely female, if it's any consolation.

Dear Mr Coren:

I am having great difficulty in coming to terms with this new proposition, given some of the, well it has to be said, quite *beastly* things that God has done. I mean, I realise of course that they had to *be* done, one has to take a firm hand with some people, look at the miners, but one or two divine actions do seem to me to smack of the male touch. For example, did She really slay all the Egyptian first-born? It seems extraordinary behaviour, even for a zealous and almighty Mum!

Lavinia Gribling, Poole

Dear Lady Gribling:

You are of course perfectly correct, and many eminent Scottish theologians are even now examining the Bible closely for what are obviously glaring mistranslations.

As far as *Exodus* is concerned, I am happy to be able to inform you that what She actually did was insist that the first-born tidy their rooms up and stop picking their nose. Provided they did that, they would be allowed to come downstairs and watch the plague of boils. Well, pimples, really.

Dear Mr Coren:

Sorry, sorry, sorry, I am just an "ordinary" housewife and not, is the word "into", feminism and so forth, my hubbie Gerard would be furious if he thought I was bothering a busy man like you with my "nonsense", but I feel sure God understands about us "little people", doesn't She? After all, Her eye is on the sparrow, am I correct?

Anyway, I was very excited about God being a lady, and all I want to know, on behalf of all of us who are beginning to "spread" a bit, is did She have Her own special secret for staying slim? Is it a question of "what you eat" or "how you eat"? Or did She take exercise, if so what form, are there those stationary bicycle efforts "up there"?

Germaine Hodge, Bromley

Dear Mrs Hodge:

Goodness me this is a bit of a poser! How often you "ordinary" folk turn out to be not ordinary at all and ask just the sort of tricky question that puts us so-called experts right on the spot!

The fact is that now we are pretty certain that God is not, as was previously believed, an old man with a long white beard, what is She? Clearly, not an old woman with a long white beard, but beyond that we do not have a great deal to go on, except that She made us in Her image, so we all look a *bit* like Her, and it's quite clear that couldn't be possible if She were not fairly average, probably about five feet five, slightly swarthy skin (although of course free from blemish of any description), and with manageable hair, which she does Herself.

As to build, this really is unknown territory, one can hardly begin to conjecture: She could be an absolute knockout, She could be more sort of comfy and maternal, but whatever She is, that is the way She stays, since She does not eat anything, being divine, and does not take exercise as you and I would recognise it, being omnipresent. I suppose we shall all just have to wait until that glorious day when we at last gaze upon Her face and are not dazzled.

I hope that answers your question.

"It's sad, just when he was getting the hang of it."

Larry's *Firemen*

Basil BOOTHROYD

Litigating Circumstances

AT a guess it would be two years since I broke a foot coming down absurdly designed stairs at Temple Tube station, with consequent loss of earnings, train and dignity; perhaps four or five since a Cretan waiter, on a shaded drinking terrace, bowed me to a chair with several legs poised over the ridiculously sunken surround of an ornamental tree with consequent backward somersault and a frozen shoulder I still feel in frost.

Property as against personal damage is harder to date, unless of recent memory. From a witness box, which I've never been in and never intend to be, I could only name the summer of 19— as the time when I braked for an amazed Poitiers pedestrian, in defiance of local custom, and had my rear-light assembly stripped by the man behind. Consequent loss of no claim bonus and the last ferry from Dieppe.

He was at my window, throwing down his beret and jumping on it, before the glass stopped tinkling, accompanied by what I took to be a passing *juge d'instruction*, who left the scene as soon as I'd settled out of court.

Of recent memory, or the equinoctial gales of March, is the disappearance of my garden wall into the neighbour's garden. This was my first intimation that he had secured a gnarled wistaria to his side of it by ring-bolt and three-strand flex, causing loss of privacy and a builder's bill for £167.07p. It may have been the 7p that stung me to rare legal action, or at least its preliminaries, such as ringing the next-door bell with the bill at the ready, getting no response, and writing to his house agents, who responded with the response that he had moved to Rugby, the matter was not within their purview, and they returned the bill assuring me of their best attention at all times.

There the matter rested.

Also the other matters hereinabovementioned, notwithstanding and whereas. That has always been my way, and I only regret that isolated and foolish departure. What got into me, apart from the 7p? And the £167 that went with it, of course.

Things happen. They cost you. That's life. Shrug out your cheque book. It's either that or accompanying the judge and jury to measure the depth of the Temple Tube steps, let alone fighting a case through to the European Court of Human Rights, with expert witness testifying in Greek, French and Wistaria.

If my breakfast eyeballs hadn't yesterday fallen on three converging items in *The Times* I wouldn't have bothered you with any of this. Given just one headline, "Roof Fall Man Wins £9,500", I would have turned the page, a thing I can do thirty-two times per bowl of bran-enriched cereal, and move on to read the packet's grand holiday offer of free bucket, spade and windmill. But when the same page also carries "Council Must Pay for Tree Damage" and "Severed Arm Man to Sue", that's different. Different from me, anyhow.

Granted, the parallels are wobbly. Though we hear from time to time of the faulty diagnosis, a severed arm is not a broken foot. A roof fall man is not to be equated with a chair fall man. A wistaria is not a tree.

It struck me all the same, as it must you by now, my hard-headed friends, that a resigned complacency over life's backhanders can be carried too far. In a grudging admiration for those who don't carry it at all, I may have to consider suing, a word I shun, and not only from a lifetime's uncertainty about whether it should have an "e" in the middle.

The Russells, of Barnet, when the borough oak trees "sucked the moisture from the soil under their house", with consequent loss of horizontals and market value, point me the way. Whereas I would have moved to Rugby, or anywhere but Purley Oaks, Sevenoaks or even Okehampton, they put it to the Council that they were due £55,000, and got it, Mr Justice Tudor Evans and eight years' resolute litigation intervening. You need only the time, resolution, and eight years' breakfast reading of lawyers' stupendously embossed correspondence.

Had I been in the position of Mr Murphy, of Barnes, which was on the pavement with his leg broken after the roof fall, well, I don't know. From the very best of motives—in the words of Mr Justice Popplewell four years after the event—he had climbed on the roof to let in a Mrs Van Praagh who had locked herself out. There are fine shades here. Was there hestitation by Mr Murphy

"Sister acts always flop on the northern circuit, Branwell."

before the rosy glow of a neighbourly act faded into the prospect of a £12,666 award for his, as you might say, pains? He didn't get it. The presiding Popplewell knocked it down by a quarter, telling him that he should have the sense to spot a slippery roof when he saw one.

I call that humiliating. Just the kind of thing, remembering my 7p, that I could see myself su(e)ing over, standing up there in the public glare and being told I was a chump, and more than three thousand quid short into the non-bargain. Take into account future bad feeling between the Murphys and the Van Praaghs, the latter now stuck with locking themselves out and lumping it, I would put this, at least in emotional terms, as an even more painful situation than that of Mr Roy Tapping, of Bledlow, Bucks, otherwise a possibly good place for Mr Murphy to move to.

Mr Tapping, for whom universal admiration has been rightly expressed since a baling machine sliced his arm off, which he tucked under the other one and admitted to hospital for a successful reunion after a tiring walk across ploughed fields, was probably not, during the actual walk, thinking of any firm sum in which to mulch, if I don't mean mulct, Mr Richard Markham, the employer of the baling machine. The thought may have come to him later, with the bedside grapes, especially if his solicitor had brought them.

He may have re-thought even then, Roy's arm having already cost Richard £1,300 in fines and £1,000 in costs for not having an arm-proof machine. At the moment, says the report, the two men "have remained on good terms and there is a possibility that Roy may return to his old job". Now that he's got his old arm back.

He should also, in my view, think about this. Reading between other lines which only say that he "is making" a claim for compensation, I fancy things may not yet have gone too far. Shaken down for arm money Markham could have a re-think of his own and advertise a baling machine vacancy in *Farmers Weekly*, knowledge of agricultural machinery preferred.

Even aside from the likelihood that Roy wouldn't get a bean through the courts until 19— earliest, at current rates of plaintiff, spending many an hour in legal chambers reading EXORS, H. de Q. BLUFFLER, DECD. painted white on shelves of deed boxes, I would strongly recommend him to hold his arm. Back on the farm with a cheery "Morning, Dick," from him, and a "Morning, Roy, let me take that heavy bucket," from Dick, it could be like old times with knobs on.

Meanwhile, returning to my own affairs with all the spring of a released wistaria, I see that my dustmen have been today, substituting for my new plastic bin an old tin one with the handles broken off. If they hadn't also regarded, and taken, as rubbish, my outside double-brush boot-scraper, I might not have considered penning a stern note to the Rural District Council.

This I have done. Have, that is, considered, but left it at that.

Unlike many, I don't want trouble.

"Escape? Are you crazy? In sixty-five months, twelve days, five hours and seven minutes, the governor's seeing me out at the main gate!"

"... And now, if you'd care to hold this piece of bread between your teeth."

"When are you going to tell us about the birds and the bees and the hydrozoan polyps?"

Richard BOSTON

COLD COMFORT

I have never cared very much for ice-cream. The only one I have ever really enjoyed was in a bar in Sicily on June 17, 1958, a date which is not so much seared into my memory as recorded in the diary I kept at that time. I was in the company of a girl called Graziella Fedele whom I was madly in love with for several weeks. She had a terrific bust, and I only wish I had seen more of it. That I saw the little I did was entirely due to the ice-cream. Not that I ate it. She ate it, but she did give me one spoonful, putting it in my mouth with her own hand. She leant forward to do this. Gosh, it was wonderful. The ice-cream. For weeks afterwards I lay awake at night thinking about it.

Otherwise, I have never cared very much for ice-cream. Even as a nipper I never joined in the cry of "I scream, you scream, we all scream for ice-cream." Not that it would have done any good, since, as far as I remember, there wasn't any ice-cream just after the war. In those days the big treats were Radio Malt, Cod Liver Oil and the Ministry of Health orange juice which made our generation the Titans we are. Strict sugar rationing ensured that we didn't develop a sweet tooth, as a result of which our palates remained unsullied and able to appreciate, a decade and a half later, the exquisite and bitter delights of Campari, Punt e Mes, Cynar and hop-

flavoured drinks. I may very well be the only person who can not only drink Fernet Branca without a hangover but who actually likes it.

What with the aftermath of war and living in the country in days when fridges were things you saw only in American films, ice-cream made a late appearance in my life. My brother and sister were some years older than I (they still are, come to think of it. Will I never catch up?) and they could remember, or claimed to, pre-war ice-creams, for which they made extravagant claims. I was pretty blasé at the age of six or seven or whatever I was when finally ice-creams and I crossed paths. Even so I have to admit that my excitement would have been better concealed if the experience had not been delayed for some minutes by an urgent need to have a pee. I nearly had to go again when faced by the totally unexpected and absolutely torturing choice between cornet and wafers. I can't remember which I finally plumped for (my Lett's Schoolboy diary for those years was laconic to an extreme: a typical entry reads, "Rained. Played Beggar-my-Neighbour. I won."). What I do remember was that the ice-cream was a big disappointment. It tasted like cold margarine. I didn't even like warm margarine. I didn't like any food much. It was so cold that it made my teeth hurt. It

also caused a pain in a nerve behind my right eye-ball. I have no idea why this should have been so, but I didn't like it. When ice-cream became more frequently available I took to swapping it for stamps, playing cards, Dinky toys, marbles and other really useful things.

What I did crave was candy-floss. As on most important subjects other than Beggar-my-Neighbour victories, my diary is silent on the subject. This doesn't matter because my memory needs no jogging to bring back the first sight of candy-floss one fine day in Yarmouth. I remember it as though it was yesterday. (Incidentally, what *did* I do yesterday? I remember it much, much better than yesterday.) I had never seen a colour so beautiful or a texture so mysterious. I knew more certainly than I have ever known anything that my whole life would be transformed if I could get my hands on some.

There used to be an advertisement in the *Eagle* (the best publication ever, apart from the late *Vole*) which depicted the adventures of Tommy Wall. Eating ice-cream and making a W out of his thumbs and index fingers brought about in him the kind of change effected by Clark Kent when he went into a telephone kiosk and turned into Superman. I had tried it for myself and it didn't work. This reinforced my dislike of ice-cream and laid a healthy

"I think it's time we told him that you're not his real social worker."

foundation for a life-long distrust of advertisements.

But it would work with candy-floss. I knew it. I would just eat the candy-floss and make my thumbs and index fingers into a C and before you knew it I would be weaving in and out of skyscrapers with the crowds in the streets below looking up and gasping, "Is it a man, is it a bird? No, it's Richard Boston."

It was not to be. The grown-ups said that the candy-floss was too expensive. And there wasn't time before the bus went. Too expensive! Admittedly the price was something horrific like fourpence, but what was fourpence or a missed bus against the opportunity to zoom around like Superman or Tommy Wall? My word, how I screamed. I've never screamed so much in my life. And I've never eaten candy-floss. I could probably afford to buy some for myself now, but the risk of disappointment is too great. Suppose I bought some candy-floss today and it turned out that I couldn't fly after all? One's few remaining illusions have to be protected carefully. They're an endangered species.

Do forgive me. The above trip down memory lane was prompted by the news that someone has launched a Campaign for Real Ice-Cream, the latest in a line of succession that started with the Campaign for Real Ale, which was followed by the less successful Campaign for Real Bread and Campaign for Real Cheese. The late *Vole* magazine even launched a Campaign for Real Life, but that got nowhere. Life has continued to become more unreal all the time.

Be that as it may, I thought I should find out what these campaigners for real ice-cream were belly-aching about and accordingly sallied fifth (that's allowing for inflation) and bought some of the stuff. You have to admit they've got a point. Probably a belly-ache too. The freezing cabinet of the first supermarket I came to held a bewildering choice of things with names like Dracula, Funny Feet, The Finger and Funny Faces. The one choice I didn't have to make was between wafers and cornet because there weren't any. The nearest to a cornet was a Wall's Cornetto, but this turned out to be not at all like the real thing. It's securely wrapped in paper, which means you can't bite the bottom off and then race your way down before the ice-cream starts coming out of the hole and dribbling all over your sleeve. The Cornetto struck me as pointless. It didn't even give me a pain behind the right eye-ball. The only authentic bit was that it tasted like cold margarine.

The tubs were just as disappointing. The best bit about tubs was the little wooden spoons that used to come with them. These were terribly useful and could be carried around in your pockets for weeks. The only way I could tackle the modern tub was by making the cardboard lid into a scoop, but I don't like the taste of cardboard very much, and have absolutely no intention of carrying ice-cream-smeared cardboard about in my pockets. Even off a real wooden spoon the Two-Ball Screwball would have tasted disgusting. This raspberry ripple-flavour ice-cream (contains non-milk fat) with two bubblegum balls, also contains the following ingredients: skimmed milk, sugar, dextrose, vegetable fat, glucose syrup, whey solids, gum base, emulsifier E471, starch, stabilisers E405, E407, E410, E412, citric acid, flavouring, colours E102, E122, E124, E132, E133 and E171. That's an awful lot for an ice-cream to contain. Far too much to leave room for cream and egg yolks, which my dictionary says are the proper ingredients (what, no E102?).

I sampled a number of these modern ice-creams before the danger of nausea caused an abrupt conclusion to my research. Even so, I consumed enough to realise that the Campaign for Real Ice-Cream has a strong case. A Cornetto would never have got Tommy Wall off the ground. What it would have done to Graziella Fedele doesn't bear thinking about. ✺

I KNEW A BANK WHERE THE WILD THYME BLEW

DONEGAN

A "gourmet restaurant" for dogs has opened in Nice. Three-course meals costing up to £10 or £11 are served on china.

Daily Telegraph

PEDIGREE CHUMS

KILL-IT-YOURSELF BUFFET

"We'll have the rats. Medium live."

"Right, that's five cats – one roast, one tartare, two sauté à la Nicoise and I'll have the Tom au vin."

16

"What the hell do you mean, 'You don't do a business lunch'?"

"Bury these for me, will you? I'll have them next week."

"Have you any idea how long it takes me to make this kind of money?"

"Read it to me. I forgot my glasses."

"American Kennel Club? That will do nicely."

PUT OUT THE SUN!

A Masque of Summer
E. S. TURNER

Scene: a grand amphitheatre, decked out as a forest clearing. Suspended above is a gigantic golden glitterball, representing the sun.

Enter, in a clapped-out Popemobile, the Master of the Revels, followed by the People of Britain—a representative array of common law wives, doctors of philosophy, discharged football managers, vision-mixers, hen-stranglers, invisible darners, progress chasers, minders, moonlighters, sperm donors, disconnection officers, brokers' men, laboratory raiders, systems analysts, Kremlinologists, brothel-fitters, menu-wipers, student princes, kneecappers, ethnic awareness enforcement officers, pregnancy-testers, Belgrano bores and Monsignor Kent.

Dionysian music throbs and swells. The People of Britain begin a half-hearted baying and swaying.

Master of Revels:
On with the Masque! Let summer madness reign.
As frantic fancies seize the torrid brain.
Apollo's beams incite the willing flesh.
Unmarried fathers push their luck afresh.
The jaded rich seek out *recherché* sins,
And barren wives line up for test-tube quins,
While devil-dons with lank, disordered hair

Jump up and down and clap their hands in air.
Begone, Tranquillity! Silenus, enter!
I've seen more action in a garden centre.
Shall we dance naked on the Doomsday silos?

A Greenham woman: *(Disgustedly)*

Master of Revels:
Why not? Or lose yourselves at sea on Lilos.

Enter a tipsy fairy, tripping over her wand.

Fairy:
I am Good Sense. Pray help me to prevail.
Though, truth to tell, I'm feeling somewhat frail.

Master of Revels:
Beshrew me! 'Tis indeed a wayward floozy.
(Leers) I'll try her mettle in my new Jacuzzi.

Good Sense tries to prevail, but is led off by Prudence, Chastity and Temperance, all rolling drunk.

There is a great blaring of motor horns. Enter six coachloads of investigative reporters.

Master of Revels:
Who are these headstrong and scorbutic knaves
That mar our jollity?

A reporter:
We seek mass graves.

Chorus of reporters:
Mass graves! Mass graves!
We can't meet the demand.
In Salvadorean caves,
In Matabeleland,

In Israel, Argentina, Muswell Hill,
While shines the sun, we'll poke about until
      We find what Fleet Street craves:
      Mass graves!

Master of Revels: Avaunt! Much toleration have we shown.
If graves you seek, then go and dig your own.

The coaches roar off.

On with the Masque! Let not Reality
Intrude again. Dear God, what's this I see?

Sound of tuckets and pickets. The crowd divides. Enter King Arthur and a train.

A herald: Our King approaches. Aye, but watch him, brothers.
Observe how irrepressibly he smothers
With kisses all your sisters, wives and mothers.

King Arthur, shaking off female adulation, points dramatically to the sun.

Arthur: What means that furnace blazing in the height?
PUT OUT THE SUN! Put out that flaming light!
We are the creatures of the Sacred Pit.
No form of energy do we admit
Save what is quarried from a Stygian hole.
Sun, oil and fission all must yield to Coal.
Some crazed MacGregor up there in the sky
Is out to butcher us—but let him try!
      Begone! Have done!

Dissenting voices: You've jumped the gun.
We've had no ballot on the sun.
      A shower of Trots,
      Egged on by Scots,
Means nothing to the Men of Notts.

Arthur: O less-than-brothers, do you fear to fight
The cause of Chaos and Eternal Night?
We do not ballot or negotiate.
We sit round tables only to dictate.
A howling host I'll call from underground
To shake Creation with the Yorkshire Sound.
To those who crave the sun, in distant lands,
We say: Belt up, support our just demands.
Now, altogether lads, in one great shout – –
Our message to "King" Sol is OUT, OUT, OUT!

The sun: Not wanted, am I? I can take a hint.
I'll ration Planet Earth to one pale glint.
I'll cool their lusts. I'll freeze their sinful sweat.

The light begins to fade.

Voice of BBC: There is a fault. Do not adjust your set.

The amphitheatre is now in almost total darkness, from which rise the sounds of weeping, wailing and gnashing of teeth.

Enter, dimly perceived, Recrimination, Contumely and Rumour.

Recrimination: Who slays the sun?
Contumely: Some four-eyed git.
Rumour: The Leith Police dismisseth it.
Echo: The Leith Poleith dithmitheth it.

Enter a freckled Welshman.

Welshman: King Sol, farewell!
      O wicked crime!
I'll kick up hell
      Next Question Time.

Who blacked the sun?
      The NUM.
But clearly one
      Can't censure them.

I'll hide behind
      The loony fringe
And bleat and bind
      And whine and whinge.

Spotlight on Margaret Thatcher, attended by Faith, Hope, Flattery, Subordination, News Management, Mammon and Victorian Values. The phone rings.

Thatcher: Give me that phone. No need to smirk and smarm.
      Who seeks an audience?
Subordination: The Cowboy, ma'am.

Another spotlight reveals the President of the United States, telephoning from horseback.

Thatcher: Hello there, Ronnie! Did your sky go black?
We've lost the sun. I'm trying to get it back.
Reagan: The Reds have done this, Maggie. Holy cow!
I've got my finger on the button now.

A third spotlight shows the President of the Soviet Union, telephoning at desk.

Chernenko: Your CIA has sabotaged our sun.
Ten, nine, eight, sev'n, six, five, four, three, two, one.
Thatcher: Stay! Let me handle this domestic matter.
I'll call the sun myself and have a natter.
Yes, yes, I promise not to drag my feet.
I'll ring you back before the ice-caps meet.
First David: If all is doomed, we can't just stand and stare.
The SDP must lay a wreath somewhere.
Second David: I too will lay a wreath with my good friend.
In staunch Alliance we'll salute the end.

Roll of drums. Margaret Thatcher seizes a microphone.

Thatcher: Auspicious sun, that shone in like degree
On Charlemagne and Caesar, shine on me.
Think of the days on which you never set
On Britain's Empire.
The sun: How could I forget?
That glorious passage in the waste of Time?
Thatcher: Let not the world revert to frozen slime.
Shine on our owner-occupying land
Where cuts and closures help us to expand.
Shine on the isle that snubs a continent.
Shine on our civil servants, well content
To sell their unions for a bag of lolly.
Shine, if you must, upon North London Poly.
Shine on Technology, which lifts the yoke
Of labour from so many decent folk.
Shine on the GLC, that all may know
How ratepayers' cash helps deviant groups to grow.
Light up the moles among our mandarins,
Illuminate those dread banana skins.
Shine upon Cecil, once more striding forth,
Shine on the South, but don't forget the North.
Shine on the pit that yawns for Liverpool.
Shine on *The Sun*, our brashest, bluntest tool.
Give us this day a sky of Tory blue,
And blaze for Britain as you used to do.
The sun: And Arthur? Will you trade him clout for clout?
Thatcher: No. We have active plans to sit him out.
The sun: Then I relent, Prime Minister. Ere long
My light shall stun you like a brazen gong.

The amphitheatre lights up again. King Arthur and his train have vanished. The People of Britain are emerging from a chill torpor. Small bands of hunt saboteurs, Hell's Angels and Spurs' supporters are going round exterminating each other. The investigative reporters are back looking for mass graves.

The mood changes excitingly. There is a sound of wild shrieking, as of nymphs pursued by satyrs.

Enter two hundred romantic novelists, baring their starved bosoms to the sun, chased by two hundred demented social scientists.

Enter, from the opposite direction, four hundred overclad policemen, who good-temperedly push everybody out of the arena.

A constable: O frabjous day,
      Calloo, callay!
      The things we do
      For double pay!
Master of Revels: So ends our Masque, before it ever started.
But stay, good people, be not broken-hearted.
At least the sun is back in all his glory.
As for what happened, well, you voted Tory.

Michael BYWATER

Dolly Mixtures

ANDREW CRACKNELL next door keeps bending my ear about his appalling desire to be famous, and the way things are going, he might just make it.

Mind you, he's not my type at all, being what you'd call cheerful and extrovert, with a tendency to play cricket, whereas I like them dark and soulful and yearning and, indeed, *female*. His wife Pippa is much more my sort, and I would have no objection at all to THWACK but THUD no, no, CRUNCH, help!, SMACK, oooh! WHOP.

Aaah—the old nostalgic sound of willow on flesh. And if that makes me a pervert, what about these women? You know the ones, the International Bachelor Women's Society, a fishy-sounding bunch of hoodlums who, hungry for publicity, have issued a list of the world's ten most desirable bachelors.

Among the hunky manhood considered ripe for the nibble of an International Bachelor Woman's bridgework is a thing called Boy George, and that's why I postulate that Cracknell, if he hangs on to his teeth and hair, may well find himself a celebrity.

For every revolution there's a lashback: the Empire women walked about with their norks hanging out, for example, and therefore it wasn't long before the Victorians rolled up, with draped table legs, high necklines and the presiding image of Poor Old Albert dutifully boffing Her Majesty through a hole in a monogrammed sheet, with a grim set face, moiling and toiling away for Empire and Alliance, with one cerebral hemisphere fixed on Tiny Tim and the other on *Ein' Feste Burg ist unser Gott* ... then snuffing it, bonk, and turning into a bloody *monument*, for heaven's sake. (Did you see that, by the way? The Albert Memorial? Some bugger's stolen the chain. He'll never flush the thing now. Terrible.)

In other words, a lashback, counter revolution, backswing of the pendulum.

Can't happen soon enough, if the Bachelor Women are anything to go by. I mean, really, *Boy George*? Have you *seen* him? Walks around looking like a parrot that someone's been potting at with a 9 mm anti-vermin shotgun. Wears women's clothes. Talks like a berk. Which was the paper that ran some snaps of him early in the morning, without his face on? Ha ha ha. He looked awful, like a gay stevedore the morning after a rough night on the waterfront. And yet the Bachelor Women weren't put off. If that's the sort of taste they have,

no wonder they're unmarried.

The sad thing is that in the same week which saw this damned list, the TUC started whining about "challenging the media's treatment of women as sex-objects ... pin-ups, pop or film stars" with one of those daft pamphlets (this one called *Images of Inequality*) that they so much love turning out. This Boy George stuff is going to make their task harder, in much the same way that the Vegan League would be discomfited by a pamphlet from the Factory Farmed Animals Association saying, "We like being stuffed, cooked and gobbled all up. One for Mummy, one for Daddy, down the red lane! That's what we say!"

Mind you, Boy George isn't the only one whose face peels off at night. I used to know a male model whose face was his fortune, rugged good looks, chiselled features, hungrily hollowed cheekbones like oxbow lakes in the sculptural umber geology of his face. But it was all painted on. He went before the cameras under half a pound of slap and pan-stick. A high wind vectored to catch him just beneath the ear, at the interface of *maquillage* and blanched epidermis, would have pulled his entire "face" off and sent it gusting and flapping down the street, frightening the children.

You'd see him at the pub on his days off, and it was dreadful. Moon face? It was *luminous*, like some terrible world ... the sort of sodden planet where all the inhabitants had died from drinking too much

*"But we vampires have always drunk blood, Kevin—draining people's sinuses isn't **natural**."*

water. He didn't so much engage you in conversation as *loom*, drawing you into ineluctable silent orbit, so that you'd whirl around, humming, waiting for the intercontinental drift to start, nose creeping off up to the hairline, part of an eye floating off to start an independent existence as an offshore colony, corners of the mouth becoming an archipelago ... no man is an island, except in parts.

Who else do the Bachelor Women like? Would you believe Johnny Carson, who is an American television "personality" of about 178 years old who has a team of twenty gagwriters yet remains embarrassingly unfunny? He's another one of the make-up brigade, appearing on your screen late at night with that curious, expressionless gamboge mask that American newsreaders have, and which we can't imitate (except for David Frost, and his was natural). "We've been going to bed with Johnny for years," says an International Bachelor Spokeswoman, which perhaps explains Carson's blank, shagged-out appearance and also the immense consumption of narcotic drugs by America's womanhood.

Would you believe, also, "designer Xavier Roberts, brains behind the Cabbage Patch Doll craze"? What's the secret of his inclusion? Perhaps, like his vulgar little dollies (which crazed Americans fight to obtain, so starved of love and destitute of natural instincts are they), he has an infinite number of faces, all different, all plastic, all designed by computer for the sole purpose of making a lot of money.

On it goes. Next on the list is whacky urbane lumberjack-leader Pierre Trudeau, who clearly knows how to make women happy, as is seen by the fact that his wife, having gone somewhat barmy, ran away from him. An actor called Gregory Harrison. A *really* dreadful comedian called Eddie Murphy, who reminds me of the guys they used to use in old Myrna Loy pictures for comic relief, and whose scenes would all be cut when it came to the final editing. A producer called Jon Peters, but what does he produce? And when? An American TV star called Mr T, which says it all really. Someone called "former first son John Kennedy Jnr", which suggests that his older brother was born after him, a phenomenon which would really violate all laws of nature but which, in the context of this preposterous list, seems peculiarly natural, like the rubbish they give you in dreams.

Oh dear, oh dear. A picture is beginning to emerge of these International Bachelor

Women, sunk in melancholy like John Donne in his shroud, craving any form of novelty, however bizarre, as they sit before their television sets, twiddling their knobs, hunting for any man so egregious as to accept, in fantasy anyway, even the least beguiling of invitations.

I picture them lying in their double-size sunken bath tubs, floating in scented oils, their expensive hairdos wound in protective designer towels, making themselves beautiful for Boy George, Eddie or Mr T, repeating dutifully "I am unmarried by choice, a free and happy International Bachelor Woman," before retiring to their King Size, satin-sheeted, under-heated beds, alone with late-night Johnny, blowing a blushing invitatory kiss at the screen as the white dot shrivels away.

Can't help feeling they've got the wrong idea. There seems to be nothing in common between the unhappy members of this beastly list apart from pretension, television, a pair of testicles and a woodwork O-level, and I always thought there was a bit more to manhood than that.

If I was a woman, I wonder what my list would be? Something like this, I suppose:
M Paul Tortelier
Sr Jorge Luis Borges
Prof Sir Eric Laithwaite
The Pope (*ex officio*)
Sir Ranulph Fiennes (*Capt*)
Mr Graham Greene
Prof Umberto Eco
Gen Sir John Hackett
Mr Auberon Waugh
The Rev Joseph Christie SJ
(*Reserves*)
Sir Peregrine Worsthorne
Mr Canaan Banana

Mind you, the problem is that they're all married, in one way or another. Perhaps I'm just the sort of girl who likes unattainable men. But one thing is certain: I haven't filled my list with a lot of silly show-offs, and perhaps that's the point: perhaps any man who has shown off enough to make himself notorious, and who at the same time is not married, is bound to be either homosexual (which excludes him from the selectors' consideration) or peculiar in some way.

Some good may come of it, though. I predict that all the silly sods who want to be "desirable men" will immediately start trying to imitate the berks on the International Bachelor Women's list. Then the International Bachelor Women will rebel, being surfeited. Then people like Cracknell, too indolent to follow fashion, will suddenly find that, being clean-limbed Englishmen, they are Internationally in demand.

"*Cui bono?*" you may well ask, and "We thought Cracknell was married. What about his missus?"

My answers respectively, (1) Me, and (2) So what? No man could resist the temptation of the International Bachelor Women. He'll run off with one or more of them. Then I'll be round next door like a THUD WHOP ouch! BASH leggo! CRUNCH WALLOP rats, rats *rats*.

"*We're all that's left of the Dean Martin Fan Club.*"

"*Certainly, we have world cruises. In fact, if you hurry, there's one leaving in about twenty minutes.*"

"*That's his shrink.*"

"Ladies and gentlemen—here is a special announcement for those passengers who ordered the salmon à la florique . . ."

"Remember the name, Captain—Millweed. I expect to represent the passengers should there be the slightest deviation from a happy, carefree and friendly cruise."

"Surely there must be somewhere else that's not a trouble spot?"

McMurtry: LINER TYPES

"Good Lord, no. My husband and I come cruising every year. Isn't that right, steward?"

"But Mrs Fortescue—it could be months before you get a second opinion on your specimen."

"I'm sorry—I think we must be passing through the Bermuda Triangle."

"Don't panic. We're trying to locate our deck quoits champion now."

"I've never known so many burials at sea."

Janet St.CLAIR

AMERICAN aficionados of the Wild West have always been able to tell Lawmen from Outlaws. But differentiating between Good Guys and Bad Guys is quite another matter. National history and legend is framed around motley collections of social misfits; and our heroes, as likely as not, are desperados. Seems the only thing that binds us together is our subversive insistence on individual liberty. Pard'ner, this is Outlaw Territory.

And now, into the Wild West of this strange nation, comes a new heroic outlaw—the high-rolling, gun-slinging marijuana grower of the northern California mountains. Known and revered from sea to shining sea, he is nevertheless dogged and harassed into vigilant armed watch, by the merciless and inflexible Forces of Order of the western hills.

Were we unpatriotically to set rhapsodic glorifications aside for a moment, however, these modern bucolic cultivators of California's No. 1 cash crop might perhaps be found just the teeniest bit lax in their observances of the romantically venerable Code of the West. The guerilla warfare tactics they employ to protect their remote garden plots—such as hanging fish hooks at eye level from the boughs of surrounding trees, and digging bamboo pungi-stick pits in nearby forest paths—often do little to inspire a lyrical poetic fancy in the hearts of their hapless victims.

Never mind their Uzi submachine guns, land mines, vicious person-shredding dog patrols, AK-47 rifles, range fires, and plastic explosives. And murders. At least fifteen bodies associated with the local marijuana industry have been found in these rugged mountain ranges in the last two years. But one shudders to speculate on how many remote ridges might be spanned, were the actual sum of cannabis crop-connected cadavers laid end to end. Gruesome tales abound, for instance, of illegal Mexican aliens who are hired to cultivate the large plantations, then murdered after the harvest, the better to ensure their sealed lips. Facts and rumours such as these tend often to tarnish the romantic image of the outlaws of the Eighties in the eyes of the more discerning of social observers.

But don't let's be hasty in our judgements: these champions of individual liberty, after all, have a considerable interest to protect. "California Homegrown" is the new sensation that's sweepin' the nation. And cashing in on American fads, as the Pet Rock people will freely attest, is no idle enterprise. An ounce of quality California sinsemilla—Spanish for "seedless"—will

"These armoured farmers with the fat bankrolls are typically the gaunt urban hippies and impoverished peace activists of the Sixties."

fetch $250 in trendy, laid-back East Coast circles. Formerly fashionable Acapulco Gold and Maui Wowie is presently painfully passé; anything beneath your premium Californa "skunk weeds", such as the celebrated Mad River Kush and Humboldt Skunk, is definitely nothing but low-grade "shake", any way you cut it.

And since a single bush wholesales at up to $7,000, small high-quality family gardens proliferate. It's estimated that three-

"Look here, Blenkinsop, I've got enough on my plate with the Animal Liberation crowd without the staff starting."

Pot Shots

quarters of the northern California crop comes from these modest little ma-and-pa plots, from each of which an annual harvest of ten to fifty thousand tax-free dollars is reaped. The other one-quarter, though, is grown on Strictly Big-Time marijuana plantations, backed by Southern California investors, and tended by sharecroppers. Up to 8,000 plants, worth an estimated $48 million, have been found on a single plantation. Obviously, there's gold in them thar hills. Even after the confiscation of tons of illegal pot, the state's annual harvest is estimated at up to $2 billion.

Ironically—but isn't that just Life for you?—these armoured farmers with the fat bankrolls are typically the gaunt urban hippies and impoverished peace activists of the Sixties. Now, they live in glamorous solar-panelled split levels built on scenic hillsides commanding panoramic woodland vistas, and loll about the beaches of Bali between autumn harvests and spring plantings. How gratifying it must be to the likes of former Governor Ronald Reagan, that these upstart no-goodniks have finally developed a mature appreciation for the virtues of American laissez-faire capitalism!

Nevertheless, to look at them, you'd think nothing much had changed in the intervening years. Except for the infrequent business trips to San Francisco that necessitate the expensive three-piece pinstripes, the gentlemen farmers and their families dress—or not—just as they did when they left the hippie commune a decade ago. They still eat soy grits and tofu, and they still do their mantras, religiously.

But, most of all, like placid, peace-loving Candide, they tend their gardens. And—excepting, of course, the sporadic shoot-outs—these gentle outlaw businessmen make good neighbours. That is to say, their business is good for the neighbourhood. Northern California's economy, back in the olden days when the occasional American could afford the interest rates on a mortgage, was based on the lumber industry. These days, the timber trade having toppled totally, few hungry lumberjacks and lonely shopkeepers are particularly vociferous in their opposition to the savoury smell of skunk. Prosperous little ex-logging towns that should have long since expired, still speckle the local forests. Main Street chainsaw repair shops of yore are now gardening centres featuring high-tech fertilizers and specialised cultivation manuals, and Rosie's Café now serves gruyère and alfalfa sprout omelettes with bran muffins and herb tea. But it is perhaps in these backwoods Safeway supermarkets, where entire aisles are stocked solely with small plastic bags, that the untutored most seriously suspects the secret source of these little towns' salvation.

Justice, under the kindly guidance of local lawmen, remains at least purblind. Times are tough enough in those rugged woods without squandering scarce tax revenues and manpower merely maiming the goose that lays all those lovely golden eggs. It's not as if they could stamp out the outlaws, even if they wanted to. There are only one thousand rangers to oversee the 20 million acres of remote, mountainous public land that ensconces these little gardens. And even if one of those rangers should somehow sidestep the bear traps, slide under the electronic alarm system and evade the Bengal tigers guarding somebody's shrubbery, he's unlikely to find it in the best interests of either his health or welfare to bring the matter to anyone's particular attention.

Of course, now and then there's a Grandstand Operation of the type from which the former Attorney General and present Governor harvested such rich political rewards. But while intrepid flak-jacketed posses, politicians, and television camera crews sweeping out of the skies in armoured helicopters to make daring marijuana plantation raids are good for the occasional 6 o'clock news splash, John Law tends usually to prefer a rather lower profile. There have been more than a few unofficial admissions that local survival depends on our President's trickle-down theory of economics being permitted to operate unhampered in these mountains. And at least two counties have rejected hefty federal grants for marijuana eradication programmes, preferring not to have scads of pesky US narcotics agents poking around and stirring up trouble.

Nevertheless, where there's smoke, there's bound to be gunfire. Outlaw growers paranoically prowl the perimeters of their private plots in the light of harvest moons, toting the sort of artillery one typically associates primarily with Audie Murphy movies. But it is not the long arm of the anti-outlaw they fear in those small nocturnal hours of autumn, but the sudden sieges of ubiquitous bands of heavily armed thieves. With tens or even hundreds of thousands of dollars at stake in these midnight games of crops and robbers, neither side betrays any particularly debilitating compunctions about blasting out the black hearts (never mind lungs) of their vicious adversaries.

The West never could have been much Wilder. Latter day lawmen of these wide-open ranges have been known publicly to endorse legalisation of marijuana cultivation, seeing that as the only hope of restoring local law-'n'-order. The growers, however, content with their current profit margins and tax status, are among the staunchest foes of such legislation. So the convoluted battle to weed out the outlaws continues.

Sort of. But the people who follow this sort of thing still can't seem to agree on who the Bad Guys are. 🔄

"How long would the company survive, Miss Hobson, if we _all_ stapled our ears with the firm's materials?"

"1972 was a very good year. That was the year they invented twist-off caps."

"Oh dear, it's that dreadful Ramsbottom person."

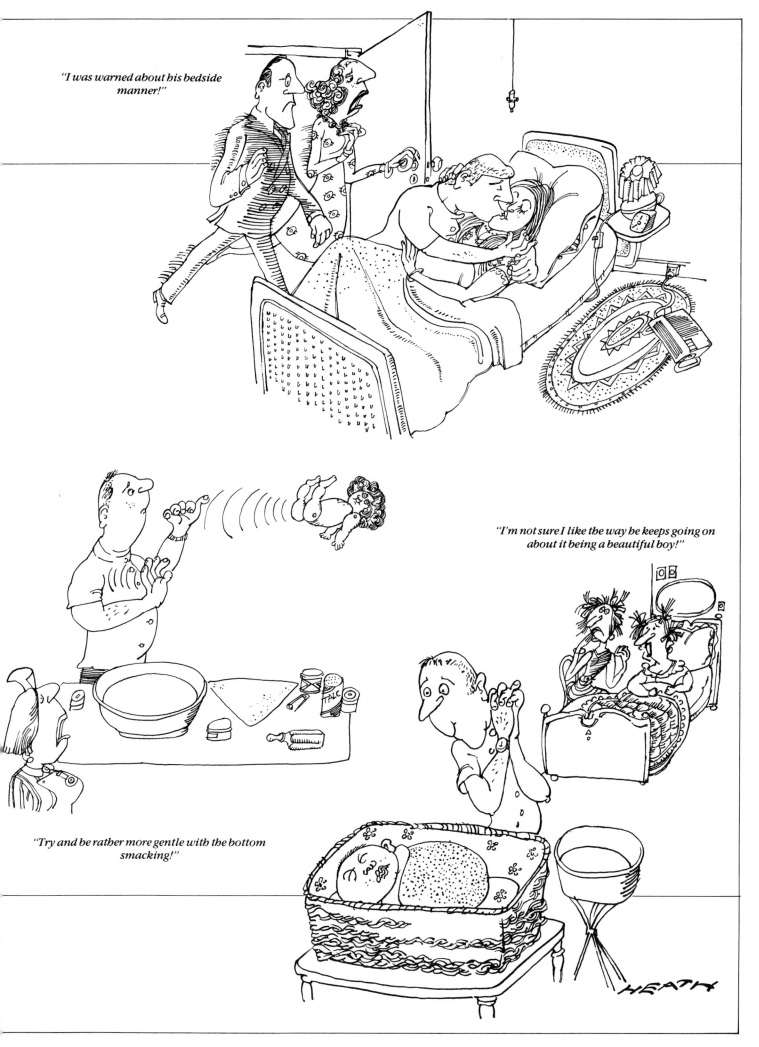

"When that Jacuzzi salesman comes round again, we'll have him for manslaughter."

DUNCAN

"I had no idea he was depressed."

"What's happening to us, Howard? Have we stopped caring? We never seem to be trying to give up something anymore."

"But _am_ I a person, Cynthia?"

TWENTY-FIVE THINGS YOU DIDN'T KNOW ABOUT WINTER

Keith WATERHOUSE

1 The well-known quotation, "If winter comes, can spring be far behind?" is grammatically wrong. To suggest that the probability of spring is conditional upon the possibility of winter, Shelley ought to have written, "Should winter come, might not spring be far behind?"

2 The world's largest snow-flake, the size of a dinner plate, was photographed by Mr Matthew Jebbings of Bull Creek, Nebraska, in February 1972. Allegations that what Mr Jebbings had there was a Hallmark paper doily are put down to jealousy on the part of slow-witted neighbours who observed the snow coming at them like frisbees yet failed to get out their cameras.

3 There is strong medical evidence to suggest that the common cold is caused by self-pity. Research among nearly six thousand sufferers over a three-year period revealed the single common factor that they all felt extremely sorry for themselves.

4 Double glazing was invented by the Earl of Sandwich who, feeling a draught down his neck while at the gaming tables, instructed a servant to get some warm air and put it between two sheets of glass.

5 During the Great Frost of 1672, Sir Christopher Wren proposed building a church in the middle of the Thames where skaters and ice-fair vendors might worship. He went off the idea during the Great Thaw of 1673.

6 There is no recorded case of any eye-witness ever giving the correct size of a hailstone. To arrive at the truth the following conversion table should be used: Hailstones the size of golf-balls = hailstones the size of marbles. Tennis balls = golf balls. Footballs = tennis balls. NB. An alleged hailstone the size of a beachball which bowled over a postman in Skipton, Yorkshire, last year, proved to be the dislodged head of a snowman which had rolled downhill.

7 Contrary to popular belief, heat does not rise—otherwise there would be no need to lag the cistern. Heat evaporates. The process is caused by high temperatures—a paradox that has scientists so baffled that instead of admitting their ignorance they go on pretending that heat escapes up the chimney like Santa Claus.

8 Nostradamus singled out the coming winter for special mention: "There will be a great gale in 1983, In which hundreds drown'd will go to Eternity, Followed by scatter'd showers clearing up in most places by noon, Temperatures down there in the low forties Fahrenheit (around six degrees Centigrade) but with bright intervals quite soon."

9 Flavoured snow that could be scooped up in cones and served as a dessert was developed by an Illinois farmer who went up in a crop-spraying aircraft and sprinkled the snow-clouds with sarsaparilla. The experiment fell foul of the public health regulations and a plan for fudge-coated hail had to be abandoned.

10 King Canute is credited with trying to abolish winter by ordering the calendar to recede. The annual ceremony of turning the clocks back is in commemoration of this foolhardy gesture.

11 In Lapland it is regarded as unlucky to talk about the long winter. Tradition has it that the last Lapp to complain, "Oh, bloody hell, is it only half past October?" got a bunch of fives.

12 The expression "Brrr!" as a comment on the cold weather is peculiar to the British. The French, for example, exclaim Bwww!" and the Japs "Blll!"

13 The first known snow-woman was built by a feminist snow-sculpture workshop in Islington in the winter of 1982, with the aid of a GLC grant. The snow-woman had a roll-up ciggie instead of a pipe, coal ear-rings, and a snow-baby in a sling in place of the traditional muffler. The first known snow-woman joke appeared in a *Daily Mail* leading article the following day.

14 The reason so few Roman buildings survive in Britain is that most of them were constructed of packed snow. Arriving in the long hard winter of 55 BC, Caesar's troops had never seen snow before and mistook it for a local mineral. The melting of the St Alban's Coliseum in 54 BC was the signal for terrible reprisals on the indigenous population who were lined up and snowballed.

15 The first ice-skates were inverted flat irons held in position by leather straps, by which means the unlicensed itinerant garment-pressers of Amsterdam used to speed along the frozen canals looking for custom, while incidentally lightening their burden and at the same time confounding the beadles of the Garment-pressers' Guild who were empowered to seize the tools of any unauthorised person practising their craft.

16 The reason alcoholic spirits do not freeze is that they give off invisible fumes which are absorbed by the cold air until it does not know whether it is coming or going.

17 Two Eskimos, frost-welded to one another while traditionally rubbing noses in sub-zero weather, were hired as Siamese twins by Phineas T. Barnum who happened to be in Alaska at the time. Their contract was cancelled when the show reached Southern California.

18 Hannibal, while crossing the Alps, experimented with primitive skis made of tree bark. Unfortunately the elephant selected to try them out was given no practice on the nursery slopes and was last seen descending the Matterhorn at an alarming speed.

19 It is a myth that no two snow-flakes are alike. A flake plucked at random out of a blizzard in northern Canada two years ago was found to be identical in every respect to the specimen symmetrical crystal hexagon shown in the Encyclopaedia Britannica. Unhappily, it melted under the arc-lights while having its picture taken.

20 Shivering is caused by cold air entering the body via the ears, nostrils and other orifices, and whistling around it rather like water gurgling through a radiator. Having been warmed by the bloodstream, the air is then expelled in the form of steam—hence the illusion that one's breath is visible in frosty weather.

21 In winters past London was renowned for its "peasoupers", which deadened all sounds except the clip-clop of hooves, the trundling of hansom cab wheels on cobbles, the blood-curdling screams of prostitutes having their throats cut, the shrill blast of police whistles, and footsteps retreating into the fog. All this is now illegal under the Clean Air Act.

22 In the winter of 1719, Jabeth Sprack, a self-employed muck spreader, hit upon the idea of hacking small pieces of ice out of a frozen-up duckpond, mounting them on twigs and dipping them in sugar, and selling them to yokels at two for a farthing. Owing to their disastrous side-effects these confections came to be known as "iced cholera". Sprack himself, who by now had had his tongue cut out for contravention of the Food and Drugs Act in allowing more than the permitted quantity of frogspawn into his product, unwittingly corrupted this to "iced lolly". Thereafter, until hanged on the gibbet for giving short measure, Sprack used to patrol the village ringing a bell and crying, "Iced lollies! Glet your iced lollies!" and the name stuck.

23 Why is ice slippery? Scientists are not sure, but the answer is probably that the water from which ice is formed is itself slippery, in order to help it move more easily when finding its own level, running out of taps etc.

24 The practice of stamping the feet in cold weather has its origins with a queue of Norwegians waiting for the last bus into Oslo one frosty evening. By the time it came their feet had frozen to the ground, and the conductor refused to keep the bus waiting while they wrenched themselves free. The story was picked up by the newspapers, one of which advised its readers to hop up and down if they wished to avoid finding themselves in the same predicament. Sailors spread the habit to Britain, though it has been said that in their case they were more likely doing the hornpipe to keep warm.

25 Countrymen have a saying: Frost in December, snow in January. Frost in January, 24-hour Emergency Plumber in February. ✿

"That was close—she's coughed up the fly . . ."

A la Recherche d'un Turkey

Monsieur: Je désire un turkey.
Shopman: Bon, monsieur. Pour Thanksgiving ou Noël?
Monsieur: Thanksgiving? C'est quoi?
Shopman: C'est le jour où les Américains célèbrent la liberté et l'égalité avec la massacre de 100,000,000 turkeys.
Monsieur: Quelle horreur. Non, pour Christmas.
Shopman: Bon. Quelle sorte de turkey?
Monsieur: Quelle sort vous avez dans votre grand freezer?
Shopman: Nous commençons avec le Whopper, puis le Superwhopper, et le Giantwhopper et aussi le Banquetwhopper.
Monsieur: Vous avez un petit turkey?
Shopman: Oui. Le Whopper est petit. Il tourne les scales à 40 lb.
Monsieur: 40 lb, c'est petit?
Shopman: Oh, oui. Il faut se souvenir que les turkeys, aujourd'hui, sont un super-race. Un peu comme les athlètes Olympiques.
Monsieur: Avec le training, les muscles, le jogging et tout ça?
Shopman: Non. Avec les stéroides diaboliques, les drogues, et tout ça. Le next step, c'est le sponsorship commercial pour les turkeys.
Monsieur: Mais je désire un tout peitit turkey, un turkey minuscule. Jour de Christmas, je dîne tout seul sur mon tod. Donc, un turkey pour un. 40 lb, ça va me donner 39½ lb de leftovers.
Shopman: Ah, monsieur, je regrette, mais nous ne faisons pas le one-man turkey. Nous avons le turkey-leg, le turkeyburger, la rissole de turkey . . .
Monsieur: Yuk. Vous n'avez pas un baby turkey?
Shopman: Non, monsieur. Voilà un grand mystère de la nature. Le baby turkey n'existe pas, seulement le Whopper.
Monsieur: Vous pouvez faire un arrangement sale-ou-return? Je prends le 40 lb, je mange 1 lb, je retourne 39 lb?
Shopman: Monsieur, pour nous, 39 lb de turkey sur le Jour de Boxing, c'est un nonnon. Impossible.
Monsieur: Vous n'avez pas de wild turkeys? Les oiseaux sauvages sont toujours plus petites.
Shopman: Le wild turkey n'existe pas. Un wild turkey est un dead turkey . . . J'ai une suggestion. Si vous dînez seul le jour de Christmas . . .
Monsieur: Oui?
Shopman: Venez dîner chez moi! Joignez le party! Un slap-up meal pour £7 inclus!
Monsieur: C'est très gentil. Mais je vais déranger . . .
Shopman: Pas du tout. Il y a déjà 27 customers qui demandent un petit turkey comme vous, qui viennent maintenant chez moi. ✿

Help-the-victim sentence plan

by Martin Kettle

CRIMINALS could be made to meet their victims, to offer personal apology for their crimes, under a new approach to punishment now being planned by the home office.

Other ideas under discussion by ministers include offenders giving assistance to victims with such chores as gardening and cleaning, repairing damage they have caused to property or broken window panes, and personally returning stolen goods.

Sunday Times

Formerly the New Cross Ten, serving fifteen years apiece for defrauding the borough of £26,000,000, these men were recently released after the personal intercession of Ken Livingstone, and are now the GLC Ways & Means Committee. ▼

Little Sean McCafferty may still look a little uneasy, but he has nothing to fear! For Sir Anthony Cork-Futtering, until recently The Beast of Wandsworth Allotments, has turned over a new leaf and now really *is* a talent scout for St Jude's choir. Well done that magistrate, we say!

Having libelled Lesbia Greenham by referring to her as a housewife, ITN newsreader Myfanwy Preston was required not only to pay punitive damages but also to help her victim overcome the terrible insecurity the libel has caused, by visiting her twice-weekly. Here, Ms Greenham (*right*) tries to explain her problem to Miss Preston.

In 1978, Arthur Thorncroft, now 26, strangled Mr E. J. Nardson, a Bromley lithographer, after an argument about shirts, and was sent to Pentonville. Last week, however, he was paroled, on condition that he spends each breakfast-time with Mr Nardson's widow, Janice, exchanging pleasantries by throwing his voice through Mr Nardson's skull.

"It is wonderful," confirmed Janice. "It is just like having Ernes back, with none of the unsavoury bits."

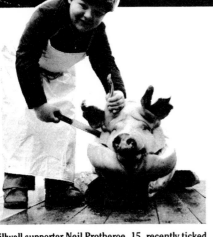

Millwall supporter Neil Protheroe, 15, recently ticked off by the juvenile court for stealing eight cleavers from his local Dewhurst's prior to an away match at Rotherham, is happier than ever now that his Saturday afternoons are spent in compensation rather than the Den. As soon as he has mastered his trade, he told newsmen, he plans to become a Leeds United supporter.

Not all the experiments have been totally successful. Phonebox vandal Denis Mussorgsky was bound over on the understanding that he would spend forty hours' community service telephoning messages on behalf of estate-dwellers whom he had previously deprived of twelve instruments. Now charged with making 1,368 obscene calls, fraudulently ordering 6,000 foxtrot lessons, and causing 900 tons of horse manure to be delivered to Ealing Magistrates' Court. Mussorgsky said that he had always been a fool where 5p pieces were concerned, and blamed society.

Boxed In

"GOOD morning, everyone. Morning, Trevor."

"Mmm. Ahh. What? Umm. Poor ball, poorer shot, reasonable catch. Zzzz."

"Morning, Sir Frederick."

"Well, ah gi' oop, ah really do. Beggared if ah know what's bin goin' on aht there f'lasst three days. That Bob Willis. Ahm lost f'words, ah really am. E'en wi' a mickle an' a mookle, mah dog, William, could place 'is field better than yon."

"Morning, Blowers."

"Mornin', Johnners, old thing. Frightfully good to be here, I must say. Oh, look at that pigeon flying near the roof of that spiffing red 39 bus . . . or is it a 54?"

"Morning, Alderman."

"Mebbe f'some. Call that place an 'otel. Ah knew better at Nagpur on '82 tour."

"Right, everyone, chocky cakers for the old double one-ers—elevenses. Golly, look. Two glistening pink cherries on the chocky. Reminds Blowers of Barbados, what."

"Tee, hee. What-ho. Nudge-nudge. Say no more."

"Make with the bubbly, Boil."

"Leggo. Yaroo. I say, you fellows, let's not leave any for that swot, CM-J, what?"

(In the distance, a smattering of applause.)

"Coo, cripes. Some diminutive chappie must be out. Is it little Vishy? Or that tot, Gavaskar? Or one of those teeny weenies from, what's the new name for the place, Sri-Lon? All look alike to me. Tell us, bearded wonder."

Frindall reads the scorecard, after which Bailey says, "Mmm. Ahh. What? Umm. Poor ball, poorer shot, reasonable catch. Zzzz," to general background effects of giggles being stifled with handkerchiefs and occasional spittled chocolatey pellets exploding on the microphone. At last, Johnners pulls himself together and expansively, even sexily, pops a glistening cherry into his mouth. He wipes the chocky from the toe of his spats, and says:

"Now let's go over to Wimbledon to see if it's stopped drizzling yet."

Cricket's Prudential World Cup competition starts this week and the boys from the Remove are back in their little dorm above the pav. The final will be played at Lord's on Saturday, June 25, after which the New Zealand side remain to play a four match Test series against England. For the BBC radio's *Test Match Special* ball-by-ball commentary team it will be an important summer. After more than half a century of basking in the nation's esteem, they find themselves this year as an institution being sniped at. By their own kind, too.

For a year or two in *Radio Times*, and last summer in both the *Times* and *Guar-*

"The boys from the Remove are back in their little dorm above the pav."

dian, there had been letters of complaint from the cricket buffs about the suddenly juvenile standards of the broadcasting team. Then, in the October edition of *Wisden Cricket Monthly*, three whole pages were given over to the debate, with "Distraught of Tunbridge Wells" mixing it something rotten with "Leave Well Alone of Cheltenham".

"I say to the whole sniggering, wine-bibbing, self-backslapping rump of a once dignified institution, 'For God's sake go. You have been with us more than long enough'," wrote a Mr Heald, of Canterbury. His sort was answered at once by Mr Edsett, of Somerset: "They should watch their bloody television instead"—or Mr Crisford, of Lewes: "Send them a cake to cheer them up, and let's have the smoke from Fred's pipe coming out of their radios." While the correspondence was balanced, the very fact of criticism might well have undermined the seemingly cheery composure of the chums. Bonhomie treads dangerous ground once it has to watch its step—especially in this case when, like most long-running serials, the cast in "real life" are not half as matey or unbitchy as they seem to be once the compelling little red light goes on, and the signature tune starts up.

Test Match Special had bathed in the warm waters of cultish applause for a long and, I would say, deserving time. Now here was their own "in house" magazine printing reams of abuse from cricket lovers, which included such wounding sideswipes as "*It's a Knockout,* on a bad day", or "I listen with disgust, not having heard anything like it since the fourth form", while others fumed at hour upon hour of "puerile comment" with Trueman's "sour grapes", Mosey's "boredom", Blofeld's "ignorance", and Johnston's "jokes, sweets, and concern for trivial side issues" while in the background the sacred sound of leather on wood "is drowned by the clink of ice cubes and the fizz of tonic water".

The bridge between national institution and national bore is thin and rickety. Ask David Frost, Anna Ford, the Editor of the *Sunday Times*, or even Ted Moult and his ruddy double-glazing outfit. In hindsight, *Test Match Special* was going to be up against it from teatime on the final day of the Lord's centenary Test a couple of years ago when the players, even, paused to salute the broadcasters' eyrie high above the pavilion. It had just been announced that John Arlott was making his last broadcast commentary. And when he got up, turned his back on the cricket, mopped his brow with a great big hobo's red-and-white spotted handkerchief, and looked for a glass of wine after saying, "And after Trevor Bailey it'll be Christopher Martin-Jenkins," it really was era's end.

Arlott had begun his cricket broadcasts long before every ball was covered in every home Test Match. His first commentary, I think, described the Indians at Worcester in 1946. I first heard him some time in that golden summer of 1947. I was nine. Was it Jack Martin, of Kent, who was bowling? Or Harold Butler, of Notts? Anyway, I remember to this day Arlott's description of the lumbering walk-back, the turn, the twirl of sleeve and "one-two-three-four-five-six-seven-eight-nine-over-she-goes . . . and he's bowled him". You have to read it back with old Hampshire's mellow growl. I can give you, just about verbatim I reckon, Bradman's last knock at the Oval in 1948. Again, pretend you're gargling with the water of (appropriately) the Test. "Bradman plays forward and it goes in the direction of the House of Commons . . . it doesn't go that far, of course, but just to Watkins at silly mid-off . . . Hollies again then . . . and he's bowled . . . Bradman—bowled Hollies . . . nought . . . well, what can you say in such circumstances?"

When Arlott finally hung up his vowels after the centenary Test, the BBC's cricket producer, Peter Baxter, could have gone out to replace him just as, say, Selina replaced Anna. But as a broadcaster, Arlott was up on the plinth alongside Murrow and Cooke and grandfather Dimbleby. He was one-off, irreplaceable. So Baxter and his team soldiered on, but now without Arlott's overwhelming, melancholic, Wessex gravitas, the joky jollity was thrust downstage and, more crucial, without the eminence around, the carpers and critics dared at last to come out and play.

A very good broadcaster, surely, can only be himself. Nobody could remotely charge Brian Johnston with putting on an act. Though he is remarkably experienced and "professional", he is the one who alters his personality not one jot when the little red bulb lights up. Johnners talks just like that in real life. He has a permanent smile on his face. His autobiography was called, simply, *It's Been A Lot Of Fun.* He genuinely sees his role as anchor man at a transmission "of four or five friends who would be at the Test Match anyway, just sitting around and chatting about it". It just so happens that microphones are live in front of them. I don't know if Johnners actually likes chocky cake, but he certainly thinks it's a good enough jape if there are two glistening, pink cherries plonked on the top of it. He particularly enjoys anything ambiguous that he can get away with about "balls", and relishes the day when someone is moved in the field to short-leg so he can stand there "with his legs apart waiting for a tickle".

Yaroo. Yippee.

Good morning, Johnners. Morning, Sir Frederick.

Morning, Blowers, old thing. Morning, everyone. Welcome back to one of the nicest sounds of summer. Make with the bubbly, Boil.

BANX

"No one calls the Concho Kid a has-been and lives."

"Something's wrong, George—you don't normally drink when you're on duty."

"It's your turn to prune the bonsai."

TINTIN'S ODYSSEY

Tintin is racist, says Brent Library.
So **MAHOOD** has redrawn the
strip, just to keep them happy.

Hot-footing it through the Duty Free Compound at Lagos International, former Presidential aide and palm-oil narcotics executive Field-Marshal Ibrahim Tomato boarded a Libyan Airline Ingotstretch-er to an undisclosed destination, pursued by creditors and nomadic CIA tribesmen. Tomato, rumoured to be amongst Africa's top ten richest bankrupts, brushed aside suggestions that he plans to join an Abidjan cable consortium and maintained that he was leaving on a private holiday to the World Bank.

Looking fit and bronzed despite his recent punishing round of pro-celebrity tournaments in the Latin American World Semi-Finals, veteran international chat-show anchorman HENRY "Game For A Laugh" KISSINGER was pictured in transit at Managua, momentarily unable for the life of him to recall off-hand whether it is Gate 27 for Honduras and Gate 5 for El Salvador, or Gate 25 for Nicaragua and Gate 7 for El Salvador via Managua, except Tuesdays and Thursdays when it is Gate 2 for El Honduragua, or possibly vice-versa. He was urged by fellow-travellers to read the time-table as a whole.

Recuperating still from what many doctors believe to be the stubbornest head cold of all time, Soviet premier YURI ANDROPOV was pictured dis-embarking from an Aeroflot SuperANTHRAX bar-gain excursion to his Siberian dacha. A spokes-man with the escorting SS-20 battery issued a statement confirming that Andropov, despite continuing discomfort in one sinus, was alert and carrying on with "business as usual" from his air-conditioned pallet.

GS Another busy week for Punch's airport papparazzo
DAVID TAYLOR

Confirming his glittering reputation as show business's most snappily-dressed, top-of-the-bill escapologist, designer boiler-suited YASSER ARAFAT cut an unmistakable dash amongst passengers waiting patiently for the fog to lift at Yemen's Terminal Two.

Offered a complimentary 7-Up by the airline, a day-dreaming Arafat was for a minute non-plussed into supposing that he was being ambushed for *This Is Your Life*, but quickly regained his composure and struck a deal with our photographer that he would allow one posed snap provided he was then left in peace to enjoy his shooting holiday unmolested.

Her Majesty The Queen Mother (arrowed) delighted passers-by when she commanded her nearside window be wound down for an impromptu radiant chat. The incident occurred after Her Majesty, en route to Sandringham from RAF Brize Norton, was bogged down in rush-hour traffic around the Wandsworth Gyratory System. Over-the-moon Luton call-girl Michele Gabor and her common law friend, Mick, an unemployed terrorist, told reporters that Her Majesty had graciously asked them what they did, but before they could answer "Happy New Year, Ma'am!" the lights changed and a dream-of-a-lifetime situation had passed. A spokesman for RAF Brize Norton later confirmed that the aircraft had waited.

Pyramids and so on are the latest assignment for fashionable society lensperson ELSPETH HOWE, one of the jet set who is always on the go taking snaps for her coffee-table album, *Some Rather Super Things One Has Spotted Whilst Abroad*.

Checking in the baggage at Riyadh departures is her shy assistant, BOY GEOFFREY, who likes to string along and meet a few of the locals between a busy schedule of sightseeing engagements.

Amidst Hollywood buzz that he and dapper RONALD "MISTER PRESIDENT" REAGAN may soon sign for a big-budget goodwill re-make of *Singing in the Rain* for MURDOCH BROTHERS, superstar showman ZHAO ZIYANG (pronounced *Zh-ao Zi-yang*) flew in to a ticker-tape welcome at Washington's fashionable JOHN FOSTER DULLES airport and quipped to waiting newsmen: "Taiwan to be alone!"

Widely tipped to be a coast-to-coast sensation on THE JOHNNY CARSON SHOW, Zhao, recently named *Cutest Chinaman of the Year* by prestigious *McDonald's* magazine, would not be drawn on whether he planned during his vacation to date sexy Sinophile SHIRLEY MACLAINE.

Breakaway North Staffordshire winders RON GROSSETT and SID HOLDCROFT take advantage of the current deadlock with face-workers to join the thousands of other disenchanted trade unionists currently undertaking Caribbean cruises. "There's a lot of block-booking on fact-finding tours this time of year," revealed Ron, "but we mentioned Arthur Scargill's name to the captain and secured a victory for common sense."

39

Hunter DAVIES

Cheque, Mate

I SUPPOSE it had to happen. All this feminism was bound to have an effect. I should have put my put down when it started, knowing it would all end in tears, probably my tears.

Over our glass of Guinness at lunchtime, and our evening cocoa at night, the subject has been the same for the last three years. Boring old feminism. My lady wife is working on this history book, which means we're all working on this history book. Flora starts humming when the subject comes up, which drives her mad. I just bang the newspaper loudly, which is how I read newspapers, hitting them into submission, getting the print to lie down, knocking the headlines into shape. This also annoys her. But no, on she trundles, telling us for the thirteenth time about the Contagious Diseases Act of 1864.

No, she hasn't had a crew-cut, not yet anyway. Nor has she gone to Greenham Common. She does spend a lot of time at the Fawcett Library where they keep all the feminist archives, but she hasn't yet applied for a job there.

Look, what's so special about feminism? Why can't I call it boring? Bloody hell, you're all so sensitive. It's just another subject, like fretwork or philately. You say my stamps are boring so why can't I give a yawn when Josephine Butler comes into the conversation. Oh come on, that was a joke about crew-cuts. OK, it was a rotten sexist sneer joke. That's the sort I like.

My mother got it in the neck last evening. She is still living in our street, with my sister, and comes round here most afternoons and then has supper with us. It's the return of the extended family, back to the cave age. They say that would suit the way I eat. They are going through a phase at the moment of imitating me eating. Even Jake does it, going chomp chomp, grunt grunt, whenever I start a mouthful. I can't help my jaws.

I don't really know why they have it in for me, though at the back of my mind I remember my own father annoying us when he was having a meal. And at the front of my mind I read somewhere recently that the reason teenage girls leave home is to get away from the sound of their father eating. We won't go into all that. Not now. Crew-cuts, dear God.

When you think of the remarks *I* have to put up with in this house.

Anyway, my mother was asked if she wanted some more casserole. She looked round politely, being well brought up, and said perfectly pleasantly, "Have the men had enough?"

I thought it was a nice thing to say. I liked the courtesy of calling us "men". I felt quite horny-handed, son of the soil, after a hard day digging in the typewriter, shovelling out the words; Jake does come back from doing his A-level Politics essays as if he's been down the mine, his hands filthy, his brow lathered, his limbs aching.

But my wife nearly had apoplexy. Listen Grandma, I asked *you* if you wanted some more. There is no earthly reason why men should ever get served more than women. That's what was wrong with your generation, brain-washing yourselves into thinking, bla bla, oh do stop humming, Flora.

My mother just smiled, perhaps even dis-

"Goodness! I didn't know the aroma of Falafel could waft up 36 floors."

---

played a trace of a sneer. She quite likes being attacked. She knows she's not going to change. Not now. Had there perhaps been a trace of a joke in the reference to men which we had all missed? I'll save that thought for the cocoa tonight.

In the meantime, what has happened with all this feminism talk is that when I came down for breakfast this morning my wife put down *The Guardian* and looked at me defiantly. "Why haven't I got my own cheque-book? Answer me that!"

Who've you been talking to, I said. Is it that German Greer. I told you not to talk to her. Wait till I see her Dad. I don't want you mixing with that crowd. Or was it that Irish Murdoch. She's a bad lot. You're not going to her party ever again. I'm ringing the head-mistress at once.

Ha ha, very funny. Seriously. I'm the only woman I know who hasn't got their own cheque-book. Is there any reason why I have *not* got one?

None at all, my petal. You were there when the jobs were given out 23 years ago. You got all the easy jobs, cooking, cleaning, washing, ironing, houseworking, mothering, talking to the Miele, being kind to the Potterton. I got the really hard ones, like answering the telephone, and I'm just about fed up with that, all last week it was for you and I rushed to answer it then when I screamed downstairs you wouldn't even leave your rotten desk. I do have my limits, you know. I can be pushed just so far.

Then, of course, there's the finances. If you want to, my sweet, you can deal with all bills and money matters from now on. Be a pleasure. Count me out of counting out.

I just want my own cheque-book, she said, that's all. I would like from now on to be treated as an individual, not your appendage. No, that wasn't the word. What did she say? That's the trouble with not listening properly.

I broke in to say that she *did* have a cheque-book. We have a joint account between us, Mr and Mrs, so it says on every cheque, and she can sign the cheques just as much as I can. So what's the problem, dear heart?

OK then, it's my own *account* I want, something which is personal and private to

LET'S PARLER FRANGLAIS!

me, nothing at all to do with you and nothing to do with the household accounts. I would like to be able to spend money, *my* own money, without you knowing about it.

I see. It's come to this, has it. I have suspected that French onion-seller. He came again this morning and I heard her buying two enormous strings of onions when the kitchen is already a mass of onions with green shoots sprouting all over the place. It's like having to fight your way through the hot-house at Kew Gardens just to find the jar of Gold Blend. I always maintain he is not French, but a Cockney cowboy, and that once our front door is closed, he puts his old bike in the boot of his Volvo.

Those onions are household expenses, she said. She doesn't mind me knowing about *them*. It's when she buys presents for people, such at Caitlin, that she doesn't want me analysing all the cheque-book stubs and screaming at the prices.

"Look, there's an advert here. I could join this scheme."

It was a whole page advertisement for the Abbey National Building Society, who are starting a new scheme with cheque accounts. You have probably read about it. I studied it closely and it did look quite good. They pay you at least 4% on your current account. Sounds really good. Better than the Midland.

"Everybody in this house has got a bank account, except me. It's about time I got one. I should have done it years ago."

I offered to fill in the form for her, to write away and get the particulars for her, investigate all the possibilities, but she said certainly not. She wasn't completely incapable. She could do it all on her own, thank you very much.

It is not quite true about the accounts. Flora hasn't got one, though she has National Savings Certificates. Jake hasn't got a bank account either, being only sixteen, but he has other accounts. Jake is our hope for the future, the only one so far to show any financial sense. He has two deposit accounts at the moment—a Savings Bank Account and a Building Society Account with the Abbey National. The precise sums are confidential, and I have recently signed the Official Secrets Act, but he went out last week and bought a new pair of trousers for £20—and paid for it out of his annual interest.

He has his weekend job, which helps, plus my allowance which I give him, currently £55 a quarter, out of which he has to buy everything. He manages it all so beautifully, with his expenses and income neatly tabulated. He used to keep it under his bed in a tin box, but that led to problems. He thought at first it was mice. He would hear this rustling sound in the middle of the night, but

think nothing of it. Two days later he would look in his money box and find a torn bit of paper. "IOU £15. Luv Cait."

About a year ago, fed up with being a money-lender, he got a big barrow and wheeled it all round to the Post Office. I don't know how Caitlin manages now. I dare not ask. I have done her this covenant for Art College, which she receives monthly, and I think on paper she is reasonably well off, but she never has a penny. She never had a penny. So it goes. It is one of the mysteries of the Western World. These women. Sorry, just slipped out. You know I don't sneer.

So off to her little office went my little wife and filled in the form at the bottom of the page, very pleased with herself. Joined-up writing as well.

Half an hour later, Jake shouted up to me from the hall. He had noticed the envelope laid out to be posted, to the Abbey National, Freepost, 180 Oxford Street, London W1.

I came down and picked it up and saw that she had put a 15½p stamp on it. I knocked at her door, politely, I do know my place, and then pointed to the stamp.

You are so mean, she said. You would have put on only a 12½p stamp. I want it to get there quickly. The sooner I start looking after my own money the better.

It's Freepost, my loved one, I said.

She looked rather bemused. I think she thought Freepost was a suburb of Liverpool. I explained it all in words of one syllabub that no stamps were necessary. It goes for free. Gorrit. Free post.

Oh, gosh, what fun. We men. We did rather chortle . . .

P.S. This was a sexist column. Not suitable for Sisters. ◗

"Good news, Mr Thomas. You're not dyslexic at all—you're Welsh!"

Dans la Pizzeria

Dineur No. 1: Moi, je prends la pizza Stromboli.
Dineur No. 2: Moi, je préfère la pizza Jacuzzi.
Dineur No. 3: Pour moi, la pizza Cosa Nostra.
Garçon: Bon. Et pour vous, monsieur?
Dineur No. 4: Mmm . . . Je ne sais pas . . . C'est difficile . . .
No. 1: Mais non, c'est facile, Jim! Prenez un pin—stabbez dans le menu.
No. 4: La pizza Monteverdi, c'est quoi?
Garçon: Monteverdi, c'est tomates, mozzarella, mushrooms de bouton, anchovy et oignons.
No. 4: Hmm. Et la pizza Moderato Cantabile?
Garçon: C'est mozzarella, tomates, oignons, anchovy et mushrooms.
No. 4: C'est la même chose!
Garçon: Avec un pinch de basil.
No. 4: Oh dear. La pizza Juventus, c'est aussi tom, mozz, mush, anch et oignons?
Garçon: Oui. Mais avec l'addition d'un rind de bacon.
No. 4: Toutes les pizzas sont les mêmes, presque identiques.
Garçon: Mais non! La pizza Bambina est différente.
No. 4: Dites-moi les ingrédients.
Garçon: Junket, confiture de strawberry et blancmange . . .
No. 4: Yuk.
Garçon: . . . avec tomates, mozzarella, etc.
No. 4: Double yuk.
No. 2: Jesus pleura, Jim, décidez-vous!
Garçon: Il y a le pizzaburger, monsieur. Ou le pizza kebab. Ou le croque-signor.
No. 4: Croque-signor?
Garçon: Comme un croque-monsieur, mais c'est un toasty pizza.
No. 3: Jim, pour l'amour de Moïse, nous ne sommes pas sur un fast jusqu'à la mort!
No. 4: Reste cool, Keith. OK, je prends la pizza Monte Cassino.
Garçon: Cela, monsieur, c'est avec oignons, anchovy . . .
No. 4: Ne, me dites pas! Qu'elle reste une surprise!
Garçon: Bon, monsieur. (*Il s'en va.*)
No. 1: Non, mais, Jim, vous êtes pathétique.
No. 4: C'est difficile, la cuisine italienne. Tenez, par example. Vous avez vu les posters et les commercials pour les Spaghetti Shells?
Tous: Oui. So quoi?
No. 4: Spaghetti est long et mince. Les shells sont petits et ronds. Alors, un Spaghetti Shell est nonsense. C'est comme soupe dans le basket, ou steak et kidney sorbet.
Garçon: Voilà, messieurs. Quatre pizzas.
No. 1: Mais . . . elles sont identiques!
No. 4: Naturellement. Une pizza est une pizza est une pizza. Gertrude Stein. ◗

So the Bisto kids are to make a 1984 comeback—but isn't it time some of the other greats were

dusted off and revamped?

So much for people who say I can't smoke and write at the same time! And by the way, these pens are really cool, rich, and satisfying.

Ronald Reagan

see RONALD REAGAN starring in "HONG KONG" a Pine-Thomas Paramount Production Color by Technicolor

Vote DEMOCRAT in '84

"Of course there's no harm in your knowing!"

THE GUARDIAN

My Goodness My VALIUM

GLC FOR A GREATER LONDON

AN "island of health" where tired businessmen could enjoy fresh air and the simple life is being suggested for Islay, off Scotland's west coast.

Daily Telegraph

"Must be good here—Irene was the first woman in the Stock Exchange."

"Only one on the island and that was vandalised just before the Amersham business."

"Y'know, Donal, sometimes I think she makes deliberate typing errors just to get you across here!"

"Whisht, man! To hell with the Phantom Piper of the McDoons!"

Bill Tidy
THE SAP ALSO RISES

"I'm feeling the benefit already—carrying these boxes on the beach . . ."

"Consolidated Ores has taken over Chemco and United Packers. They're all ordering porrage this morning."

"Morag, a little more whisky on the stones please!"

"Well, well, well . . . Patrick Sergeant."

Skin Deep

I HAVE never forgotten the first time I used make-up. I sat down in black-and-white, facing a mirror which covered an entire wall, and I got up in Technicolor. Before, I had been just a grey, ghostly bit-part player in crowd scenes, indistinguishable among the cut-outs except to my mother. Afterwards, I was a star, apple-cheeked, blackberry-eyed, rose-lipped, outlined in glowing neon. I thought to myself—this is the real You.

I was only seven-and-a-quarter.

The occasion was a children's festival at the town hall where our junior school was booked for a ten-minute enactment, to recorded music, of *The Teddy Bears' Picnic.* Until the day before, I had been cast as one of the six bears in identical hairy costumes, rejected for the leading role as Holiday Boy because, as the Headmistress told our form teacher, I had "no soul". It was probably the truest thing ever said about me, and I felt, when I overheard it, quite pleased with myself. My mother, however, being a Christian woman who took such spiritual rankings seriously, was outraged.

For the only time in my education, she challenged the decision of the authorities, storming up to school and demanding that I be de-classified as a pagan infidel. It must have been an impressive exhibition of maternal indignation and religious zeal because the Headmistress backed down, claiming that she had only said I had "*no music* in my soul", an even more perceptive and exact summing-up.

Anyway, the result was I became once more the only one of the troupe who would show his face on stage, hence the application of rouge, lipstick, and various sweet-smelling bars of coloured wax, in the dressing-room. Elated by the transformation, I decided to give my public all I possessed, improvising various routines not previously glimpsed outside my bedroom, dancing, clowning.

The item over-ran by at least a quarter of an hour, but the audience, I thought, loved it. Not so the teachers in the wings, who stamped their feet and shook their fists, obliged to play the record over and over again, while I innocently avoided catching their eyes. Eventually, the irate and envious

bears had to re-dress in their costumes and come on to drag me off, still milking the applause.

Since then, I have resented the apartheid of gender which denies the Western male the panoply of cosmetics to improve on nature while allowing the female to change the colour of her hair, re-site her eyebrows, enlarge or diminish her mouth, add an extra skin, and generally operate under a disguise. In the years of obscurity following my debut, I used to sit in our council house kitchen watching my sister adopt and reject half a dozen different images of herself while all

"*You've lost seven pounds since you were last here—gosh, that's really terrific! What diet are you on—the Scarsdale? Yes, it seems to work really well on most people . . .*"

that was available to my three elder brothers, one of them at twenty almost bald, was the choice of various-size dollops of Brylcreem or the number of layers of Vaseline. Vanity, for women, was a social imperative. In men it was a secret vice.

The best they could hope for, under the grease, was a glistening, smudged replica of the dago gangster, like a fly-blown George Raft. In later, posher days, I discovered that the better-groomed the man, the more he was expected to look like all other men, escalating on gala occasions to an evening-dress as regulated as a uniform, while the women were encouraged to rise to heights of individuality personalised enough for even their husbands to pick them out in a crowd.

But now at last, so I read in the Women's Pages of the Sundays, many British males, long covert users of their wives' and girlfriends' beauty products, were following their American counterparts out of the closet and into the parlour, at places like the Aramis Clinic in Harrods and Selfridges. I decided to join these pioneers, hoping that, following years of neglect of facial potential, I could offer myself as a Before and After model.

I saw it all like a TV commercial. Enter a stooping, stocky, seventeen-inch-neck figure, grateful to be dubbed "middle-aged", eyes webbed with converging tracks like a desert oasis, cheeks mottled with blood-vessels about to burst into super-novae, receding hair and sprouting beard dusted with white like a politician who had just run a gauntlet of flour-bombs. Exit a willowy, athletic, mature sex-object, stripped of his bulbous peel, coiffeured with chestnut waves, skin ironed to a pinky sheen, cheeks highlighted, eye-sockets glittering with silver lacquer, possibly even with the tweeds freshly pressed and the shoes shining.

THE first thing I noticed is that the companies involved in these campaigns are clearly sensitive to any fears that its customers may have of being thought unmanly. The word "Clinic" is itself a give-away, suggesting that a masculine interest in appearance is really a concern for health rather than beauty.

The men's section at Harrods is located in the Pharmacy, where the floor is conservatively carpeted, the lighting subdued enough to reflect only vague outlines, the array of bottles and packages suggesting expensive wines or liqueurs rather than cleansing lotions and creams, hardly a hint in the air of anything resembling flowers or fruits. By contrast, the women's section has bright lights, set even in the eaves under the counters, disseminating a shadowless glow which

'S LONDON

"It is a rare female who lacks the courage to study her appearance with the pitiless scrupulousness of a gynaecologist, or a corset-fitter."

bounces off the shiny floor, bathing the department in swimming-pool radiance, so that the shoppers seem to be floating like naiads in a bath of fragrance. Whether this is designed to make everyone feel new-washed and semi-nude, or grubby and over-dressed, I could not quite decide.

Certainly the few men I saw trespassing among the feminine mysteries seemed restless to leave, as though afraid to be caught on *Candid Camera*, their eyes evading the magnifying mirrors which lined the counters like distorting lenses in a fun-fair.

In Selfridges, on brash, battered Oxford Street, Aramis operated in the open, soliciting the men passing by to take up the offer of free shaves and facial massage in full sight of the public. In the discreet opulence of Kensingtonian Harrods, the free treatment and advice was by appointment only, through a recessed door in the corner. It was here that in a small, intimate cubicle, I beseeched the young lady consultant to tell me the truth about my looks. But I soon realised that, despite the publicity, no woman really believes that the male is yet ready to see himself as he really is. In vain, I pointed out all my flaws, some of which I had noticed for the first time that morning when I made the mistake of examining my face in the bath-room mirror with my glasses on.

It is a rare female who lacks the courage to study her appearance with the pitiless scrupulousness of a gynaecologist, or a corset-fitter, always seeking to sell herself some major device for improvement. The male starts out totally confident that all is for the best, wondering at most whether he is being let down by some tiny error, such as the wrong tie, or a superfluous chevron of dandruff on the epaulettes.

All that my adviser would admit to me was that I looked "experienced" with a face that was "lived-in". With a polite shudder, she denied any possibility of Aramis advising a hair tint, a dab of colour, a squirt of sexy smell, anything that could be interpreted as being included under the taboo heading of "make-up". She did convey, by an occasional intake of breath, that I had been punishing myself by using the same soap for face and body, by washing my hair only once a week with anything in any bottle which came to hand under the shower with my eyes closed, by using an electric shaver which unless manipulated with extreme care would drag the bristles against their natural angle of growth, by sprinkling an eau de cologne on newly scraped skin.

I said I thought that Aramis was an inventive name for men's preparations, presuming it to be named after the dandyish, spoilt-priest in *The Three Musketeers*. But nobody had heard of him. Instead, I was told, it was taken from "the Turkish root" on which the basic formula was based.

So far as I could make out, my face was washed with "a deep cleansing face bar", somehow not to be confused with soap, lightly treated with "a clear skin pack" followed by "a clarifying face formula", covered with "a maximum moisture lotion", and my "heat areas", known to the rest of us as the neck and the armpits, dabbed with "a fragrance" said to be "the aura that surrounds the man of elegance".

I went away with a set of samples to continue my inclusion in "the class of men who are most at ease amid luxury" and studying them back home I see from the legends on the packaging that the key words are "absolute comfort" (the shaving cream), "invigorating" (the body shampoo), "nourishing" (the moisture lotion), "sporting" (the cologne), and "custom blended" (the superior J.H.L. cologne recently created by Estée Lauder especially for her husband, Joseph "Harry" Lauder).

"And how is Mr Lauder looking these days?" I asked.

"I'm sorry to say he just died," said my consultant.

DESPITE the publicity from America informing us that such virile stars as Paul Newman, Dustin Hoffman and Robert Redford are not embarrassed to use beauty parlours for men, at least for the British market the emphasis is still on health, fitness, hygiene, neatness and cleanliness. The products sound more like natural foods or organic drinks (all the shampoos are "malt-enriched") than short-cuts to handsome good looks.

I came out into Knightsbridge, no doubt sporting a nimbus that "speaks of a classic style and presence", a living semaphore of "the statement that affirms a standard of excellence ... luxurious, distinctively masculine, in a class by itself." The blend of "138 natural essences" gathered from around the world—"thyme from Spain, cardamom from Guatemala, sandalwood from India, lemon from America."—made me quite a dish, even if one more appropriately roasted in an oven than toasted in bed, a Carrier rather than a Le Carré creation. I was laundered deep enough in every visible pore to feel no shame in being knocked down and rushed straight into the operating theatre.

But I could not make out that I was at all improved in looks, or heightened in attraction. No heads turned. "Elegance"—the term used by gossip columnists when they do not want to say a rich woman is actually plain—is not enough. I was hoping for something nearer "gorgeous" or "smashing" but it seems no groomers of the male are willing to offer even the illusion. Time is yomping along.

Isn't there anybody willing to stage a revival of *The Teddy Bears' Picnic*? I know just the man to play the Holiday Oldster. ❧

"Well, we've got the final report on your infection, Mr Northcote."

Jonathan SALE

The Dogs of War

SNOB the Dog was certainly old enough to fight for his country. In fact he fought for two countries, first on the Russian side in the Crimea and then, sensing that his owner's corpse would not be much good at providing walkies, for the British. There haven't been many animals "turned" le-Carré-style (Tinker, Taylor, Soldier, Snob the Dog) but this one served the Queen loyally until death, when a full military funeral was provided by the mourning regiment, complete with pall-bearers and three rounds of ammunition fired over the grave.

Don't take my word for that, check the stuffed hound in the exhibition *Animals in War* at the Imperial War Museum near Lambeth North Tube. Perhaps you will be able to answer something on my mind: if the dog was given a Christian burial, how come its carcase is Exhibit No. Eighteen in the third case on the left? If this is another Hitler's diaries scandal, Lord Dacre should be called in to verify it isn't a fur and skin forgery. (And then we consult an expert.)

There is no doubt about Judy the Pointer, the only animal ever officially registered as a POW, who was sentenced by a Japanese camp commandant to be placed on the menu but who escaped to have her photograph taken for the exhibition, yet never starred in a remake entitled "The Bitch on the River Kwai". Air Dog Prince No. 6073 is represented by a certificate commemorating his posthumous Silver Medal for Gallantry awarded by the People's Dispensary for Sick Animals, won in Libya in 1964.

The highest award for dumb friends (and some of them have been very dumb, like Wojket the Bear, who followed the Polish Army and was on twenty fags a day, which he preferred to eat, a practice doubtless picked up from his captors) is the Dickin Medal, the "animal's VC", which has gone to thirty-one pigeons, eighteen dogs, three horses and a cat.

The cat's contribution to the war effort escapes me but the pigeons certainly deserved their gongs, to judge by the tiny parachute behind glass, and, dangling from it, the stuffed but still embarrassed pigeon, clearly feeling as uncomfortable as a fish with a snorkel or a giraffe on high heels. This was a WWI wheeze that involved dropping trussed birds into occupied France with a note asking passing peasants to fill in the attached form with details of any troop movements they happened to know about and release at once, *merci beaucoup.*

Jacob the Goose is a hard act to follow. Saved by a sentry from a fox near Quebec in 1838, he repaid the compliment by chasing off a band of marauders too timid to say boo to him. Tirpitz the Pig was another honourable defector, this time from the rapidly submerging *Dresden* (the first example of pigs leaving the sinking ship); he joined up with *Glasgow* and later transferred to the Whale Isle Gunnery School, though not, we hope, as a target.

The exhibition, which was opened by Sefton the Hyde Park horse, a pelican from RAF Central Flying School, and Barbara Woodhouse, should have taught us that we have inflicted quite enough damage on conscripts from the animal kingdom. But the last room of *Animals in War* reminds us that some dolphins and bedbugs are being drafted for military purposes, heaven help us, and indeed heaven help them.

The only consolation for bedbugs is that they are not listed in the latest in a series known as the IUCN Red Data Books, devoted entirely to species with the skids under them. The volume *Invertebrates* (£14, World Wildlife Fund) is a list of creatures involved in a war not with humans but against them. Or rather, the humans are, one way or another, stamping them out. They are all perfectly ghastly, the insects, that is, not the humans.

Take the Dusky-headed Tailless Whip Scorpion (but only with a pair of stout gloves). This creature was once common in the outside lavatories of the state of Florida. Alas, now that the houses there have been poshed up, outside loos are a thing of the past and the scorpion has not evolved a brain capable of getting inside.

Worse, it has also forgotten how it survived in the days before there were dwellings, and outside lavs, in Florida, so it is going into a decline, not to say dying out. Its only consolation is that its fellow Dusky-headed Tailless Whip Scorpions in Mexico are going from strength to strength, so watch yourself when using the smallest, or any other, room South of the Border.

The words "endangered species" summon up something spectacular like the whale or the big cats. No one is going to walk around in a T-shirt proclaiming "Save the Earwig" (except perhaps an earwig) but we should add that garment to our wardrobes, particularly in view of the state of play as regards the world's largest specimen, eight nasty centimetres long. This is found in the Mid-Atlantic island of St Helena. At least, it was found there in 1798 but was lost again until rediscovered in 1965. Since then, a man has been looking for it again but with no joy so far.

The World Wildlife Fund has, you will recall, for its symbol the cuddly panda, hence the Godalming HQ's name, Panda House. It does not refer to its premises as "No-eyed Big-eyed Wolf Spider House"— but that thing too has its problems. The spider in question is blind, leaps on its prey without bothering to spin webs and is suffering from tourists who drop cigarette ends all over its Hawaiian caves. It could join the millions of species that become extinct—some of them so obscure they've never been scientifically catalogued or had a date with David Attenborough.

Scientists are worried about this and so is the Zuiderzee Sea Slug, whose reaction to the Dutch damming programme can be described as both sluggish and damning. We are all sorry about the whole process, none more than the Penitent Mussel of Alabama, which has never been the same since they started messing around with the drainage system.

At first sight, the Pygmy Hog Sucking Louse has a fine time of it, being a parasite for whom the object on which it lays its head is also breakfast, lunch and supper. It is riding high on the hog, you might say, until you learn that the Pygmy Hog itself has survival problems. threatening both the premises and meal-ticket of the louse.

We are all conservationists now, but, even so, few of us lose sleep over the (very) Boring Clam, scandalously over-fished by the Taiwanese, or its relative, the Small Giant Clam, which tends to be recycled as Philippino birdbaths. The Giant Small Clam, if such there be, seems to have kept its shell down when the fishermen sail past.

Sources close to the Scarce Large Blue Butterfly report that it is soon to become the Very Scarce Large Blue Butterfly. If it becomes the Ex-Large Blue Butterfly, it will never be conscripted for military service and hence never featured in exhibitions in the Imperial War Museum. Still, it would never manage to take off with all those Dickin medals clanking round its neck. ✪

albert nobbles the

"Longest trial in legal history."

"My client would like time to pay his bribes!"

RHESUS NEG COURT 7

jury

"I think we can forget the obscenity charge."

"I slipped the foreman two quid and they found me guilty of insulting behaviour."

M. WANG English Chinese meals.

WE HAVE YOUR ALSATIAN

JURY ROOM

"In the Crown v Simpson, Nineteen Sixty-Two, the jury got fifty pounds each."

The KRUM

Comrade Dimitrov:

Last week, shortly after I had completed my report to you, the place was suddenly awash with rumours to the effect that Miss Dora Petkov, our National Women's Singles Champion, would be arriving shortly to compete at Wimbledon. Big Rosa broke the news, her face pale with excitement.

"I have seen the cables," she told me in a tremulous voice. "She is to stay with us, here at the embassy. Oh, Krum, isn't it thrilling? To have a living legend sleeping under this very roof? I actually saw her at Plovdiv last year, in the final of the Konk Canneries Unsweetened Pear Halves Tournament. She won a magnificent victory. What power! What finesse! And yet she behaved with such sweetness and decorum. There was, as I remember, only one disputed call—a smash down the tramlines that raised a cloud of chalk but was in by *miles*. The line judge managed to return to her duties later, after they'd fixed her up with splints and iodine and a few strong pain killers."

Grigoriev put his head around the door and said the Old Man wished to see me at once. He also seemed all of a twitter.

"I think," he said, "you are going to have the honour of meeting her at the airport, you lucky devil."

I went to Excellency Blok's study and found that, alas, the high pollen count had wrought its customary havoc. He was slumped over the desk, Vick inhalers protruding from either nostril like a pair of tiny tusks. His eyes, brightly veined, were watering so profusely that the pupils, when he attempted to focus them on me, looked like a couple of tadpoles swimming around in a jam jar.

"You will have heard about our unexpected guest," he said. "I have been ordered to Heathrow to welcome her in person but, as you see, I am not a well man. You will go in my place. She arrives this evening, on the 6.35 Bulgarflot flight from Sofia."

He sneezed violently, sending his inhalers ricocheting wildly off the desk. One hummed wickedly past my ear, the other struck the chandelier high in the roof and rang it glassily, like a chime of small bells.

"You are to treat Miss Petkov with every courtesy," he added. "There is considerable resentment at home that, while players from other Warsaw Pact countries—your Navratilovas, Mandlikovas and Lendls—are bringing glory to their respective nations, we seem to achieve nothing. But it is felt that this Petkov girl will redress the balance. She is, by all accounts, a potential Wimbledon winner. I mean, her serve travels in excess of 150 kph. And that, of course, is the reason she cannot use Bulgarian tennis balls. When struck with that kind of force they burst and waft gently

> "When I serve I shall toss the ball up to the height of a four-storeyed building. While waiting for it to come down I will distract my opponent by enquiring about her sex life."

down over the net, mangled fragments of gutta-percha, oakum, shoddy and mungo, each painstakingly inflated by the lips of the old buglers of Wonk."

"Quite so," I said.

"Show her plenty of deference, Krum," he said. "She carries the hopes of the nation with her. Also, she knows people in high places. That is why we are preparing the VIP guest room for her." He waved me away. "Off you go now," he said, snuffling miserably into a towel. "It wouldn't do to be late."

In the event, it was she who was late though, watching her flight taxi in, it wasn't hard to see why. Bulgarflot had sent their old Yak biplane with the goggled pilot sitting high up in his open cockpit, white silk scarf flapping in the slipstream. The ancient Merlin was shedding its customary trails of oil across the tarmac as he gunned it for the final time and the big, twin-bladed elm propeller spun to a halt. The cabin door opened and an air hostess in

olive green battle dress sprang out and began chucking suitcases into the attendant lorry.

Miss Petkov marched out of Customs & Immigration an hour later, having spent some time with the sniffer dogs of the Anti-Terrorist Squad. It was evident that she was less than pleased. When I introduced myself she merely grunted and seized a baggage trolley which, in the usual Heathrow way, was stuck fast to a long, stacked line of other trolleys. She gave it a savage tug and they all began to move in unison, swinging sideways like a giant gate and cutting a swathe through the hordes of waiting meeters and greeters. As we headed for the Zim I examined our champion covertly, from the side of my eye.

My first impression was one of size. She was a very big lady, at least one axe-handle across the arse and two from shoulder to shoulder. And even on tip-toe, my eyes only came to the level of the Heroine of Socialist Sport and National Living Treasure medallions glittering on her lapel. Her hair was tinted and boyishly cropped while her hands, their backs darkly hirsute, were bunched into fists and stuck in her pockets, giving the impression that she was carrying a couple of frozen chickens about with her.

In the Zim she relaxed and became confiding. "I have a secret tactic designed to beat Navratilova," she told me as we swung onto the M4 and rattled away towards Willesden. "It was devised for me by our Psychological Warfare Department. The attack is three-pronged. Firstly, when I serve I shall toss the ball up to the height of a four-storeyed building. This should unsettle my opponent. While waiting for it to come down again I will distract her further by chatting a bit, enquiring about her sex life or asking if she likes dogs. The second prong is the classic North Korean stratagem which involves hitting all returns straight at her feet. This upsets her equilibrium and eventually leads to confusion and panic. The third is to place a box of leeches at the foot of the umpire's chair. When they start crawling up his trousers his attention will begin to wander. It is then that you start disputing his decisions. And he, seeking urgent medical attention, will be unlikely to argue."

She sat back, lit a small cigar and beamed at me.

Minutes later we drew up at the embassy. Springing from the car, she seized Excellency Blok's hand and squeezed it warmly. He winced and placed it in his armpit. Once indoors, she took the stairs to her room three at a time. When she appeared for a pre-dinner drink she threw herself down in an armchair, her left foot resting carelessly on her right knee. "Gin, please," she said. She wore a pink ra-ra skirt and a sleeveless bolero. On her forearm was tattooed a pair of screaming eagles and the word "Kill!" She had the kind of calves you see on rickshaw drivers. Lifting her glass she blew Big Rosa a kiss and emptied it with a single swallow.

"My, my, that hit the spot!" she exclaimed, handing it back for more.

Excellency Blok leant across to me, looking deeply troubled. "Her voice is basso profundo," he murmured. "And what is that smell?"

"Brut," I said.

"Ah. And whenever she rubs her skin there is a harsh scratching sound."

"Yes," I said.

He nodded and beckoned me closer. "I think, Krum," he said, "*that she is a man*."

I stared at him, stunned. That had simply not occurred to me. Later, after she had consumed an entire saddle of ewe at dinner, I shared our suspicions with Stambouliski, who promised to take a look at her in the shower. But she caught him peeping while stripped only to her camibockers and fetched him a blow to the throat that had him bedridden for days. As for her performance at Wimbledon, well, you know about that already. She too fell victim to the pollen count and, with swollen, streaming eyes, went down in straight sets to a pretty little Aussie blonde on some obscure outside court.

I place these facts before you, comrade, simply in the interests of sport and our country's good reputation. They are suspicions, nothing more. Make of them what you will. I can only add that, after the match, she took her opponent out to dinner and returned, staggering, at three in the morning with love bites all over her neck.

Fraternal salutations,

Simeon Krum
Fifth Secretary

"*OK, while you're on your knees, let's try a few simple exercises to tone up those flabby tummy muscles.*"

"*Well, here we are with our personal computer, ready for any twists and turns the conversation may take.*"

THEATRE: HEWISON

MASTER CLASS DAVID BAMBER *as Shostakovich* PETER KELLY *as Prokofiev*
JONATHAN ADAMS *as Marshal Zhdanov* TIMOTHY WEST *as Stalin*

A STREETCAR NAMED DESIRE SHEILA GISH *as Blanche Du Bois* PAUL HERZBERG *as Stanley Kowalski*

STARLIGHT EXPRESS   JEFF SHANKLEY *as Greaseball*   FRANCES RUFFELLE *as Dinah*
RAY SHELL *as Rusty*   GARY LOVE *as Dustin*

DANCIN'   Some of the troupe

SCHWADRON

"I like you, Griswold. You never waste time with long explanations when a simple 'yes' would do."

"You thought I lacked the guts to do this, didn't you? Well, *you're fired, Brewster!*"

"And I got this one for not being afraid to have a good cry once in a while."

"Step aside, please! AIDS victim coming through!"

"Look at the bright side, Mr Dow. You're damned for an eternity, but eligible for parole in an aeon."

"I was a former zillionaire until I was convicted of trifling with decimal points."

Mike MOLLOY

MY HITLER YOUTH

"Any Communists here?" he shouted. "You two, go and get a band."

AS it is the fiftieth anniversary of his coming to power, the government of West Germany is spending millions of Deutschmarks explaining to the younger generation the adventures of Adolf Hitler. They should have come to me.

I only have to hear somebody humming the *Horst Wessel* and my mind starts to throw up information about him with the precision of a digital watch.

It isn't that I *want* to remember the grisly old bastard, it's just that I took in the facts at an impressionable age and now they're tucked up there along with the verb *avoir*, six verses of Gray's *Elegy* and the plot of *Casablanca*.

A woman in Swansea got me started on Adolf. She wrote to the *Sunday Pictorial* claiming that her husband bore a remarkable likeness to the Führer, and enclosed a snapshot as proof. Now as any reader of newspapers will know, there is nothing that quickens the blood of a letters-page editor faster than the claim that a certain person is a dead ringer for somebody else:
Sir, has any other of your correspondents noticed the remarkable resemblance that Kenny Everett bears to Benjamin Disraeli?

Bung in two photographs, and another page is ready for press. Our man was no exception. "Perfect lead letter," he said and sent me to the library to find a picture of Adolf that exactly matched the face from Swansea.

Supercharged with enthusiasm, I set about the task with a fanatical thoroughness that would have earned the approval of Albert Speer.

The reason for my devotion to duty was common to those who are called to newspapers at an early age. I had the bug. Every time I entered the building, the smell of newsprint got so far up my nostrils it made my eyes water like an attack of hay fever, and if I didn't actually have printer's ink in my veins, quite a lot of it was daubed over my clothing. Had I been captured by accountants and grilled over a fire of blazing ledgers, I would have kept the faith as vehemently as a Tudor Christian. An exact picture of Hitler was wanted—I would not fail.

At two-thirty the following morning, I stumbled away from the picture library, my ink-stained clothing now impregnated with the dust of a thousand files, and caught the all-night bus home. As it ploughed its way westward with its strange cargo of night people, images of the last seven hours played in front of my mind's eye onto the darkness of Holland Park.

Hitler as a political agitator, statesman,

soldier, lover, adored leader, conqueror, madman. Hitler on holiday, having tea, destroying nations, decorating children, adorning postage stamps. Photographs of him with Hindenburg, Edward VIII, Göring, Goebbels, Röhm, Himmler, Eva Braun. Thousands of faces floated past Notting Hill Gate. None, however, resembled the man from Swansea.

But I was not defeated. Tomorrow I

would try the agencies: Camera Press, UPI, Fox Photos, PA, Hulton's Picture Library, the Imperial War Museum. Somewhere in London, nestling in a filing cabinet, was the photograph I needed.

It was going to be a busy day. I had already arranged to take Pauline, a girl of stunning beauty and deep political convictions, to the Anarchists' Ball at Fulham Town Hall. It was a last-ditch attempt to impress her with my own political savoir-faire. So I had a seven o'clock deadline on the problem of Adolf if I was to get to Fulham Town Hall in time for the first jive of the evening.

At six-forty-five the following day, I trudged towards the offices of Fox Photos in Farringdon Road with all the jauntiness the Wehrmacht showed on its return trip from Russia. A full day of failure lay behind me. As I drew near I pulled the copy of the Swansea snapshot from my pocket and gazed upon the features once more. They had now taken on the elusive, enigmatic qualities of the Mona Lisa. I began to think I could detect a faint hint of mockery in the staring eyes.

Waiting for me at Fox Photos was an unsealed manilla envelope of portraits but I was too dispirited to look inside. Instead, I stuffed the envelope into my pocket and made for the District Line. The only thing that could bring balm to my battered spirits would be the love of Pauline. What better opportunity could I possibly want to win back her waning affections than a political jazz dance?

A damp night-haze bathed Fulham Town Hall in a pearly light and there, by the steps, she waited for me. As I approached her, my stomach began its customary rumba. Despite a tendency to trivialise our more intimate conversations with chatter about the class struggle, her mere presence could transform the mundane to the romantic. I suppose it was the drizzle on the street but to me Fulham Broadway looked like Venice. Taking her gently in my arms, I kissed her proud lips. It was like embracing a barbed-wire fence.

We entered the Town Hall with a straggling crowd and hung our coats in the unattended cloakroom. Following the mob, we found ourselves in a hall where absolutely nothing was happening. After a few minutes some kind of commotion began at the far end of the room and we could hear raised voices. Pauline set out to find the source of the disturbance and I followed. Pushing through a fringe of spectators, we discovered a dark, powerful youth who seemed to radiate energy shouting at a ▶

defeated-looking figure who was tugging nervously at a long beard.

"It's always the same with you bloody anarchists," shouted the dark youth. "Where's the frigging band?"

The bearded one shrugged his shoulders sadly: "We thought one would sort of emerge," he said.

The dark one clapped his hand to his forehead so hard it sounded like a car door slamming.

"Any Communists here?" he shouted and several hands shot up, including Pauline's. "You two," he ordered at random, "go and get a band. The rest of you," he said addressing the rest of us in the hall, "go to a pub for 45 minutes."

We did as we were told and sure enough, on our return, the bandstand was occupied with a fully-equipped Traditional Jazz band. Pauline and I jived the rest of the night away but I did notice that she managed to dance in a particularly provocative manner whenever we whirled near the dark revolutionary.

Eventually the last notes of *The Red Flag* echoed through the Town Hall and the crowd drifted towards the cloakroom and a problem; a couple of hundred people with no tickets and no cloakroom attendants crowded the corridor trying to recover their coats.

The mob started to get angry but salvation was at hand. "Pass me over your heads," shouted a now familiar voice, and the Trotsky of West London was lifted over the crowd and deposited on the cloak-room counter.

"Any Communists?" he called again and this time Pauline bored through the pack like a conga line on New Year's Eve. She joined him at the counter where together they threw coats to the waiting owners.

As they struggled together, bringing hope and order to a failed political system, they exchanged glances of triumph and mutual admiration like workers in an Eisenstein epic, and I knew that Pauline had forsaken me. When it came to my duffel-coat, the dark victor hurled it in the direction of my upraised arm and the manilla envelope parted from the pocket. Portraits of Adolf scattered on to the floor and I did not even have to bend down to see how little they resembled the Welsh Führer. I just walked away and left them to be trampled underfoot by the dispersing crowd.

The next morning I presented myself, sore of heart and low in spirits, to the Letters Page editor and confessed my failure.

"Show me what you've got," he demanded briskly.

Miserably I produced a selection of Hitler portraits. He studied them for a few moments, then spoke: "Tell you what," he said brightly, "get the retouchers to make Hitler look more like this Welsh berk."

It was a lot to take on in 24 hours. Disillusion with a goddess and the first crack appearing in my unquestioning faith in Fleet Street. But I managed.

*"You say you've gone and made **what** in your image?"*

"Incidentally, passing the buck is your responsibility."

"We don't know what it is but it eats table scraps and bums."

DER FLIEGENDE PICKETER

ARTUR, ein Surface Arbeiter ...*Baritone*
MARGARETHA, die Führerin.....*Soprano*
ALTER BILL, Polizeikommissar ....*Tenor*
HERRN. McGREGOR VON STEEL,
der Meister ....*Bass*
GRAF ALASTAIR BURNET, Nachrichten
Am Zehn ....*Tenor*
ZWEITAUSEND KOHLARBEITER (das
Hoi Polloi)
EIN DUMMKOPF IN DER STRASSE
DER BRITISCHE VOLK

ZEIT: Die Dunkel Ages
LOKATION—Die Mittelländische
Kohlfelden von Derby, Nottingham und
Nord Staffs (*Mit Streikposten besetzen*)
und das Dartford Unterpass
(Einbahnstrasse)

AKT 1

ZWEITAUSEND KOHLARBEITER:
"Ho-jo-he! Ho-jo-he!
Wir sind Hundert Prozent!
Ho-jo-he! Ho-jo-he!
Der Sieg wird unser sein!
Thatcher aus! Thatcher aus!
Kein pits geschlossen!"

ALTER BILL:
"Stone uns!
Hier gehen wir noch einmal!"

ARTUR:
"Schweine! Schweine! Polizei skum!
Immer, immer das NUM!
Ich bin krank als ein Papagei!
Hier haben wir Sud-Afrikaanische Typ
Gestapo Taktiks!

Or I'm a Dutchman

A Wagnerian Nasty in Three Acts

(UNFINISHED)

Unser Lads wird nimmer unter ein
Toryische Jackboot sein!"

GRAF ALASTAIR BURNET:
(BONG!)
"Guten Abend
(BONG)
"Das Kohlkrisis—Mehr blütische
Konflikt
(BONG)
"Herrn Artur sagt 'Up seine!'
(BONG)
"Der Alter Bill antwortet 'Das Recht ist
Das Recht. Wir nur tun unser Job'
(BONG)
"Und ein Komment von Zehn
Downingstrasse: 'O Weh!' "

DER BRITISCHE VOLK:
"Gott give us Kraft!
Was ist auf Kanal Vier?"

GRAF ALASTAIR BURNET:
"Mehr uglische Szene auf den
Picketlinie heute. But wir haben keine
dramatische Aktion-Bilde. Unser
Kameramann war auf den Kopf gebifft.

*(Ein Krankenwagen: hee-haw, hee-
haw!)*
"Und nun, dramatische Aktion-Bilde
von last Woche."
(Ein uglische Skuffel.)

HERRN. McGREGOR VON STEEL:
"Ouf!"

EIN DUMMKOPF IN DER STRASSE:
"Hat er gefallen?
Oder hat man ihn gepusht?"

ARTUR:
"Kein Way meine Lads sind
hooliganischen Kraft-Arm Bully-Junge!
Das ist alles Media Rubbisch.
Das recht-wing BBC und ITN, Die
Sonne, Der *Post am Sonntag*, Der
Tägliche Telegraf, Der *Spiegel*, sie haben
es in für mich.
Es ist ein Plott gegen der arbeitende
Mann.
Schweine!
Faschisten!

Tory Henchmänner!
(usw)"

ALTER BILL:
"Wir sagen, genug ist genug.
Der Yorkische Fliegende Picketer, zB,
must nicht mit Autobus nach Kent
fahren.
Wir haben Polizeipanzerwagen im
Dartford Unterpass.
Wir haben, wenn need be, zehntausend,
hunderttausend, eine Million Koppers!"

DER BRITISCHE VOLK:
"Und Christ Allmächtig!
Das kostet eine Million per diem!"

ZWEITAUSEND KOHLARBEITER:
"Ho-jo-je!
Ho-jo-he!
Es ist only Geld!
Der grosse Britische Publik ist Hundert
Prozent hinten die Kohlarbeiter auf
dieses!"

DER BRITISCHE VOLK:
"According zum *TV Zeiten*,
Es ist Torvill and Dean in fünf
Minuten."

MARGARETHA:
"Wunderbar!
Sie wissen, Sie sind so wunderbar!
So absolutely wunderbar!"

*Donner und Blitzen. Gross Britannien ist
doomed to Nacht after Nacht of dies bis
nach das Ende von Zeit.*

REMEMBERED TO TELL THE VATMAN YOU'RE AWAY?

Every quarter, thousands of sole proprietors or other duly authorised signatories return home from holiday to find their self-employed person's premises a shambles. It's a sickening feeling when it happens to *your* business—output files ripped open, your schedule of inputs in tatters, previous month's under-declarations strewn about all over the place.

According to one weary Customs & Excise operative: "They just never learn. They just go off without so much as a mention as to whether they may be importing bonded steam hoists, partially-coated floorcoverings, tinned peach halves or zero-rated marzipan men—you name it. It is the duty of our personnel to make periodic what we term swoops and of course if we have reason to suppose that the registree is off out of it we must effect an immediate forced audit."

Remember—unless you make the proper return to Southend-on-Sea WD40 EMC2, the heartache of months on end of readjustments *CAN* happen to you. Ask a neighbour to keep an eye open for tell-tale buff envelopes which can give up to 24 hours notice of inspection, otherwise when the worst happens they may just assume you've got burglars and not want to get involved.

HOW TO LEAVE WOMEN
LORD CRICKLEWOOD, as told to Henry Kelly

In this hot weather, women tend to go off. This is a well-known fact.

As a happily married man, I have had various assorted women over the years, and have always looked after them. Being something of a traditionalist, I keep them in a bijou residence in St John's Wood, nothing fancy, but a nice bathroom and a lot of drapes everywhere. When I say *them*, I mean one at a time, that needs to be made clear.

Most of the time, they do not need a lot of attention: I see to them once a week, all right, four times a week, and they have a small personal account at Waitrose and the Golden Dragon Elite Take-away, also I get their teeth done in Wimpole Street, I do not like to come home to a mouthful of date-stones, that does not seem too much to ask.

Holidays, however, are a problem. I like to take a family holiday for four weeks with the wife and children, and I have found it essential to make sure, over the years, that my women do not go off while I am gone. Here are a few tips I have been invited to pass on:

1) Get someone in to see to them. In my own case, Errol from the Wood Karwash comes in and does it for nothing, but that may be because my women give no trouble. If you have a difficult one, or something a bit horrible, you may have to pay a small service charge.
2) Turn off all joint bank accounts at the mains.
3) Leave the keys with the police, and tell them to keep an eye on the place. If they do, my experience is you can forget about 1).
4) *Never* chain them up! This can make them very excited. I once made this mistake, and Errol was off work for three days with his back.

CALLING ALL CATS!

Two very special Reader Offers coming up from *Behind*

For the younger or more sensitive cat, unused to unsavoury whale or treadmill exercise, a fortnight in a cattery can prove an unsettling experience. Often it can lead to some subsequent loss of confidence, characterised by foaming shrieks or a yearning for the feral life in sewers or an abattoir's boiler room.

But now the conscience-stricken cat-owner can rest easy whilst on holiday thanks to two amazing spin-off products of space-age technology.

Fashioned from finest hand-galvanised tin, the Portakat convertible scuttle is easily fixed to willing pensioners and leaves sometimes arthritic hands free to attend to such everyday chores as changing litter or opening fiddly tubes of worming tablets. At only £19.99 plus VAT, you'll wonder how you ever went away without one.

And new from Buxton's Plump Grade A Foster Hens, specially-trained brooders can be bought direct from the free-range Hendon Cattycare Centre (batteries NOT included) or hired by the fortnight on a leaseback scheme which includes all the eggs your gerbil can eat. Limited numbers of foster geese are also available for use in inner-city crime blackspots. Cats love the change of being looked after by another silly old hen—and at £29.99 for 7 days (plus breakages) this is an offer no caring cat-owner can afford to miss.

TORTOISES AND THE LAW

In law, the tortoise need not be licensed and is treated as a domiciled insect. With no statutory entitlement to tenancy, and in the absence of any clear EEC ruling on tortoises' common rights, these often shy and forebearing creatures are therefore vulnerable, as are certain locomotive snails and most sponges, to being carelessly abandoned to "fend for themselves" whilst their heartless owners cavort on holiday.

It is this "loophole" which encourages unscrupulous catteries to discriminate unfairly against the domesticated tortoise and the lame excuse of "We'd like to help you out but the last vacancy has just been filled by a skunk" is all too common in this uncaring day and age.

Local councils' obligations towards the welfare of tortoises are, alas, confused. As a result of recent spending cuts, many authorities have dispensed altogether with social work amongst tortoises. In a recent test case, Nat the Tortoise *vs* Hillingborough and Weaseldon UDC, Their Lordships ruled that the prosecution's allegations of wanton neglect towards Nat—deprived for fourteen nights of close human contact or even so much as a lettuce leaf—could not be upheld in the light of reports. Public Health Officials had maintained that there was little hard evidence that Nat, who was at the time dormant under a hedge-

row *not adopted by the local council*, had noticed to any appreciable extent that his owners were not about. Neighbours moreover testified that the plaintiff had never so far as they knew touched lettuce during the months March to October inclusive, when it caused him to perspire.

Health and Safety at Work Regulations do not, as a rule, apply to itinerant tortoises, though as a matter of common sense they should be lacquered before being left exposed to wet weather and, in the event of any risk of thunderstorms, *must* be properly earthed.

DISGUISE THAT SKIP! advises Sir ROBERT MARK

Some famous writer, I forget exactly who, once said: "You leave a skip outside your premises for half an hour, and suddenly it is full of old lavvies."

That is as true today as it has ever been. Just where all these broken khazis come from has baffled New Scotland Yard since records began. Do people, I used to ask myself after I became Commissioner, have old bog-pans hanging around their house, waiting for a skip to appear so's they can all come out at night and run through the streets to dump them?

Who can say, but I remember once, the Serious Crimes Squad did one of their lightning raids on South London containers, and in one skip alone they found the dismembered remains of fourteen low-flush suites, together with sundry pipework and ballcocks etc. According to one Chief Superintendent, "It

was like an Aladdin's Cave in there!"

The only answer, if you are leaving a skip outside to go on holiday (you, not the skip), is to disguise it. Many Crime Prevention Officers advise painting wheels on it, luring Chummy, as we call him, into attempting to drive it away; usually, after a few goes at starting it with jump-leads, they will pack it in. Not bad, but personally I would paint big teeth on it, and affix some kind of hairy tail: most villains will think twice, especially at night, about throwing old lavatories into a big dog.

It is just not worth the risk.

I am convinced this could be a major contribution to holiday happiness!

YOU WRITE . . .

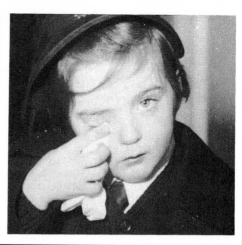

Dear Behind,

Last holidays, Our Rene, 9, comes home and says the school had fixed her up with ten days off our hands on an exchange in Cologne. Naturally, we were over the moon as French is her best subject, plus she likes to smell nice and could do worse these days than grow up to be a Hello girl.

Anyhow, no sooner had we seen Rene off from King's Cross, when my husband turns to me and says as we come up the drive, "Hullo! got a squatter, have we?"

Well, as it turned out, it was only this little mite about the size of Our Rene, only not quite twenty shillings to the pound, and all she can say is Vo Bin Ick. Our neighbours reckon she's one of them Vietnamese off a boat, but we live quite a way from the sea. Can any of your readers advise us whether this little find might be valuable? We have had no ransom demands to date.

Yours,

E. Bagnold (Ms)

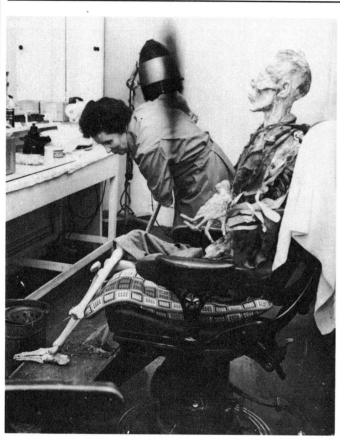

Dear Behind,

I am a ladies' hairdresser. Last July, I got eight cheese labels in the correct order off of a thing they had in Tesco and won a Glorious Holiday For Two In Sunsoaked Chad. I was so excited, I just run off, leaving Mrs E. R. Werbs waiting for her comb-out. When I come back a fortnight later, well! I enclose a snap. I am the one sweeping up fallen teeth. I just thought I'd mention it.

Hannah Rees-Mogg,
Willesden.

Dear Behind:

As we put our Dobermann in kennels when we go off, I always like to leave something on the lawn to frighten off burglars. I take pleasure in enclosing a snap of my wife Deirdre putting the finishing touches to this year's Plasticine number.

Yours truly,
R. E. Bonte

KROOKSTRIP No.13

HOW TO DEFLECT THE BURGLAR AWAY FROM YOUR MOST PRIZED POSSESSIONS

These stick-on 'doors' disguise your favourite Stradivari cello as a fun cocktail cabinet....

Blue-tack your Meissen figurine to a 'Tatcade' porcelain base

A Present from BLACKPOOL

Worried about your Modigliani? Convert it into a temporary pop-poster with 'Washoff' graffito inks

STICK-ON HOLES FOR YOUR MESHED BOKHARA RUG

QUIK SAFEGUARD Display a letter from a leading London auctioneer confirming that all your art objects are genuine......

GREEN PEACE

For millions of us hortiphiles, going on our "annual holiday" can be a nightmare!

Be we in Benidorm or Rhyl, when we wake up to our "morning cuppa", however lovely, our first thought is usually for our little green friends who we last saw staring out of the window as we drove off. For us it was "getting away from it all", but for them it was the beginning of misery and not knowing if the rat-faced old cow next door would remember to come in with their daily drinkies. Especially with this "hot spell" we have all been having; millions of us will come home from holiday to find our little friends all brown and dead.

How, millions of you ask me, can we avoid this from happening? Well, a good way is to put all your house-plantpersons on the floor and leave a tap running. This way, they will not only stay fed, they will be happy, bobbing about and floating to different places "around the home". Another way is to take them on holiday with you: the AA-Readers Digest Book of Really Desperate Boarding Houses (£7 to members taking advantage of Double-Glaze-Your-Caravan's-Cedarwood-Extension Offers) gives a handy checklist of seaside landladies that put pot plants first, but make sure they are all in by 9 pm. If any of your plants wishes to have a "a real night out", a notification in writing usually suffices.

One "note of caution": avoid vegetarian establishments! A close friend of mine took all his succulents to Lyme Regis, only to find that they had become vichyssoise while he was out enquiring about Krazy Golf facilities.

SHOPPING AROUND
with
TINA CANTUAR

Leaving elderly relatives is a problem for many of us, but now Gericare Ltd have come up with a super answer! Their GRANNIBOX is escape-proof, fits easily into cellar or loft, and can be hosed out in seconds. A snip at only £89.95, to include burrow-resistant steel base and saline drip, and remember: if the inmate is a registered invalid, there is no VAT!

STOP PRESS!

New from Nattitat! The answer for all those of you who are afraid to go on holiday leaving foreign au pairs behind to look after the house—dreading that while you're gone, she and her appalling friends will use the time to throw orgies and desecrate your furnishings. *Fret no longer!* Nattitat's new range of revolutionary wallpapers mean you can take a pre-emptive strike by redecorating *before* you go, leaving the staff nothing to do but jam the waste-disposal and burn down the gazebo. Comes in Spanish, Portuguese, German, Norse, and Erse, at only £7.99 per roll (please state whether Left- or Right-wing when ordering).

SHOW me a man's garden and I will call him knave or neighbour. I am unsure whether Dr Johnson ever did say that, but if not it was surely just an oversight, for the dazzling truth of the aphorism has been apparent to sages for centuries.

Most cultures have a similar proverb. Years ago, in an attempt to solve the Rhodesian problem (as it then was), the Commonwealth Secretary, Arthur Bottomley, visited the territory and sought to ingratiate himself with the natives by quoting their impenetrable folk sayings back at them.

I remember vividly standing in the shade of a flowering tree and hearing him declaim, to a solemn but well-dressed group of local chieftains: "A man's heart is a granary." For years that worried me, for if you think about it, it makes no sense.

It was only when I started gardening in earnest that I realised the Government linguists had been guilty of mistranslation. Shona is a poor language and the words for all parts of the body are similar, while "granary" and "garden" are interchangeable. What the original mystic meant was: "A man's garden is his face."

You can tell more about people from their horticultural practices than anything else. Someone who insists on double-digging the vegetable plot year after year will be meticulous in all things. Conversely, I wonder how many people who have greenfly also have herpes? Both stem from a blithe disregard for hygienic practices. It is no coincidence that, in romantic dramas from the Restoration onwards, the prudent heroine generally insists on taking a turn in the garden before finally succumbing to the hero's seduction.

Thus, after years of horticulture on both sides of the Atlantic, an essential truth about the difference between the British and Americans has been brought home to me: we love dispensing advice, while Americans prefer to receive it. And that's why, come summer, I take to wondering what the gardeners of Roosevelt Island are doing without me.

People who have been to New York may know Roosevelt Island as that place in the middle of the East River reached by a red cable car that runs from near Bloomingdale's. What they may not be aware of is that it is one of the few parts of that frenetic city that boasts allotments—tiny ones, but allotments none the less.

I lived there for four years until 1981 and rose to be vice-president of the Garden Club—one of the highest elective offices to which a non-citizen can aspire. I earned the accolade largely because of my disinterested prodigality in offering advice.

Americans are addicted to advice of every kind—hence the proliferation of how-to books and analysis. I soon discovered that tendering advice on gardening was as foolproof as telling people how to bring up children or improve their sex lives, in that there is no absolute standard by which it can be judged.

For instance, when people asked me how to grow peas I would tell them solemnly to pop the seed in the ground and wait for it to come up. There may be better ways—pouring paraffin over the ground first or facing east and offering a sacrifice to Buddha—but since the victim would only be doing it my way, he or she (usually she, as it happened) would never know any better. And such is the vulnerability of tender produce in the inhospitable New York environment that failure could be put down to any number of hazards unconnected with my recommendations.

Yet even if worthless in practice, my advice was a necessary psychological prop for many of my neighbours who had taken up gardening mainly because it seemed benign, ecological and conducive to inner peace. It was less tiring than jogging and cheaper than analysis. So what will they do without me?

> ## "At this fecund time of year, the urge to give advice overwhelms people without warning."

A few didn't need my advice. There was a network of Korean families who grew nothing but Chinese cabbage, clearly for commercial purposes. (The Koreans control much of New York's retail grocery trade.) For the rest of us, it was mainly tomatoes. New York's hot and muggy summers are ideal for growing tomatoes but for very little else.

By August, the allotments would be a mass of scarlet, and early fears of pilfering by salad-loving muggers were changed into fervent wishes that someone, anyone, would come and take the stuff away before it rotted on the plants. Even the ravenous rats, rising from the East River, were welcome visitors.

Aware of my responsibilities I tried, like some intrepid horticultural pioneer, to extend the range of things grown in Manhattan, introducing rare British delicacies like runner beans and Brussels sprouts. But such enterprise was lost on the keen and impressionable young plantswomen who would come and inspect my plot. "Are they some new kind of tomato?" they would inquire.

"Come to my place," they would then suggest invitingly. I would follow them to their allotments where they foraged in the earth to find some unfamiliar grub they were convinced was gnawing away at their produce.

"What are they?" the women demanded. I hadn't the first idea—perhaps some earthbound cockroach, the most prolific form of wild life in New York after the tomato. But they wanted advice, any advice, so I improvised.

"Could be the Zimbabwe root fly," I would say, trying an imitation of Percy Thrower. "They come in the holds of banana boats. Spray them with betel juice." They would pad away to spread the word to their friends, huddled together and throwing the occasional glance of awe (I think that's what it was) in my direction.

Back in London the roles are reversed. I am the one who seeks advice, tendered with relish by neighbouring toilers on my London allotment and by readers of the *Daily Express*, where I write a weekly column on my gardening adventures. Whenever I admit to some dreadful natural disaster or to simple ignorance, they put down their hoes and pick up their biros to tell me how it should be done.

Who would have thought there were so many ways of making parsley germinate (sow it on the shortest day, pour boiling water over the seed) or of deterring moles (bury holly so they will prick their noses, or simply club them with a spade)? And even if there are perfectly good proprietary chemicals for dealing with carrot curl or potato pox, *Express* gardeners prefer folk remedies, like blowing tobacco smoke over them (Woodbines work best) or spraying with a mixture of washing-up liquid and Jeyes fluid.

At this fecund time of year, the urge to give advice overwhelms people without warning. The other evening I was interviewing a languid society hostess about something completely different, when we fell into talking about the demise of my cucumbers. She quickly perked up and diagnosed mosaic disease, which I had thought to be that crick in the neck you get from looking at too many Roman pavements.

On the whole, I prefer being the recipient of advice to the responsibility of offering it, even if I do sometimes miss the trappings of the office of vice-president—those earnest discussions with concerned young women as to who was last seen with the key to the toolshed, or whose turn it was to switch off the water hydrant the night before the flood.

I wonder who they're turning to now? No doubt someone with greener fingers but, I like to think, less intimacy with the insect life—and the native proverbs—of Central Africa. ✪

In the Can

"The glass companies fought a rearguard action, claiming that the cans had uncounted bugs in them."

"SORRY! We're *open*," was the engaging notice in the window of a junkshop in Pasadena, California, where I have been staying. When I got inside, I found the apologies were in order. It was evident from the stock that Americans will collect almost anything short of pre-masticated chewing-gum.

Apart from their partiality for strands of barbed wire and "cowboy collectibles", they also go for plaster table-lamps in the shape of Red Indians; 1950s wireless sets concealed by the visor of Galahad helmets; and copies of *Playboy* with the best pin-ups ripped out. And beer cans.

The existence of a beer can cult has been revealed to me by a memorable book, *The Beer Can*, edited by Larry Wright and published at $3.95 by the Cornerstone Press, New York.

It begins, with due portentousness: "The beer can, emblematic of today's throwaway culture, has been with us just over 40 short, though tumultuous years, but it has a family tree stretching back almost 8,000 years." Well, you can skip most of the first 8,000 years. ("Brewing itself was one of the first arts known to man, beginning prior to Old Testament times.") Beer first reached America in 1584. The first "canning" process was perfected in France in the nineteenth century, using specially strengthened glass bottles sealed by heat pressure. The Englishman Peter Durand improved on the French model with cylindrical canisters of tinplate: in 1810 George III granted him a patent for the world's first can. And in 1825 Thomas Kensett and Ezra Daggett obtained the first American patent for preserving foods in "vessels of tin". Use of cans was widespread by the Civil War.

The beer can came later than the food can, because canning beer required greater pressure per square inch, and because beer reacts strongly with metal, creating salts which give the brew a nasty taste. As the book says, "If canned beer tasted more like the can than beer, it wouldn't sell well in Peoria." Plastics were the answer, with the American Can Company's "Vinylite" leading the way. Even so, "the beer can faced a long uphill battle to gain public acceptance ... bottled beer wasn't about to step down from its throne," as the authors record, mixing their metaphors like Molotov cocktails. Naturally the glass companies wanted to protect their market; and the brewers had millions invested in bottling equipment. But the can was smaller and lighter than the bottle, it cost less to ship, was easier to stack, and could be junked after use—creating a "rarity factor" for future collectors. The glass companies fought a rear-

guard action, claiming that the cans, which you couldn't see through, had uncounted bugs in them. (To refute this, one brewmaster scraped the linings from three cans and consumed them—with no ill effects.) But the can was finally accepted, especially after the Second World War, when GIs became used to drinking from the cans shipped to them.

The world's first beer can, of Krueger Cream Ale, was marketed on January 24, 1935, by the American Can Company and the Gottfried Krueger Brewing Company of New Jersey. The can was a "flat-top"—the universal shape today; but many of its immediate successors were "cone-tops", in imitation of glass bottles. By the end of 1935, 23 brewers had jumped on the canned wagon.

The cone-top fell into disfavour in the 1950s. In 1962 Alcoa and the Pittsburgh Brewing Company introduced a can that needed no opener. The lift tab—a small

piece of metal that the consumer ripped in a zipper-like fashion to open the can—was developed by Ermal C. Fraze, owner of the Dayton Reliable Tool Company of Dayton, Ohio. Some consumers slashed a finger or knuckle trying to prise open stubborn tab tops; but "The consumer apparently was perfectly delighted to cut his finger on a six-pack and come back for more," said Donald V. Earnshaw of Continental Can. The safer U-tab followed and the "ring pull"—another Fraze invention—was introduced in 1965. It was later given "dimples" to make it easier to lift.

To be an expert on the niceties of beer-can collecting, now a craze in the United States, you have to guzzle down information like this from the Larry Wright book:

Crown Cork & Seal Co. produced both flat and spout top cans, but it is most

noted for both its unusual spout top (introduced in the early 1940s) and perhaps the widest variety of cans produced in the U.S. The squat "Crowntainer" was of three-piece construction: a seamless side, a bottom and a cap. It has no welded seams or tops like the Continental, American, and National cans.

The Beer Can Collectors of America (BCCA) society was born in 1970 when six men in the St Louis area, after reading an article about Mr Denver Wright's hobby in the *St Louis Globe-Democrat*, began meeting to talk beer cans and view each other's collections. It now has thousands of members, ranked according to the number of cans in their collections from "Brewery Worker" (100–249 cans) to "Grand Brewmaster" (1,000 or more cans) and divided into "chapters" with names such as "Olde Frothingslosh" and "Mile Hi". They hold "canventions" for making swaps. (The society is totally against *selling* cans.) Their registered logo is a hand reaching for a can.

The members include rabid collectors like mortician Armin "Shorty" Hotz who, when told that the club boasted another funeral director, quipped, "I'd like to get together with him sometime and share a cold one!" Or Lefty Lorenz, an Iowa State Trooper in a boy scout hat who drives round town with a row of beer cans each side of his pickup truck and a sign claiming "Beer Cans are Beautiful". One of the youngest members is Pam Woodman of Olmsted, Ohio, who was only 14 when the book appeared. ("Pam reports she often gets the 'evil eye' from grocery clerks because the first place she heads to when she enters a grocery store is the beer counter.") There have even been some romances among the cans. Bud Hack of Hartford, Connecticut, and his lovely wife Suzanne first "realised that they had more going for them than just beer cans" at the second Canvention at Lake Geneva, Wisconsin.

Perhaps the most besotted of all the beer can collectors is Clyde L. Hooker of Bimidji, Minnesota, who admits a time came when "I was neglecting my loved ones ... my wife was playing second fiddle to a beer can." But I'm not sure he is really repentant. He and his son are still raking through the rubbish dumps of America, braving the rats and snakes that live in them, in quest of venerable cone-tops.

Only once has Clyde Hooker felt a trace of embarrassment. "I had started digging through the second garbage can when a little old lady came up to me and asked me how long it had been since I last ate. 'Oh, back up the road about thirty miles,' I answered." 🍺

That's all ffolkes

*"**That's** our whale. Why be a hero for a little blubber?"*

"But this is where we landed **last** time."

"It's called Babylon and I think it has a great future. Sell the camel."

Christopher
MATTHEW
PROPERTY

Home Truths

ANYONE madly keen on finding the perfect country retreat could, on glancing through the agent's particulars, be forgiven for supposing that for once Fate had permitted itself the luxury of a faint smile and presented him with a truly unique opportunity to acquire the country cottage of his dreams.

"A charming period house ... lovely moated site set in about 3 acres ... hall, dining-room, breakfast room, sitting-room, 5 bedrooms ... adjoining cottage ... living-room, 2 bedrooms ... domestic outbuildings ... mature gardens ... grounds and paddocks ... believed to date from the 16th or 17th century ... potentially a most attractive farmhouse, it retains much of its original character and charm ... offers great scope in providing a spacious country property ..."

And all this in the heart of rural Suffolk, only a few miles from Ipswich and the A45.

All right, so it's in need of "restoration and modernisation", but then what period property isn't? And okay, so it may need a spot of re-wiring and the roof may need a new tile or two, but there's nothing that can't be improved out of all recognition with a lick of paint, a slap of plaster and a few night storage heaters. And actually, to judge from the colour photograph, it looks in pretty good nick anyway. The land alone must be worth the £49,500 asking price. In fact, it sounds too good to be true.

And, of course, any disinterested observer with the slightest experience of these things knows in his water that it is. But the frustrated town-dweller with his over-developed sense of the romantic is not easily put off in his search for his real roots. And so, with his mind teeming with half-resolved sums and his wife's with images of exposed beams and Laura Ashley prints, he sets off on the long trek up the M11.

His first reaction as he draws up on the grass verge outside the house is that all that expenditure of petrol and nervous energy has been for nothing. As his eye rapidly takes in the disintegrating roof, the nasty cracks in the unexpectedly shabby outside walls, the rotten-looking woodwork, the overgrown garden, his sums begin to look as silly as the expression on his wife's face. And even before he has set foot inside the dank, crumbling gloom of the ... what? hall? kitchen? dining-room? who knows?

... he is telling himself that once again he has drawn the short straw.

But then, the more he looks at the place, the more he begins to wonder whether perhaps, despite the peeling walls and the uneven floors and the holes in the roof and the dust and the dirt and damp, it really is quite as hopeless as he at first supposed. Provided the structure's sound and the owner's prepared to accept a cash offer of, say, forty-five ...

In fact, it was precisely at this point of the proceedings that Christopher Shaw, ARICS, of Abbotts of Ipswich was instructed to carry out a basic structural survey and valuation on the property.

Having been at the receiving end of one or two surveys myself in my time—not to say bills—and having often wondered exactly how surveyors earn their fees, I invited myself along.

Mr Shaw always kicks off with a brisk, general look round.

"At least then I have some idea how long I'm going to be there," he said, standing in the garden swinging his moisture meter. "I like to stick to a routine; that way there's

less chance of my missing something. I begin outside and work my way from the top downwards. Right, well, for a start that chimney stack needs repointing and proper lead flashing. There's probably no flue liner, so anyone burning wood could run a very real risk of fire. The roof's been patch repaired here and there, and I'm ninety-five per cent certain it won't be lined. And the timber framework needs doing, so basically we're talking about a complete new roof. The dormer window's something of a joke frankly. It's cockeyed and the cheeks have gone. Rainwater goods next—that's gutters, drainpipes and so on. Well, there aren't any on this side and there's nothing to hang the guttering on anyway except the tile battens ..."

This dismal catalogue of woe continued unabated as we strolled round to the front. En route, he treated me to a perfectly executed example of the "surveyor's donkey kick"—that's to say an accidental, on purpose hack with the heel to remove a revealing lump of loose rendering.

"Ah yes," he said. "Thought so. This is where interpreting cracks really becomes fun. Now that one there could simply mean the lintel's dropped, but in fact, as you can see, the footing's gone and corners have dropped. The wavy walls might be nothing more than a charming period feature; on the other hand ..."

Once inside, we were really able to get

"Mind you, he's a lot livelier now he's dead."

68

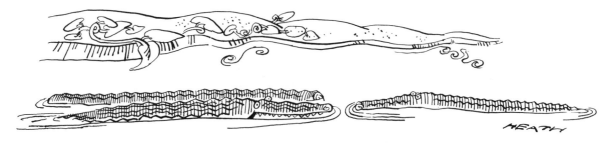

"You wouldn't have any trouble if you did what I did—I married a log."

down to business, and Mr Shaw could take a close look at the state of the timber framing upon which these sort of houses are built. We started once again at the top, in the bedroom.

"I'm not really too concerned at this stage about the general state of the floors and the plasterwork and so on. That's going to have to be renewed anyway. I'm looking beyond all that and asking myself How well is the house put together? Is the structure sound? I want to know about the joints in the framework, and whether there's been any significant splitting or cracking. Then I can start relating that to the state of the floor. Now, for example, I'm concerned that of the three main tie beams, two have been cut to make way for doors and one has been removed altogether."

He was even more concerned downstairs in the sitting-room. He pointed at the rudimentary panelling that ran along the bottom of the walls.

"Now that sort of thing immediately sets alarm bells ringing," he said. "Ninety-nine times out of a hundred it's hiding something. Damp usually. Hallo, someone's filled in behind with concrete. That's a bad sign."

The little prongs of his damp meter sank ominously into the few visible areas of original beamwork. The needle should not record more than 20%: it shot to 60%.

"I was originally thinking of £20,000 as being the sort of figure one might have to consider spending, but now I'm not so sure, not now I've seen the condition of that timber at ground level. You can't inject anything into that, for a start. More importantly, we're talking about a real loss in structural strength integrity."

Things looked even blacker, in every sense, in the dining-room, where he assured me that I'd be lucky if I ever came across a better example of how timber framing can come completely apart; and in the scullery, where his suspicions re the bulging outside wall were suddenly grimly confirmed.

Yet more horrors were to greet us in the roof.

Mr Shaw said: "I'm beginning to worry now what else my client's going to find when he starts redoing the place. Indeed, should I be recommending him to strip the whole thing down to the bare bones and start again? And yet that's the only way he's really going to know what he's in for."

Outside again in the fresh air of the orchard, Christopher Shaw made a list of major requirements and quickly re-did his sums.

It would take up too much space and make far too gloomy reading to reproduce here. Suffice to say that his earlier estimation of restoration and modernisation costs had by now leapt by nearly 100% to £35,000.

Nicely done up (and for that sort of money, it could be made very nice indeed), it would probably fetch about £75,000.

"If my client were to drop his offer by around £10,000–£15,000, I'd be reasonably happy," he said.

In the end, he pointed out, whatever his professional advice, it all boils down to why people want houses like this at all.

"A speculator might be interested in it at, say, forty. But his profit margin would probably be too small. On the other hand, if someone wants it for himself and he's really keen on it, he might well be prepared to pay over the odds. But probably not if it means spending nearly £50,000 and then rebuilding it. Actually, I have a feeling it will go fairly soon; it's been on the market for quite a while now. I must see half-a-dozen houses like this a year and they all get sold eventually. And on the whole, people make a very nice job of them."

"Things have been pretty tight lately."

LARRY DOWN UNDER

LEGAL BROTHELS FOR MELBOURNE

By Our Melbourne Correspondent

Prostitution is to be legalised in Melbourne massage parlours approved by the Victoria State's Labour government.

George MELLY

W HILE Candy and the rest of the Feetwarmers flew on direct to Canberra for our next gig, John Chilton and I stopped off at Sydney for a few hours to make our third appearance on the Mike Walsh show, a popular nationwide midday slot, and in consequence an important boost to our opening in the city the following night.

We were met at the airport by a representative of Kinsellas, the night-club who had booked us for the week, and their publicist, Ms Ingrid Berg. I already knew Ms Berg as a voice. She had rung me several times in London, usually to advise me of a forthcoming call from a Sydney journalist, and was clearly right on top of her job. Ms Berg, alias Greta Garb, alias Marlene Diet, turned out to be a large, humorous lady of frenetic energy whom I was later to nickname "The Magic Pudding" after the eponymous hero of Norman Lindsay's Australian children's classic. Needless to say, somebody told her but she was far from minding and signed all future correspondence "The Magic P".

After the television show, with Mr Walsh extremely affable and the rest of his staff seemingly delighted to welcome us back, we visited Kinsellas itself and John and I were immediately convinced that it was absolutely the right place for us. Until a couple of years ago, it had been a large undertaker's establishment trading, if that's what undertakers do, under the same name. Surrounded by plate glass windows, presumably once utilised for the display of coffins, the ground floor, including the lofty Art Deco chapel of rest at its centre, is now the restaurant; on the next floor is a long bar and offices; and above where the caskets were made is the large supper room with its low stage and elaborate lighting system. Night-clubs in the daytime tend, as Sir John Betjeman observed, to be depressing places, but not so Kinsellas. It was with keen anticipation that we returned to the airport and continued our journey to Canberra.

In the late afternoon there I gave my lecture on Magritte at the Australian National Gallery, to which Candy had already delivered the slides. It's a magnificent building but the collections are, due to such a recent start, curiously unbalanced. Strong, fittingly enough, in Australian painting and Oceanic art, the modern movements are sketchily represented except, for reasons which remain obscure to me, in the case of American abstract expressionism. The Old Masters on the other hand, presumably owing to financial considerations, may be counted on the fingers of one hand. Here the older state museums are much better endowed. The lecture, the first of several I was to give during the rest of the tour, went well. The educational staff, headed by Terry Michelin,

"They are building a new House of Parliament underground, officially to symbolise that a democracy should be 'under the feet of the people' but according to Oz cynics as a bomb shelter."

late of the Tate Gallery, proved extremely hospitable.

We played that night in a large, friendly social club where the ground floor was devoted to obsessive middle-aged ladies whose "game" was to feed a huge number of clonking one-armed bandits. We didn't see much of Canberra. It isn't, I got the impression, a city so much as a landscaped park with buildings. The embassies are built in the style of the countries they represent; a grotesque notion represented at its most extreme by a grounded gargantuan version of an Indonesian long boat. They are building a new House of Parliament underground, officially to symbolise that a democracy

"The fools are probably still scouring South America for us, Heinrich!"

Alternative Oz

should be "under the feet of the people" but in reality, according to Oz cynics, as a bomb shelter. Australia, during our visit, was working up to the election. There was, however, little sign, except on television, of any feverish excitement, even in Canberra.

Last time we played Sydney it was for two days in an obscure club and a well-kept secret. This time, thanks to the Magic Pudding, the location, and the enthusiasm of Dick Hughes, the ebullient journalist and piano-player whose only failing is to imagine that everyone needs as little sleep as he does, we opened to an audible buzz. The first night was very glamorous and we managed to deliver. The press next day was great. We had found our home.

I am no longer surprised how, in Australia, faces from my past loom up everywhere we play. That evening friends and acquaintances from the nursery on materialised out of the darkness. There was also a confrontation. Danny La Rue, as big a star in Oz as here, kindly came to see me and, while we were chatting during the interval, I was approached by another friend, an admirable feminist film producer of whom I am extremely fond but who is given to an abrasive conversational style, especially after a couple or more drinks. She and Danny didn't hit it off, to say the least, and neither, in their individual styles, proved to be inexpert at angry rhetoric. I could do little except reiterate rather wetly, "This is my first night." Both accused me of having peculiar friends and I must admit to retreating to the stifling band room. When I next rang up the film producer, I began the conversation by saying, "This is Danny." There was an appalled silence, followed, after my assurances that it was me, by generous and repentant merriment.

Otherwise, the week was a flawless delight, the young staff at Kinsellas helpful beyond the cause of duty, the owner, an enigmatic smiling personage called Fink, a nightly visitor lavish with champagne and splendid dinners, if seemingly deaf to our repeated request for some form of air-conditioning in the dressing-room. Kinsellas has allegedly and believably the best chef in Australia. Among other virtues he doesn't suffer from the principal failing of Oz cuisine, the tenet that you shouldn't be able to see the plate. He is called Tony and took a liking to us; a prejudice confirmed by the appearance of several bottles of superb Australian wine. We walked home every night down Oxford Street—Australia's penchant for British place names is a shade disorientating—in high euphoria, despite the constant demands for twenty cents from small groups of persistent green-haired punks. We stayed in a comfortable and elegant hotel called (here we go again) the Hyde Park Plaza.

►

The Magic Pudding kept me pretty busy the first few days with broadcasts, press conferences, interviews and a return to the Mike Walsh show. I was also booked to address the press club, a somewhat intimidating experience in advance but painless in the event, especially as Dick Hughes helped keep the questions flowing in a relevant direction. "There are more musos than journos," a member told the chairman and indeed, among others, Graeme Bell was there tucking into a meal which, to be truthful, paid homage to an earlier phase in Australian cooking. It was Graeme who, in the late Forties, brought his band to Britain and transformed the rather solemn revivalist jazz movement into the raucous mayhem in which I spent my youth. I was pleased, however tardily, to pay my dues to him.

I found a good friend in Sydney, a charming and very funny girl called Elizabeth who was at the first night. She has two peculiarities: one physical, the other acquired. Her eyes are a startling cat-like yellow and she smokes a pipe. She gave me a beautiful collection of tiny shells she had picked up on Whale Beach where she lives some distance from the city. She proved a splendid guide to the city, especially as Collin Bates was continuously if understandably absent in the company of the friends of his youth. We had dinner one night in China Town, where the Chinese New Year, the Year of the Pig, was being celebrated, and the streets were full of dragons and loud with fire crackers.

As things eased up, I began to have more free time. Penelope and Ricki Fatah again gave a cocktail party to which John and I were invited. It was as enjoyable as the year before and among the guests, all ravishing or funny or both, was Little Nell, until recently staying with us in London but now back to make a film in her native city, and transferred from our basement to a huge suite in Sydney's most luxurious hotel. It was no chore to sip champagne in Penelope's long, cool sitting-room overlooking the harbour and its twinkling lights.

Candy's life changed drastically during the course of the week. One night outside Kinsellas, a girl asked me how she was. I said she'd gone to bed early. The girl was astounded as she hadn't realised she was in Australia. From then on Candy didn't go to bed early again. There were, it transpired, several of her London friends very much on the town.

Our party had increased by one. Chuck Smith's wife Sylvia, who had been in Australia for six months staying with her sister, had rejoined her husband. She was a delightful addition and a most useful one. Like some Swiss family Mrs Robinson, she seemed able to produce any nostrum, whether for sunburn, insect bites, or an upset stomach, from about her small person. There was also Chuck's brother Brian who after twenty years he had re-met on our previous visit. Unhappily, halfway through the week, he had to return to Melbourne where his house, some distance outside that city, had been destroyed completely in the terrible bush-fires then raging, although his family were mercifully all safe. I also heard, with much regret, that my friend Kym Bonython, jazz impresario and gallery owner, had lost everything: Victorian family house, fine pictures, irreplaceable record collection, in the blazing hills above Adelaide.

Perhaps the most magic day in Sydney involved a visit to the zoo with Candy, Elizabeth, Penelope and her enchanting three-year-old daughter Paloma. The koala bears snoozed like elderly club men in the branches of a tree silhouetted against a view of the distant harbour bridge under the cloudless Australian sky. We ate a late lunch in a courtyard brasserie where Paloma gave vent to her only vice; a rapid but thoughtful striptease executed before her mother had time to dissuade her. We visited the huge studio of Brett Whiteley, a constant visitor to Kinsellas, who is painting brilliantly these days, his small Harpo-like person galvanised by activity both physical and mental. That night, outside the club, I spent the interval watching the floats of the all-gay Mardi Gras applauded by this tolerant and civilised city. Next day, at noon, we left for Melbourne. 🐟

"They must be nearly ready to sail."

THE MARX COMRADES

The two great philosophers celebrate Karl's centenary

Mahood

THE LIFE: KARL MARX WAS BORN IN TREVIRORUM IN 1818

"Where did it all go wrong, Groucho?"

"You got off to a bad start, Karl, the three wise men had a hard enough time finding Bethlehem!"

HIS ORIGINS WERE JEWISH BUT HIS FATHER BECAME A LUTHERAN

"You don't *have* to be Jewish to be a Messiah ... but it helps!"

"Perhaps I should have been a Moonie?"

HE STUDIED LAW AT BONN UNIVERSITY AND BEGAN TO ASK THE ETERNAL QUESTIONS

"Why are there only twenty-eight days in February?"

"Does God suffer from headaches?"

"Only if he exists!"

"Have you ever spent February in Siberia?"

"What has got four wheels and flies?"

"Meals on Wheels on a hot day!"

IN 1843 MARX MARRIED THE ARISTOCRATIC JENNY VON WESTPHALEN

"Lucky he didn't have to take her name - can you imagine anyone taking Vonwestphalenism seriously?"

JUST MARRIED

PARIS

ENGELS MET MARX IN 1844 AND THEY DECIDED TO WORK TOGETHER

"He waltzes divinely, for a philosopher!"

"What a pity he isn't called Spencer!"

"QUICK, QUICK, SLOW ..."

"Not only is this meeting historical ... it's hysterical!"

THEY WROTE THE 'COMMUNIST MANIFESTO' WHICH SLOWLY BEGAN TO CREATE WORLD WIDE ANXIETY

"A spectre is haunting Europe - the spectre of Communism. All the powers of old Europe have entered into a holy alliance to exorcise the spectre: Pope and Czar, Metternich ..."

"His 'Das Kapital' will have we rolling in the aisles, your Maj!"

"We are not amused!"

AFTER BEING EXPELLED FROM GERMANY HE LIVED IN LONDON IN DIREST POVERTY

"Writers of the world unite, you've nothing to lose but your clothes!"

"He's a true revolutionary, he's worked himself up from nothing to a state of extreme poverty!"

ENGELS HELPED TO SUPPORT HIM WHILE HE WAS WRITING HIS REVOLUTIONARY BOOKS AND ARTICLES

"I'm calling this one 'The Poverty of Philosophy'"

"Wouldn't 'The Philosophy of Poverty' be better, Karl?"

"If he hadn't been ahead of his time he would have been swamped with grants from the GLC!"

MARX SPENT THE LAST TWENTY-FIVE YEARS OF HIS LIFE WORKING ON HIS MAJOR WORK, 'DAS KAPITAL'

KARL MARX SUFFERED FROM MIGRAINES, PLEURISY, BOILS, HAEMORRHOIDS, NERVOUS DEBILITY, PULMONARY ABSCESS, BRONCHITIS, INSOMNIA, AND DEEP DEPRESSION HERE 1849-83

"the canary had yellow fever!"

"How were things otherwise, Karl?"

Katharine WHITEHORN

Dilated Pupils

IT is my great pleasure today, as chairman of the newly-formed Board of Governors of Slipway House, to give you as parents or potential parents—I mean of boys and girls in this school, ha-ha—some idea of the thinking behind this new venture, this great voyage of discovery on which we are about to embark.

But first, I would like to introduce to you our two Heads—and to explain, perhaps, why we decided from the beginning that we needed two. This was not to ensure sexual balance, or even (as in ancient Sparta) to prevent tyranny; it was a matter of simple practicality. P. G. Wodehouse always said there were two sorts of Headmaster, the workers and the poppers-up-to-London, but he was talking of a bygone age. Nowadays it is essential for a school of any standing to have a visible Head who will appear on chat shows and give interviews on such matters as education, the future of prisons, job multiplication, golf or the state of British theatre; not only does this leave him, often, with less time than he would wish for actually running the school, but it might mean that we would be forced to turn down, for her lack of media credibility, some tough old boiler with thin lips and a greying bun who might in all other respects be ideal.

This way, we can have both; and lest anyone should think this strange, we would remind you that the *Île de France* was said to have had two Captains, one to run the ship and the other to chat to the passengers over dinner; when it became increasingly hard to fill the latter post, they were apt to offer it to those who would otherwise be in for a long stint on Devil's Island. In America, too, it has frequently been found useful to

> **"Punk rock music is to be taught and practised every day, there being some hope that by term's end the kids will associate it so closely with school that they will turn to Brahms and Mozart in the holidays."**

have two editors for a newspaper, one to edit and one—should occasion so require—to go to jail.

We are agreed that pupils of all ages shall spend a part of each day learning poetry by heart, as they would otherwise emerge totally unprepared into the modern world, replete as it is with committees, airports, watching other people's TV and traffic jams. Sport is not to be made compulsory to anyone over the age of ten. The primary purpose of ball games below that age is to give small boys something to kick besides their mother and each other, an aim in which we heartily concur. Over ten, however, sport is supposed to be there to ensure that the adolescents will have no energy left over for sexual yearnings; but as the Governors, after a short, reminiscent pause, were unanimous that it had not worked at all in their own youth, they have no reason to suppose that it would do so now.

Moreover, it seems to us absurd that the

just ambition of one master, who wishes to propel his pupils through exams, should be thwarted by the equal and opposite ambitions of another master, who wishes to score a maximum number of Away wins against schools chosen for their social acceptability regardless of distance; so that a boy is kept out till ten at night by one master, and reviled for not having written his essay by another. Parents will be pleased to hear that punk rock music is to be taught and practised every day, there being some hope that by term's end the kids will associate it so closely with school that they will turn to Brahms and Mozart in the holidays.

On the vexed question of school uniform, your Governors were at first divided: there were those who felt the pupils should be allowed to use clothes as a means of expressing their individuality, and those, on the other hand, who felt they were better off in the identical jeans, T-shirts, and black leather jackets of their group, without wasting time bending their school caps, narrowing their school ties or muddying new shirts to look as if they'd been passed under a hedge. On balance, considerations of cost were held to be paramount, and all pupils are to wear a uniform of grey trousers or skirts and white blouses obtainable at Marks and Spencer; at least there was no disagreement about refusing to bolster the fortunes of some mouldering small-town outfitter with garments modelled on something one of the founders once saw chasing a camel in Cairo, as is apparently the case with the djibbahs of Downe House and Roedean.

It is with some amazement that we remember that there was once a time when it

was thought that boys should be educated only with other boys, whilst girls would profit from co-education, since it is now so evidently true that it is the other way round. Girls need to be battened under the hatches during the years when puberty first informs them that they can get by on charm, not work. Boys, on the other hand, need some sort of corrective to the massive macho myth-making of their peers if they are to be any good at human relations in later life. We propose to resolve this dilemma by teaching girls and boys in separate classes, and making entry to mixed school events obtainable by high marks alone—at least for the girls. This will stop them thinking that if they show signs of being able to add two and two together to make anything other than a tutu, their boyfriends may think them too brainy—if that's the way they think, they will never meet any.

In this context we feel obliged to remind parents, who may still cherish hopes of a sheltered girlhood for their daughters, that times have truly changed. Time was when any parent wanted a daughter to be either dumb and pretty enough to snare a millionaire (thus ensuring her parents every comfort in their old age) or dumb and plain enough not to snare anybody (thus ensuring that at least there was someone around to fill their hot water bottles). As daughters nowadays are increasingly reluctant to perform this chore and those who marry millionaires rarely stay married, the best hope for the self-interested parent lies in having a high-earning daughter who will at least, in her own right, be able to afford to pay to have them cared for in luxury.

We come finally to the matter of food; and here we have firmly decided to make no attempt to make the stuff palatable to the young. It is to be good for them: and not just because the current fashion in healthy food—lentils, porridge, baked potatoes and so forth—is so amazingly cheap; but because it then leaves the parents in the position of being able to curry favour with their young by providing food that they actually enjoy eating. For too long have schools, in the name of progress, taken on the easy task of pleasing the young, demanding little of them and putting psychology before physics; it was never fair to leave to the parent the unenviable task of telling them to close their mouths while eating and listen to the other side of the argument. In this as in all other respects we hope to make this school so relentlessly good for the brats that each one will see his or her home as it was actually meant to be—a haven.

And finally I would like to make you a promise—that each of the teachers will, at least once every year, mark a report card with the words: "Could not try harder". Every teacher every term marks most of the reports "Could try harder"—and indeed the ones who could, are not difficult to identify; the ones who actually, whatever they did, could never improve, provide, as the teachers in this school at least have realised, by far the greater challenge.

"Hot? This? You should have been here **last** week."

"Doctor Livingstone, I presume?"

"I noticed he winked when he excommunicated you."

"Let's face it, his career's gone downhill since he took up Pro-Celebrity Darts."

"Don't lie to me—you've been removing blonde hairs from your collar."

"One day, lad, I'll tell you how I lost my other stilt."

"I don't know what you're into or why, Mr Jenkins, but we'd like you to stop it."

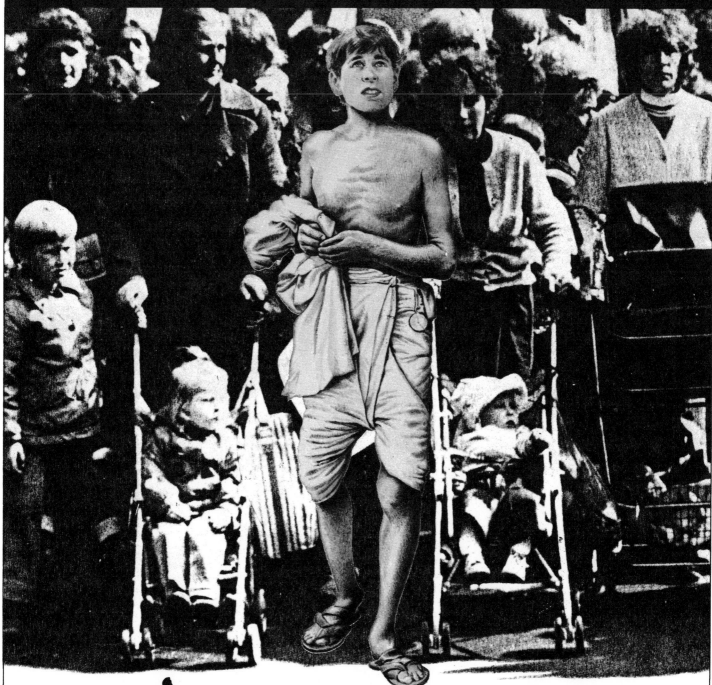

Bath Time

SPRING is in-fil-trating sneakily across the slopes of Wilt-shire parkland as the March-morning sun melts away the chiffon scarves of mist that wrap 400-year-old Longleat House, unwrapping it, strand by strand, like an early Easter present. Longleat's owner, the 79-year-old Marquess of Bath, speeds jauntily along his two-and-a-half miles of drive, under the broad-leaf English trees he admires so much he lists them in *Who's Who*, the gilded light sweeping in bars across that gent-leman-pugilist face, a cross between C. Aubrey Smith and Victor McLag-len, his six-foot-odd frame folded into the little car like a gold umbrella into a push-cart.

He inherited this Arcadian palace in 1946 but has not lived there since his first marriage in 1927. Now, with his second wife, Virginia, he occupies a cottage on the outskirts of the demesne called Job's Mill. On our way from the station, I happen to mention how everyone seems to pronounce it with a short "o", as in "big jobs", instead of after the Biblical Job.

"You religious?" he asks, steering through one of his own "No Entry" signs, and down a side-path marked "one-way" in the opposite direction. I say I am not but I do read the Bible.

"Well, I am and I don't. Read the Bible that is. Brought up in a house with 40,000 books and never read one. Not proud of it, you understand. But no one ever made me," says the peer educated at public school (Harrow) and university (Christ Church, Oxford).

Courtesy and candour are his two most noticeable qualities. "M'Lord" they may call him around the estate, and in the surrounding villages. But he addresses all strangers as "Sir", like Dr Johnson, until he gets to know them, when he addresses them as "My dear", like Laurence Olivier. Later we stand silent for five minutes, in the shadows of one of Longleat's many great book-filled chambers, while he waits with patient punctilio for a secretary to finish her conversation.

At the station, on my departure, he eels, despite his age, and a gammy leg, out of the car like a hooker, begging me to keep my seat, while he quizzes the booking clerk to check the train.

His conversation is punctuated with phrases like "Of course, I'm rather stupid ..." or "I don't know anything about these things..." or "I'm a bit immature for my age ..." He claims, rather convincingly, to have always been "very shy". He has never much enjoyed going out, being in society, getting around. He has always felt he had nothing to say anybody wanted to hear.

I point out that he was, nevertheless, the MP for the neighbourhood constituency of Frome, from 1931 to 1935. He looks at me, brows knitted, as though I had dug up some youthful scrape, stealing a policeman's helmet on Boat Race night or the like, best forgotten.

"Well, yes, they made me, you see. My father said I ought to do something instead of just lounging about the estate. The Chairman of the Conservative Party, forgotten his name, used to come down and talk to me about my duty *for two hours*. So I took the nearest place, nursed it, made a speech in each village every fortnight—same speech, of course.

"Read it out. Can't make the shortest speech today without having it written down. Like the Queen. Well, it was '31. A fly would have been elected for the National Government. I'd wasted my time.

"Wasted my time in Parliament too. Made a maiden speech, about tea I think it was, and probably never spoke again. Most frightful lot of people you meet in the House of Commons. Quite put me off politics forever."

Come, come, I say, hasn't he been seen often enough on television, weren't we once on a programme together?

"That's different. The interviewer chap has to keep the ball rolling, asking you things. Remember once, in the Beatles' days, when they'd just got an honour from the Queen. This fellow says to me—'Is that really a life's work, looking after Longleat?' 'No,' I say. 'My real ambition is to get the OBE'."

I laugh. He seems gratified. "None of *them* thought it funny. I didn't think it was too bad. OBE—do you still call it the Order of the Bad Egg? We used to. Bit childish, I suppose."

IT'S hard work, trying to dislike Lord Bath, even when the old, unreconstructed, patrician reactionary rattles his bones beneath the costume of the eccentric, charming, overgrown schoolboy in worn brown cords and indestructible ginger-tweed jacket. He is an almost comically emblematic super-patriot, distrustful of foreigners, Jews, blacks, and Communists, down to the slightly bloodshot, periwinkle eyes which I realise are literally red, white and blue. Just when I think the naked prejudice is peeping through rather alarmingly, he disarms me with a naive, endearingly dotty aside.

Downstairs, he shows me some of Longleat's priceless bibliographical treasures, an array of the earliest books ever printed, including ten Caxtons, and Britain's first cookery book, dated 1500, in which a variety of Tudor notables are thanked for their recipes, among them "the King's second son, the Duke of York", better known as Henry VIII. He is much amused by the use of the long-S—"Read that aloud ... '*then fuck up the gravy*'." Afterwards, we take the lift to the top floor, a suite of rooms in the eaves he keeps for his personal collections. "The public never come here."

We won't bother about the pictures—"all rather second-rate, no Rembrandts or anything". He is proud, though, of an Elizabethan edition of *Titus Andronicus*—"Never seen it, but I'm told it's an awful play"—in which a group of players are drawn in the margin. "The experts say the chap in the beard is Shakespeare. But there are two chaps with beards, and I've never been able to make out which is which."

In his personal archives, he shows me a bust of his present wife by Epstein. "It's so bad I keep it with its back to the window. I made the mistake of paying him before it was finished. Gave him £7000. I don't know if it was because he was Jewish but he never came back. I'll know better next time. Or perhaps not. That's the trouble with me, I never know better next time."

And he directs my attention to the brass plate he has fixed on the plinth reading, "This is nothing like my wife, I promise

"Looks like the high-fibre diet for us, Sam."

---

you," signed Henry Bath, 6th Marquess. "I owe it to posterity. I do everything for posterity. That's why I plant trees I'll never see fully grown."

He collects shells, thousands of cowries, like tiny sharp-toothed mouths, in great glass jars of the kind you used to find in old-fashioned chemists' windows. "I don't know why really. They're all the same. But we go to Herm every year and spend three days doing nothing but gather them off the beach. I look forward to that more than anything in my life. Complete relaxation."

He collects books, the centrepiece a complete set of first editions of the boys' storyteller, G. H. Henty. "I may have read some of these when I was young. I seem to remember one called *With Clive in India*."

Then there are the complete works, also in first edition, of Graham Greene. "Now

some of these I have read. I send each new one to him, he signs it and sends it back. I can't think what he gets out of it. It must be an awful bore."

WE are coming near to his Valhalla and the shrines of his heroes and heroines. A cubicle to Mrs Thatcher, full of curios, plates, cups and saucers, mugs, thimbles, flags, even toys, all bearing her name and face. "Not a large collection but I don't think I've missed anything. Wonderful woman. I have total trust in her. It's like being in love."

A room to Winston Churchill, with two wax figures of him in siren suits. "Those are really his clothes. The secretary gave them to the second gardener to burn. You wouldn't believe it, would you? I bought

them. Here's the authentication, signed 'Boakes'. That was the gardener."

An alcove for the Duke of Windsor, stuffed with exhibits, including the only E-VIII-R red pillar box outside the Post Office Museum. "Look, here's his hunting boot. Got it for ten bob from his bootmakers. He refused to accept them because they hadn't made the foot bold enough to show off the slimness of his leg. I worked for him for a while in the Duchy of Cornwall office before he was sacked. He sacked me, because he said I wasn't any good. Too shy you see, couldn't speak to anybody."

Finally Hitler, a display of uniforms, regalia, weapons plus some sixty of the Führer's early paintings. "They said he was a house-painter but he wasn't. All of these are genuine. A lot he painted while copying postcards to sell in cafes. Not as good as Churchill, didn't have the flair. I don't agree with everything he did. But as the Duke of Windsor once said to me—'You can't deny it, the man must have had something'."

Lord Bath says he imagines I think all this hoarding rather silly—"We've always been young for our age in this family." But then I have to remember he has never in all his life really had a job—"I've worked. I still work. But it's not a job, you get my meaning? I could go off to the Bahamas now if I wanted to. You see, I was brought up with forty servants. You couldn't get anything for yourself, you *had* to ring for someone to fetch it. If I'd been born in another family I'd have been happy standing at a bench putting tops on bottles, chatting to my friends, not straining the mind."

People think he has always been grand and famous. "Our family was never famous. They never did anything important, won battles or ruled the country. They didn't even make money like those families in the north with coal mines under their land."

He's not a snob, "except about the Royal Family". Though when his daughter married the Duke of Beaufort, he couldn't help being impressed. "I went around saying, 'Look at me, my daughter's the Duchess of Beaufort.' But my youngest daughter is a waitress in Covent Garden."

He's not a racist either. Blacks are all right in their own country. Jimmy Chipperfield, who went there to get the Longleat lions, told him they wash every day in Africa, "though I'm not so sure about the Pakistanis." It's the mixing of blood he opposes—"It's unnatural, like a horse and a donkey. No, that produces a mule. Like a thoroughbred and carthorse."

He's sorry to say he's depressed about the future of Longleat, not just the falling attendances because people haven't got the money. "They will take it away from us some day soon."

Who will?

"Why, Benn and that lot, when they get into power, the Communists."

But still that will probably be after his time. Meanwhile do I have the bottle of Scotch he gave me, knowing us journalists, to accompany us on the tour? We should go down to the cafeteria where he usually has a "bun thing with cream and jam on it" around this time.

"Eleven-plus, grammar school, Oxford, Cambridge. Who knows, if it hadn't been for the lead in petrol?"

COUNTRY LIFE

For £256 per person you get a trip across the Alps by the St Gothard Pass and a week in Italy, plus, on the return journey, a night in Lake Lucerne and a Paris illuminations drive.

E. Woodhouse *(Huddersfield Examiner)*

A rare Pakistani golden eagle let out of Graham Dangerfield's animal sanctuary at Wheathampstead, Herts, by vandals last Friday, was located in nearby woods and recaptured when he hired a helicopter.

A. Hall *(Evening Echo, Basildon)*

Shopkeepers were afraid that customers might be discouraged from visiting Chesham because Woolworth will no longer be operating, even if they didn't necessarily use the store itself, she added.

M. McEwen *(Bucks Examiner)*

Man who attacked woman may have thought she was his wife.

K. Bird *(Macclesfield Express Advertiser)*

Above the brightly coloured dance shop Dot will take you into the plush cool, cream and beige sunbed suite. Coming from Denmark she has been smart to install the new computerised "Solana" sunbed from Sweden.

B. Bryant *(Solihull What Have You?)*

Councillor John Waller has intervened to try to save the Olympics.

A. Godfrey *(Surrey Comet)*

The first Findon Valley Scout Group spent two hours collecting rubbish at the Gallops in Findon Valley. In return, each was given a portion of children and chips by the Kentucky Fried Chicken food bar in Broadwater, Worthing.

J. Excell *(West Sussex Evening Argus)*

One careful gun owner requires shooting—Box 308.

L. Graveley *(The Northern Scot)*

Radio Three: 10.15: Stereo Release (s). 11.15: BBC Sympathy Orchestra in Germany (s). 1.00: News.

M. Rial *(Hull Daily Mail)*

INTERNATIONAL SECTION

But remember this. You have to be punctual—there is no question of the train leaving at *around* 5.40p.m. If British Rail says the train is arriving at 5.41, you can be sure that there will be one at that exact moment.

P. Coton *(Singapore Sunday Times)*

And now a word about the singer Annie Ross. Both Annie Ross's Scottish parents were in the theatre and her mother is comedian Jimmy Logan.

R. Felton *(Akhbar Oman)*

The Minister for Minerals and Energy, Mr Parker, plans to release the report and give people till mid-July to comment on it. The Government will then review the comments and fake a decision.

V. Clews *(The West Australian)*

Professional Electric dog drier. Ideal for long coated bread.

S. Corkery *(Canberra Times)*

Hired Indonesian debt collectors are believed to be responsible for the deaths of two Singaporeans whose bodies were found cemented in a Wanchai flower box. "We expect fresh information from our boys at the Intelligence Unit," a police source said. "We hope something concrete will come up in the next day or two."

W. Jarman *(Hongkong Standard)*

ffolkes' ffirst ffolio

"These days everyone wants to get in on the act."

"Edgar Alan's a good son. He never misses Hallowe'en."

"Name's Jack London and this is my new book."

"This is Charlotte, Emily and Anne. They all write a cracking good yarn."

"I don't think they're going to circulate."

> ## "The myth of the inner urban collapse is staked out in bombed-out blocks: the evidence is in the parts the cabs won't reach."

Bronx Cheer

THE latest suggestion in New York is to do away with the unsightly bits by flattening them and putting them out to grass. This solution has been proposed for the South Bronx, Fort Apache territory; streets which compare with those in cities ravaged by terrorism of the military and not just the civil variety.

All over New York there are quarters which make complacent copy for all manner of Leftists and communists. Behind the glittering entry port to the New World the illusion can be seen on the rocks, if not everywhere then in sufficient places to persuade a visitor that civilisation is in retreat to districts increasingly fortressed by spiralling wealth. To live at all, so the myth goes, you have to be rich; to live well you have to be seriously rich.

New York has as many myths as there are images in a hall of mirrors. It dotes on them and loves to be terrified by its grosser selves. The myth of the inner urban collapse, though, is staked out in bombed-out blocks: the evidence is in the parts the cabs won't reach. New Yorkers like nothing better than to squat on a bar-stool and spin gruesome tales to gormless out-of-towners. How this friend was mugged twice in half an hour, how this cousin ended up in the garbage, how the shoot-out worked out, how the gangs rove the unpoliced streets like packs of rats by nightmare moonlight. And some of it could be true as well. The South Bronx would indeed look much better levelled.

One consequence is that it is difficult to discover a working-class district in New York. They are either abandoned, derelict or have fled outside the city. You hear about bum rows and you hear about fat cats but what is in between? Where is that Victorian street life of working New York where immigrants crowded unmurderously in streets you had to fight your way down— but only because of the bouncy life hollering on the pavements? It seems to have disappeared altogether.

I went up to what was once known as Italian Harlem with Evan Hunter (author of *Blackboard Jungle, Mothers and Daughters* etc), also known to Ed McBain (of the *Eighty-Seventh Precinct*), born with the silver-tongued handle Salvatore Lombino. We arrived at nine o'clock on a Sunday morning. The street corners were already clustered with guys looking around for something to start the day. There seemed nothing in the beaten up or battened down buildings to provide much employment. Those shops which were not open were

steel-fronted and padlocked: those open were protected by entry buzzers—even the grocery stores. Dazed street life; sad, dangerous street life, which seemed thrown onto the pavements of the city like debris onto a shore line, was already in action at 9 a.m.

"Gotta cigarette," the lady said, wheedling, sadly insinuating. We didn't smoke. "You are the ugliest man I seen. The ugliest." There you go. "Gotta have a cigarette, then I go to church. Ain't wearin' no pants. Not when I go to church. Gotta cigarette?"

Then a man came over limping a little, bearded like a pirate, voiced by a larynx which sounded as if it had been soaked in gravel. "Are you the man? I'm the man. You the man? Whose the man? Gotta dollar?"

"There's nowhere for those people to go," said Hunter. "They're poor, they're black, they're uneducated."

He himself was there to look up the places in which he had been brought up. The house in which he had been born had been knocked down, together with the whole block. The Chinese grocery store was now a Puerto Rican garage. His grandfather's tailor's shop was cemented up. The "beautiful" doctor's house was crumbling, perhaps with the corrosive accumulation of the graffiti. The winter wind blew down the streets bringing no whispers of hope. The place lacked everything. Hunter's uncorked enthusiasm, his bubbling recall and exact rememberings threw a brief cloak over the litter but the wind soon scuffed it once more.

An energetic peasant class from Italy had come to those few blocks at the turn of the century, vivified them, and then, most of

them, bust their way out into the suburbs. Only the old Italians were left and for them, to Hunter's moved delight, there was an Italian cake shop he had known and just as it once had been; old-fashioned now, trade not so good, people round here mostly not liking the way the Italians make pastry, kept going by ice-cream in the summer and cakes for the anniversaries of the redoubt of Italians in the winter.

When you have some idea—from the books and films, from the plays and performers—of the variety of talent and the chronicles which have come from settlements like this, it seems not only a shame but a loss that New York appears no longer able to sustain that decent working class of urban life.

Yet all might not be as it seems from the bar-stool. One night we went to a Puerto Rican area—warily warned off it by the myth makers of the Big Apple who maggot away about the usual knives and muggings and strangers setting no foot. We'd heard the band was good. It was. So was the place. Good was the word.

For in the middle of what most New Yorkers would regard as one of the deepest jungles in Sick City, we found a dance hall very like the posher places we went to in the Fifties. Twinkling lights. Men in suits and ties. Women dressed to impress. Dances politely requested. Partners escorted on and off the dance floor out of politeness, not for safety. A working-class culture in full and formal swing.

Perhaps we were lucky. Or perhaps New York still has its Victorian working culture although it doesn't know where to find it. Or house it. Or mythologise it into fashion. I can see that dance hall being just too nice and enjoyable for New York's sense of its own high drama; it won't be the first time that the fashion has passed by the sign on its own front door. 🎭

"Who's he? He wasn't there this morning."

Alan COREN

SUN GUIYING, a middle-aged woman chicken farmer, was given the full propaganda treatment in China's Press yesterday as a heroine of the new peasant elite. This year she has sold more than 492,800 eggs.

Her family's profit was said to be £12,486 sterling and so she was entitled to the ultimate accolade—she was given permission to become Peking's first peasant to own a car.

Daily Telegraph

THE GREAT BARBARIAN DRAGON THAT WILL EAT UP "THE BROTHER OF THE MOON," &c. &c. &c. *Punch 1853*

RED SALES IN THE SUNSET

A SAFFRON hangnail of moon rose gently over Dao Deng Hua, tinting the corrugated roofs of its serried coops. Inside, ten thousand chickens, ranked like feathered kebabs upon their alloy perches, let out one last staccato choral cluck, and settled, knackered, for the night.

In the village Hall Of Egg Norm Victory And Reciprocal Criticism, five hundred peasants packed the wooden benches no less formally, but far more excitedly: five hundred eager faces shone above the collars of their dropping-spattered smocks, a thousand rapt and gleaming eyes targeted in on the little raised platform, a thousand hands ignored the decadent speculation as to the sound of one of them clapping and set up a keen and rhythmic beat, as the dais party filed up the steps, and took their seats.

Sun Guiying was, naturally, the last. She did not sit. The applause rose to an echoing crescendo, bringing flakes of cheap eau-de-nil distemper fluttering down from the trembling ceiling so that, for a brief time-warped moment, she became a demure virgin in an old T'ang frieze, teased by encircling butterflies.

"We welcome," said the Chairman, as the cheering at last died down, "egg heroine Sun Guiying, who ——"

"So sorry to be 47.9 seconds late," interrupted the heroine, bowing slightly, first to the Chairman, then to the audience, "but these Toyotas are buggers when it comes to cold starting. If throttle-pedal over-depressed, automatic choke flood carburettor. Soon I chop it in, get Merc 450 SEL, gimme that Stuttgart fuel injection every time!"

Below her, jaws dropped open, the bright eyes glazed. What hens were these, of which the heroine spake? What was the black smear on her nose? Why, above all, was she wearing string-backed gloves? Faster egg-handling? Anti-beak protection? In the depths of the hall, a small man stood up, shyly, and took off his cap.

"Egg heroine Sun Guiying," he said, "we, the comrade-soldier-villagers of Dao Deng Hua, congratulate you on the triumphant sale of 492,800 eggs! What is your expert advice to all those who aspire, humbly, to achieve such figures? Is it a question of enriched grit, or perhaps ——"

"Get them to throw in loose covers," replied Sun Guiying briskly. "That is my advice. Do not let them fob you off with standard PVC upholstery, you would not believe how your bum slides about when drifting through the Nu Hau Heng roundabout, I bloody nearly wrote her off, there

was this yo-yo in a clapped-out Su Shiu 205 tractor, fortunately I was able to take him on the inside, these people should not be allowed on road, also, since you raise question, do not take delivery before they have modified suspension, this is a factory job, the Toyota has tendency to rear-end lightness, at present I have compensated for this by sticking two hundredweight millet-sacks in boot, but this is only stop-gap measure since what you are doing is forcing weight down onto aft wishbone, this has knock-on drag effect on rear differential, plus sump banging on road, hence oil on nose, I have very likely shredded a gasket, the stuff is seeping from the bell-housing like loose bowel motion from broody pullet, next question?"

There was a long pause, punctuated by sporadic snores and the odd whimper. Several members of the audience had begun reading *Gizzard Parasite Leaflet Number 86*. In one of the darker corners, two elderly pluckers were huddled over a Mah Jong board, normally a hanging offence. At last, the Chairman himself said:

"Glorious poultry exemplar Sun Guiying, your dazzling achievement shames us all. I should like to begin tonight's dialectical proceedings by pointing the finger at myself. What have I been doing wrong?"

85

"You have been cycling in the middle of the road," replied Sun Guiying, "you dozy old sod. What are you?"

"I am a dozy old sod," muttered the Chairman.

"Do you think you own the road?"

"Yes, I think I own the road."

Sun Guiying turned from the Chairman to the audience.

"How many other cyclists here think they own the road?"

Gradually, some sixty per cent of the hall rose slowly and sheepishly to its feet.

"*ALL* CYCLISTS THINK THEY OWN THE ROAD!" shouted the heroine.

One by one, the rest of the audience stood up.

"ALL CYCLISTS THINK THEY OWN THE ROAD!" they shouted back, and sat down again.

"It may interest you to know," said Sun Guiying, straightening her nylon rally-jacket and sending the highlights skating across her heavy bust, "that it can take up to one hundred metres to stop car travelling at 100 kph *in normal conditions*, let alone eggs all over road, bloody chickens running off pavement without warning, droppings everywhere, it is like a skating rink, does anyone have any idea what I am driving on?"

An elderly lady, nudged to her feet by her front-row neighbours, stood up, hung her head, wept, banged her frail breast.

"No-one has any idea what you are driving on, triumphant egg champion hero," she sobbed. "Forgive us."

"Mixed radials and cross-ply is what I am driving on!" shrieked Sun Guiying. "Also two with canvas showing, one with pork-pellet plug, due to no bloody stocks up distributor, car is damned death-trap, got no toe-in, got no down-line tracing, and suddenly road full of cycling nerds wandering all over shop, have you ever costed out wing-dent repair, beat out, rub down, apply four coats metallic to match in, replace chrome trim, mastic metal-to-metal edge, re-underseal wheel-arch, make good?"

"No!" cried the old lady, and ran from the hall, scattering feathers, to hurl herself into a freezing slipper-bath, shave her head, and begin her fast.

The Chairman watched her go.

"Are we to get rid of the bicycles, incredible egg-producing paragon?" he murmured.

"And the eggs," said Sun Guiying.

"AND THE *EGGS*?" howled the audience.

"No question," replied Sun Guiying.

The Chairman bit his knuckle. One did not incautiously oppose a Heroine Of The Peasant Elite, an Idol Of The Glorious Press, a Mega-Egg Producer upon whom the great sun of the Central Committee had specifically directed a major beam. He cleared his throat.

"And what, then, shall we produce?" he murmured.

"Droppings," answered Sun Guiying.

"Chicken droppings?" croaked the Chairman.

"Are there any other kind?" said Sun Guiying. "We shall sterilise the chickens and put them on a laxative diet, and from the droppings we shall manufacture methane, and on the methane we shall run the car. That is the way of the future! That is what progress is all about!"

The Chairman sank to his chair again, and dropped his head in his hands.

"You cannot have poached droppings on toast," he muttered.

Sun Guiying looked at him, and the audience looked at her; the dialectic had reached, surely, an insuperable crux? The heroine, however, merely smiled, strangely; and when she spoke, her voice was throaty, quivering, full of dreams.

"True," she said. "But then again, you cannot go round Silverstone on an egg."

"What's our policy on the Nouveau Riche?"

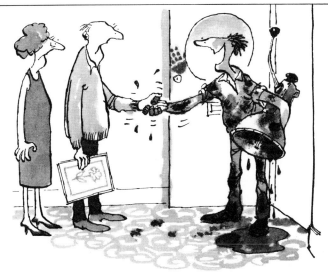

"I watched you move in and I said to Maureen, I said, there's a man who looks as though he understands Cortina gearboxes if ever I saw one."

"I couldn't care less about the full moon, just keep your bloody dog quiet!"

DUNMOVIN'
by **Holte**

"He's a pleasant enough chap—only don't let him get on to the subject of operations."

"Re-member-to learn-yer post-code, got it?"

"It says, 'Hope we're not going to have big vans parked outside all day, this is a respectable neighbourhood'."

Honeysett:
GIVE THE GIRLS A BREAK

"You won't mind if we don't use this pocket?"

RACHNUL GOLD CHALLENGE MATCH

"It's no good, Freda, the promoters have already made their choice."

"She tries to get in as much practice as she can."

"Actually I think the pink looks nicer over there."

"Any prize money she wins will go towards a deposit for a larger house."

"Before I sign you up, Miss Harmsworth, I'll have to see how well you play."

CINEMA: FFOLKES

SWANN IN LOVE ORNELLA MUTI *as Odette* JEREMY IRONS *as Swann*

ZIGGY STARDUST AND THE SPIDERS FROM MARS DAVID BOWIE

PIRATES OF PENZANCE Two Elders KEVIN KLINE *as The Pirate King*

Michael BYWATER DIPLOMATIC UNCONVENTIONS

HAVING REGARD TO the manifest and lamentable failure of the current Vienna Convention to meet with the approval and the needs of law-abiding representatives of the crushed and downtrodden worker proletariat mass Union council group workshop Jamahiriya people of the world, and **FURTHER HAVING REGARD TO** the Kalashnikov at our heads, the blood lapping round our ankles, the brains spattered on the ceiling, the hand-grenades down our trousers and the can of Brut hairspray pointed at our eyes, **WE THE UNDERSIGNED** hereby declare promulgate enact agree and undertake **AS FOLLOWS:**

1) The interests of nation states struggling for independence, nationhood and a fair hearing from the cancerous deaf goats of international manipulation and oppression (INCLUDING the Coal Board, the iniquitous viper Thatcher, the dribbling dotard Reagan, the sadistic, loll-tongued bloodlusting Metropolitan Police, the howling devils of the Vatican, sated on virgins' flesh, and the crazed aggressors of Israel BUT EXCLUDING the Greater London Council, the Supreme Soviet of the USSR and the glorious IRA) are paramount and unassailable and are hereby enshrined.

2) Whatever that means.

3) All nation states, etc., are entitled to establish free of charge embassies, bureaux, outposts, and diplomatic missions in any country whatsoever. Such bureaux, bunkers, yurts or bothies will conform to the high standards of diplomatic representation which has been so grievously flouted by the revanchist stinking priapic wolves of the West, who burn our homelands, blow off our kneecaps, eat our children, and rape our women, hurling them to the ground and leaping upon them with their flabby white bottoms bouncing up and down, ripe for the sting of the lash of justice, now stained scarlet with the blood of the Aggressor, whose black bowels coil the world like the coils of, er, black bowels, would ye ivver believe it Bigob, Insh'Allah.

4) The territory bounded by the walls (such as may remain standing) of an embassy, etc., of a nation state, etc., shall be inviolate. THIS MEANS INVIOLATE, and fraternal persuasive action will be taken to resolve such disputes through the normal diplomatic channels having regard to the laws of the host country, hereinafter called "the aggressor".

5) Where the laws of the host country, i.e., aggressor, prohibit the carrying of firearms by the repressionist lobotomised cattle of their Nazi police, this shall be respected, insofar as the existence of unarmed police may be taken as evidence of a People, mass, proletariat, membership or Jamahiriya so in thrall to the devilish manipulations of its Satanic oppressors that they are too cowed even to oppose UNARMED men.

6) The existence of unarmed WOMEN police shall be regarded as the final insult to a people, lads, workforce, Khmer, Jamahiriya or inmates crushed beyond endurance. It is therefore the clear and humane duty of all diplomats, students, freedom fighters, national executive members and Cong of all colours, provoked to fraternal sympathy, to liberate such oppressed peoples, membership, etc., by glorious acts of revolutionary diplomacy, especially the shooting of unarmed WOMEN.

7) Acts of such revolutionary diplomacy, which also include where appropriate the wearing of Shiite-smeared blankets, the burning of bourgeois stray dog holiday cottages look you, and the drinking of Murphy's stout preparatory to acts of violence approved under Schedule D attached (including gingerbread men but EXCLUDING currants, soft-nosed ammunition or contaminated Halal meat) shall be carried out from behind reinforced bars, with powerful weapons, thus demonstrating the strength of a People, Mass, Proletariat or all-powerful Jamahiriya when liberated by enlightened leadership.

8) Diplomatic bags, are in this regard to be inviolate from the prurient pryings of the evil-ridden forces of repression, ready as always to steal guns or bombs further to oppress their people, or to seize from legitimate diplomatic packing-cases the normal working tools of diplomacy, e.g. young virgins, imported from Tripoli in the normal course of diplomacy, who are seized by the vicious rank foxes of Customs and Excise and put to sex-slavery, without benefit of consultation, representation or pithead ballot, while their lithe limbs still glisten with sweat and glorious Revolutionary peoples' hairspray from the journey.

9) The following shall be regarded as acts of war:

Mucking around with the accredited students' virgins, as above.

Putting hoods on parking meters.

Severance of diplomatic relations.

Closure of uneconomic pits in defiance of legitimate right of the NJM (National Jamihiriya of Mineworkers).

Mentioning the SAS.

Presence of blatantly hostile forces in vicinity of embassy, e.g., office workers, ice cream men, people in suits who support the forces of Zionist repression, children, babes-in-arms and small cuddly animals.

Arrival of nice weather.

Attempts to collect debts or enforce legal proceedings on duly accredited students, representatives of the democratic Jamahiriya, life presidents etcetera.

10) Any other event may be considered an act of war on the completion of a secret ballot among Bureaux staff at the pithead, ALWAYS PROVIDING that in the event of an unsatisfactory vote the percentage necessary to carry the motion is lowered by (a) a full meeting of the executive or (b) the ugly one with three teeth, a scrubby beard, and a glorious machine gun, acka-acka-acka-acka! Hahahahahah!, whichever is stupider.

11) Fraternal brigade/bureau/mission/bunker comrades who are fully-paid-up may retain the right to express dissidence with any or all decisions of the glorious Democratic majority (=Jamahiriya).

12) They also retain inviolate the right to be hounded throughout the world, caught, have the hair stripped from their heads and be nailed, raw, naked and bleeding, to the embassy flagpole, as a lesson. Women will additionally be raped.

13) All embassies will retain at least one glorious democratic Comrade especially trained in the raping of women nailed vertically to flagpoles.

14) In the event of acts of war by the aggressor host country, free choccy and fags will be supplied by the aggressors, who will additionally provide an armed guard to escort the defenceless peaceful people's O'democratically elected representatives on a shoplifting spree to Harrods as compensation for the vile calumnies inflicted upon law-abiding revolutionary undergraduates, freedom fighters, pickets and other diplomatic staff.

15) All negotiations shall be conducted in an approved International Revolutionary Peoples' Tongue, e.g., Gaelic, Palestinian, Scargill, Sloganic, M'Bombast or Desperanto.

16) Disputes shall be resolved by the fulfilment of a quota, to be m'democratically agreed upon by the glorious revolutionary shop-floor minority, and the IRA will be invited to the after-the-show party to count the blood. All present will be given money raised by old, mad Americans. There will then be a post-mortem. Literally. ❦

Accept as a gift, the magic of the

ROYAL DOGS

A ONCE-IN-A-LIFETIME PUBLISHING FIRST TO DELIGHT BRITAIN'S ROYAL DOG WATCHERS

● Four fabulous, heart-warming pages of pictures which all loyal Royal Dog Family album collectors will want to cherish for all time. ● A captivating special that builds up, page by page, into a four-page treasure-house you will want to share with other loyal Royal Dog watchers, or perhaps to hand down to generations of loyal Royal Dog watchers as yet unborn.

*And remember—**ROYAL DOGS ARE NOT AVAILABLE IN THE SHOPS***

One's Best Friend

DESPITE a natural radiance and charm, they are perhaps the most private of all the royals.

Seldom interviewed by Michael Parkinson or David Frost, they have been called The Royal Dogs Nobody Knows.

Wherever they go on official duties, the Royal Family of Dogs are sure to attract a crowd of enthusiastic, stick-waving, royal dog well-wishers. Royal Dog "walkies" have indeed become a legendary part of our nation's ceremonial heritage.

Yet in their private lives at home in the royal kennels, the royal family of dogs jealously guard their regal dignity. There have been chilly exchanges with the press after a European tabloid, *Hund am Sonntag*, splashed a telephoto shot of a royal dog beside a lamp-post.

THE ROYAL DOGHOUSE OF HAPSBURG

Each and every one of the Royal Family of Dogs has his or her specially magical appeal—the warm, moist-eyed benevolence of the old-timers, some of them now well into their teens, the delightfully fluffy, pretty little lap-dog look of some of the younger royal favourites, or the ankle-nipping taste for adventure which many royal dogs exhibit to abundance as they career around the lawns of Sandringham or make a solo jump from a royal train before the delighted crowds at Victoria Station.

The names of the Royal Dogs ring out across Great Britain's noble history—Trafalgar, Spot, Agincourt, Trixie, Albert and Fluff. Their distinguished portraits line the walls of palaces and state apartments.

Grand Archduke Spot Maximilian Franz-Josef Ferdinand Georg II, a magnificent figure almost 21 inches at withers, pictured at the State Opening of Bosnia-Hercegovina Dogs' Home in 1888. Said to be Her Majesty's dogs' favourite family portrait, it hangs today in Black Vet's consulting rooms at Balmoral.

93

A PROUD TRADITION

In their courage and bearing, their dogged determination and way of putting others at their ease, the Royal Family of Dogs carry on a proud tradition which serves as a stirring example to every ordinary British pooch.

There are the fairy-tale moments of splendour, as when a royal pup is born, and there are the moments of national sadness, too, as when a royal dog takes up with some unsuitable mongrel.

When any one of the Royal Family of Dogs is pictured romping with a bone or stepping out in a stunning outfit, all Britain's dog-watchers can share in the exultation. When a Royal Dog contracts distemper or hard-pad, the British people wait anxiously for news of recovery to be posted on the Palace railings.

For in a modern age obsessed with nuclear arms and TV, the Royal Family of Dogs represents the everlasting triumphs and concerns of every British dog in the street, stands for all that is best in the British dog's way of life.

Today, we salute that awe-inspiring, right royal winning of hearts throughout the British Commonwealth of Dogs in a cavalcade of glorious pictures never before presented with such pomp and splendour.

RAPTUROUS CROWDS LINE THE CEREMONIAL ROUTE TO ROYAL HARINGAY

In her capacity as Deputy Colonel-in-Chief of The Queen's Own Old English Black-and-Tan Terriers, HRH The Princess Fluffy Alice Elizabeth Louise heads the Procession round the course before the start of the Royal Spratt's Bonio Ovals Stakes.

The traditional pomp and majesty of the daily round of official duties and stately engagements are a familiar part of the royal dog's life. Seen here inspecting a march-past by the 17th/21st Queen's Own Border Collies, HRH Prince Rover Battenburg Arthur Philip Louis sits four-square upon the noble heritage of Royal British fighting dogs. HRH Rover's great-grandfather, HRH Rex, was wounded in the tail during the Ardennes campaign.

Looking a picture of courtly grace and for many royal dog-watchers who have served in both wars the absolute epitome of enchantingly royal pedigree charm, HRH Madge Elizabeth Alice Holyrood Louise is certain of a hats off welcome wherever she roams. In this captivating study by Snowdon, the doyenne of the Royal Family of Dogs is shown resplendent at the unveiling of a plaque in the Royal Battersea Dogs' Home.

Easily the slimmest and most fashionably elegant of the Royal Family of Dogs, HRH The Spiffy Georgina Pippa Lucinda Spencer Tracey is affectionately called "Twiggy" by the loyal Royal Kennel-maids for she's never been known to manage more than a half-helping of Pedigree Chum and is, as our radiant picture shows, seldom off the scales. Perhaps not one of the sportier royal dogs, she's nevertheless a winner at every By Appointment show trial.

HRH Prince Prince, Duke of Airedale, takes the controls of an Andover of The Queen's Dogs' Flight at the start of a three-week tour of Commonwealth Boarding Kennels. HRH Prince Prince, who is also an accomplished retriever, delighted well-wishers at the airport with a characteristic snarling bark directed towards pressmen attempting to get an off-the-paw comment on rumours of a royal dog romance between HRH Prince Fido and a common poodle. ▶

THE MAGICAL MOMENT OF A ROYAL DOG BIRTH

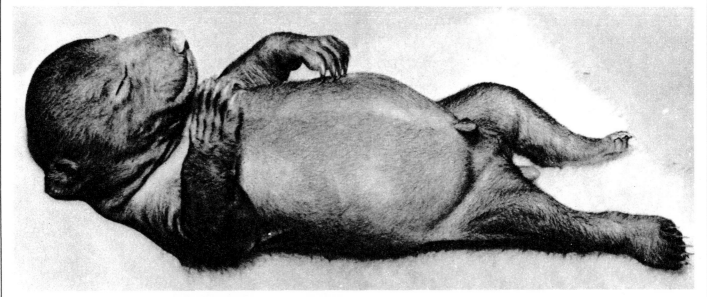

Always born under the watchful care of The Royal Family of Dogs' personal veterinary surgeon, Mr Doberman Pinker, the royal pups have always held a very special place in the hearts of the nation's royal dog watchers.

This atmospheric official portrait of the infant HRH Prince Shep was taken by Lichfield in the Bonzo Wing of The Royal Paddington Free and has since been made widely available on a fine selection of souvenir heraldic dinner dishes and magnificently embossed souvenir royal dog birth flea collars.

THE EVEN LESSER-KNOWN MEMBERS OF THE ROYAL FAMILY OF DOGS

◄ Enjoying every moment of a well-earned rest after active service in The Falklands, HRH Jet Albert Christian Edward of Annabel's furthered his popular image as a bit of a dog about town when he was pictured in *Paris Pooch* with a mystery blonde companion.

Much cherished by all royal dog watchers for her cheerily radiant way of putting commoners at their ease, HRH The Princess Snap welcomes the postman to Gatcombe Kennels.

Looking fit and bronzed after a six-month fact-finding tour of the Caribbean, HRH Fudge sets the waiting crowds alight at RAF Brize Norton with this fetchingly serene winter blouson designed for her by Royal Family of Dogs dressmaker, Hardy Rabies.

Always a one to be ready fo enjoy a jest with well-wishers in the crowd, HRH Benji shocked officials but won over all of Ayer's Rock on a recent tour of Commonwealth Defence Establishments.

The Average Person's General Knowledge Compendium

By Neal Anthony

A HISTORY OF FIREARMS

(Part One)

GUNPOWDER, like everything else—paper, printing, banknotes, bureaucracy, chow mein, outsize walls—was invented by the Chinese, and independently discovered—late, as usual—by European monks, who ought probably to have been illuminating manuscripts or ringing the bell for matins at the time.

Gunpowder is a mixture (not a compound) of sulphur, saltpetre and charcoal, all of which substances had been lying around, common as muck, for ages, until the monks and mandarins took it into their heads, for what reason God or the Tao alone knows, to mix them together and put a match to them. BANG. In less time than it takes to shout, "The enemy has breached the wall with an iron devil-machine hurling thunder-bolts!" mankind—without being consulted, as usual—had turned another corner. Just when, for instance, the English Barons had had a mere couple of centuries to gloat over having put the King in his place (*see* MAGNA CARTA), the King was suddenly reversing the process by blowing big holes in their castles, something not entirely conducive to the upkeep of baronial prestige (or of the castles).

The two basic uses of gunpowder are:
(a) hurling projectiles with great force;
(2) simply exploding, and hurling everything everywhere.

The first and second uses were often unintentionally combined, due to the somewhat rough and ropey manufacture of medieval iron tubes: all too often, the powder, instead of obligingly hurling the ball/boulder/bag of old nails straight at the target, would instead blow the gun and the gunners to bits. MAN WAS NOT DETERRED. Perhaps believing that, if God or the Tao had intended us to blow *ourselves* up, He or It would not have made us capable of hating our enemies, men applied themselves to the forging of stronger barrels. By the time that Drake was drubbing the Dons in Europe, and the Mings were mangling the Mongols in Asia, cumbersome cannon and hefty handguns were belching death across battlefields everywhere. SCIENTIFIC WARFARE HAD ARRIVED.

By the same time, firearms had already divided into their two basic sub-types:
(1) ARTILLERY;
(b) HANDGUNS.

In the Begunning, any gun consisted of a tube, open at one end, sealed at the other, with a tiny touch-hole in the top at the rear, to which a flame could be applied to ignite the charge of powder crammed behind the projectile—increasingly, a ball of iron or lead rather than a stone or fistful of bent forks. If the tube was small enough to be carried by a single complaining soldier, it was a *handgun*; and if it had to be humped about by a grumbling team, or trundled on wheels behind a protesting horse, it was a *cannon*.

Then came the Great Step Forward. MATCHLOCK handguns were marvels of technological ingenuity—for their time—and were no doubt considered the Ultimate Weapon. All the soldier had to do was remember to carry out thirty-six actions in the right order, in order to get off the staggering rate of fire of at least one shot every five minutes (roughly.) The most vital action he had to remember was not (a) priming his pan; (b) keeping his match lit; (c) cocking his serpentine; (4) planting his rest; (5) ramming his charge; (6) loading his ball; or (g) referring to the manual when confused—but ensuring that he pulled the trigger *after* the pikemen in front had parted ranks, and *before* they closed up again, lest he blow away one of his own side.

Then came the Great Step Forward. The WHEEL-LOCK, a wonder of technical ingeniousness—for its time—and undoubtedly viewed as the Ultimate Weapon, replaced the old slow-burning match with the much more straightforward clockwork spring, winding key, serrated wheel, chunk of iron pyrites, and claw to clutch this last. All was now simplified—one had merely to attach the key, wind up the wheel, bring the claw down, remember the pyrites, get it out, put it in, screw it home, do all the other things like charging, ramming, loading, ramming, priming, fixing, fuming, setting, seething, swearing—and wait for the pikemen to part. In this startlingly direct manner, it was now possible to get off at least one shot every five minutes (roughly).

Then came the Great Step Forward. The FLINTLOCK, a triumph of ingenious technology—for its time—and *unquestionably* seen as the Ultimate Weapon, replaced the old key, wheel, clockwork, clutch, claw, serrations, swearing, pyrites and precious minutes with a straightforward spring which flung a flint straight forward across a plate of steel, showering sparks into the pan, igniting the lesser charge, which flashed through the touch-hole, setting off the main charge and firing the gun. One had simply to remember to screw the flint home firmly, lift the plate to prime the pan, avoid mistaking half-cock for full-cock, bear in mind the old stuff about charging, ramming, loading, ramming, watching out for loose powder on the hand and everywhere else, return the rod, go to full cock, look for the enemy, take aim and let fly with one's one and only shot before starting the process all over again. Simple. One could get off one shot a minute like that (roughly).

At this point, the Church stepped in again. Perhaps concerned at the clergy's lapse of interest since the monks' invention of gunpowder, the Reverend Alexander Forsyth of Scotland, who ought probably to have been polishing a sermon or visiting Old Widow McGillicuddy at the time, invented the PERCUSSION system, a masterpiece of scientific innovation—for its time—and *indubitably* deemed the Ultimate Weapon. The flint, plate, pan and lesser charge were all replaced by a simple nipple—a species of nozzle—on which was fitted a brass cap containing mercury fulminate, a compound (not a mixture) which goes BANG when you hit it. A compact, simplified hammer struck the cap on the nopple, sending a flash through the nizzle and thus igniting the charge in the battom of the borrel. (BANG.)

This system was so straightforward that the ranks of the military no longer had to remain closed to those too dense to remember what to do with matches, wheels, keys, flints, pans, plates or pyrites. At last, the Average Person could join the Army. It was a Great Step Forward for democratic principles. A career in professional slaughter was open to everyone, regardless of race, colour, creed or—most of all—IQ.

The business of hurling death from a distance began to liven up.

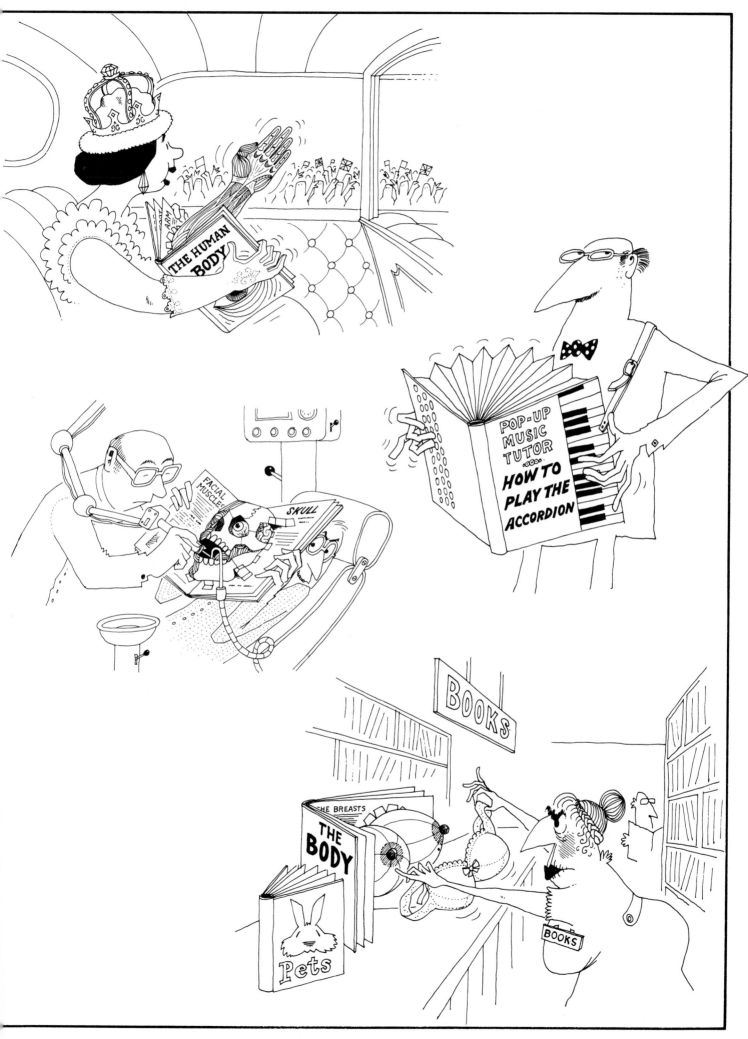

"And I'm telling you, young man, that Tom and I didn't use stuntmen to do the dangerous scenes."

Jonathan SALE

As Easy as Falling Off a Log

ALLAN would go through fire and water for a job. By profession, he is a human torch, and as a sideline he splashes around under water beyond the point at which most of us start begging for the kiss of life. If pushed, he falls down stairs. He will cross swords, literally, with any performer specified in the script.

He is on the "Probationary" list of the *1984 Register of Stunt Performers & Arrangers*, which might make you wonder what the fully qualified members are capable of. And at this point you enter a debate about what makes a stuntman, a debate which is totally unscripted and very violent, besides which the antics on London Weekend's series *The Fall Guy* are shoved into the shade (where, as anyone who has glimpsed half an episode of this American nonsense will agree, they so richly belong).

Oddly enough, considering these are men and women who could be hurled through walls bodily, leave, like Desperate Dan, an outline of their frame in the fabric and then walk away to dive 40 feet into a saucerful of water, they are very touchy. Equity, the Actors' Union which produces the *Register*, initially agreed to hand over a copy to a *Punch* messenger. Accidentally, it was given to the wrong motorcyclist; and in the time it took him to drive round the block and realise this wasn't the package he had come for, the big cheese among stuntmen in the Equity building had heard of my request, decided he did not like it, and removed the *Register* from his Reception.

I like to think of him hurtling from his room without bothering to open the door, crashing head over heels down the stairs and smashing through the glass partition to get his hands on the offending publication.

I don't like to think of his actions when he learns I managed to find a copy of my own.

The *Register* is a "Who's Who in the World of Self-Inflicted Grievous Bodily Harm". Producers flick through it in search of, say, a likely lad capable of "Car turnovers, car through plate glass, car jumps". Does he also know how to steer a power boat, not safely, but to crash it to order? It sounds as if the man we want is Frank (in a possibly vain attempt to avoid giving offence to the Stunt Committee, I refrain from surnames), especially if we also need "dog fights, fire explosions, free fall parachutist and twenty second delay falls", not to mention "driving cars by mirrors or camera". There are many motorists who drive as if they used only those artificial aids, but I take it this refers to cars in television plays performing complicated manoeuvres with no one visible behind the wheel; just under the wheels.

Stanley Baker could not be trusted to drive a vehicle through a supermarket window; Frank Finlay might find the lead round his neck in a dog fight; Dennis Waterman needs a minder when blowing himself up. For that reason, Frank has doubled for them all.

Chris, on the other hand, takes over when the going gets tough for Donald Sutherland, James Coburn, Elliott Gould, Ian Ogilvy and Roger Moore. If he's otherwise engaged, the part of Roger Moore may be played by Martin ("high falls of 100ft plus, explosions and fire"), who also doubles as Harrison Ford and Richard Harris. He specialises in "martial arts", as opposed to Fred, who is good at "marshall arts", presumably portraying sheriffs with watercolour sets.

With three million unemployed, stuntmen are desperate not to join them. Paddy says, "Have fought lions, dogs and snakes", but not, to judge by the fact that he has had acting experience of 51 years, for some time. Connie ("fights, skylight falls") asserts, "Have fallen off eighteen bridges," on purpose, we hope. She gives her statistics, too: 22 inches Inside Arm measurement, $6\frac{1}{2}$ in hats. Dorothy, with a thirteen-inch collar, has impersonated Brigitte Bardot, Liz Taylor, Joanna Lumley and Diana Rigg when the script called for "underwater shots and aerial work under helicopters and cable cars"; who impersonated them when it came to acting, it doesn't say. For them all, it was nice work, once they got it.

But who gets it? At this point, we are back in the debate from which I shied away nervously at the beginning of this article. There has been talk of some stuntmen finding more employment than others, not on account of talent but on account of belonging to an alleged Magic Circle that has entirely sewn up the business of hanging from cable cars by the teeth and fracturing skylights with the naked nose. This so-called syndicate is said by dissident wrestlers and screen Samurai to "suggest" to casting directors which car crashers and jousters should be signed up, and which should be told not to ring back.

There is certainly a fair amount of backbiting—not literally so, I suppose, though to judge by some of the mug-shots in the *Register*, teeth-marks in the spinal region should not be altogether ruled out. Equity itself denies this, stating that some actors find more employment than others and that's the way it goes. If you can't stand the heat, stay out of the fire-eating.

The pros and cons of this are best not judged by those of a nervous disposition, given that men like Clive ("height 6ft 2in, chest 44in, wrestling, magnificent physique") might disagree with whichever way they came down. Take Thomas: "Specialises in 'Heavy' parts, and fight scenes." He might take exception to opinions expressed and I should hate to cause him any distress, especially since he states ominously in his *Register* entry: "Worked sixteen years on club and dance hall doors and there were no rehearsals for bar room brawls." For rowdies finding themselves flat on their faces in an exterior setting, it was a case of "Great, we'll print that," rather than, "We'll just try that one more time, dears."

Or Bill, whom you couldn't miss across a crowded studio: "$17\frac{1}{2}$ stone, 19in collar, driving four-in-hands, caber tosser and ex-Irish Champion for throwing the 56lb weight." He specialises in "tree felling", no, not with his bare hands, but "with axe", and the chopper is just another reason why I hardly like to mention another point. But I've started, so they'll finish me off.

It does seem rather hard to achieve

"Probationary" status on the *Register*, to judge by the struggle of Tony Van Silva, actor and former wrestler. On his first application to the committee of stuntmen who effectively control entry, he was rejected. His second letter of application took six months to motivate a reply from the Committee, which was that certain qualifications in weightlifting and suchlike were essential. He is now achieving them. I should hate to be there if he ever has to call round, presumably by driving a convertible at the front door of Château Equity, to complain about a third rejection.

He probably wouldn't hurt himself. Equity Insurance tells me that since June they have paid out for only one injury, a shoulder hurt when its owner happened to be in a car into which another one was driven at speed. Stuntmen must be fully covered before they get up to their stunts. Unfortunately, there is no insurance for journalists writing about them. The scribes in question may come to wish they had torn up their articles in the first place. With their bare hands, of course. 🐦

The current price for leaving a Civil Service trade union, giving information to a racecourse gambler or standing for Parliament is £1,000.

A Thousand Thank-yous

A top-grade civil servant who
Ran signals at a key HQ
Was asked to sign a paper which,
While making him uncommon rich,
Required him, though the choice was hard,
To throw away his union card;
And what is rare among his tribe,
He bowed his head and took the bribe.

A jockey who had won the Oaks,
A riband prized by other blokes,
Was saddled with a gambler's gift.
The Jockey Club, in judgement swift,
Imposed on him a three-year ban
And made the lad an also-ran,
A punishment which somehow sounds
Hard going for a thousand pounds.

A wiser man and one who's straight,
Confronted by such tempting bait,
Would throw it down the water-closet—
Or, using it as his deposit,
Which now has risen to a grand,
Would look to Parliament, and stand
As Judas-At-The-Going-Rate
Unseated Jockey candidate.

Roger Woddis

"I've been replaced by a potted plant."

"It's just a precaution—once he tried to contradict me."

"Let's face it—what we really need is someone to take us walkies."

"Calling Patrol Base . . . Intruder . . . Number 16 . . ."

". . . and that's the flasher who frightened Mrs Latchford."

"Be careful, Sidney, it could be a trap."

"Let me through—I'm a doctor!"

"Mr Wibley! What are you doing stealing your own son's hi-fi?"

"I really do think Mr Wormleigh is taking these neighbourhood patrols rather too seriously."

Channel 4 seeks a view from the Right

by Sue Summers

CHANNEL 4, under fire for its Left - wing bias wants more Right - wing programmes, its boss, Jeremy Isaacs, said today.

Opinions, 8.30

5.30 A Full Life

JILL COCHRANE
DAVID IRVING

David Irving, historian, wit, humanitarian, talks to Jill Cochrane about his unrivalled collection of Himmler hankies, his disillusion with Ayatollah Khomeini's wets, and his own work on the revolutionary chicken-strangling machine to which so much of his leisure time has been dedicated.
TVS Production

6.00 Big Strong Bugger

A riveting, poignant, but nonetheless heartwarming documentary about Jack Anderson, born 38 years ago

CHANNEL FOUR

with all his limbs, 20-20 vision, and ears that could hear a snail cough at fifty metres, who grew to be six-feet-three of fatless muscle, capable of lifting a wheel-chaired geriatric in each hand! We talk with the doctors who have attended him all his life and never had to give him more than a sedative to stop him from punching epileptics, and we talk to the women who have had to see to his every need, frequently as often as seven times a day. We also see Jack Anderson the tireless campaigner on behalf of those like himself: for years now, Jack has worked to get the ramps taken out of public lavatories to make way for more urinals, and to remove Ceefax titles from television programmes so that the deaf will have to stop kidding themselves that they know what's going on.
RESEARCH:
GIANT HAYSTACKS
DIRECTOR:
LENI RIEFENSTAHL
An LWT/Argentina Rundfunk Co-production

7.00 Channel Four News

Peter Sissons and Sarah Hogg present television's widest-ranging news programme. Trevor McDonald accompanies them on the banjo.

7.50 Comment

Watch Channel Four's nightly soap box for a personal view on an item of topical importance. Tonight, journalist Roger Scruton puts the castrationist case.

8.00 Brookside

A snivelling wimp from the local Labour Party attempts to canvass Number 14 and is dragged around the estate behind Rodney's Jag. Fenella comes home with a new dress from Ikey Modes, and when it turns out not to be crease-resistant, hubbie Peregrine and some of his old rugger chums trot round to the shop and prove to the wily Levantine that British Petroleum lives up to its name!
WRITER:
RICHARD INGRAMS
PRODUCER:
COLIN JORDAN
Brookside Productions

8.30 Opinions

OSWALD ALDERTON
LAW AND ORDER

Continuing this popular series, Oswald, the sensible brother of Manchester's leftist Chief Constable, takes a cool detached look at the urban landscape and puts a few reflective questions to the rational viewer. Why are there no verminous limp-wristed nancy-boys hanging from our lamp-posts with their feet twitching and their purple tongues sticking out of their mouths? How is it that no modern magistrate will order shoplifting wogs to have their stomachs slit open and filled with red-hot stones? Is there no local authority in this great land of ours prepared to bring back the Iron Maiden for louts who would rather hang about Labour Exchanges insulting Her Majesty's Government than join the British Army and march off to kick the hell out of the poteen-swilling bog-Irish left-footers?
RESEARCH: JILL KNIGHT
MUSIC:
INSTANT SUNSHINE

9.00 NEW SERIES

THIRD WORLD FOCUS

SOUTH AFRICA

In the first part of a searching series of investigations into the underprivileged peoples of this often unequal globe, we look at the beleaguered folk of South Africa: hugely outnumbered by the teeming aliens within their borders who have made no secret of their murderous hatred, snubbed by Commonwealth and UN alike, cut off from decent spin bowling and nuclear protection, the courageous and noble descendants of Rhodes and Botha still manage, by sheer hard work, guts, and superior intellect, to scratch a living from the land they love.
NARRATED BY
J. ENOCH POWELL
RESEARCH BY IAN SPROAT
WRITTEN AND DIRECTED BY GRAHAM GOOCH

9.30 FILM Films For Women:

The Dam Busters

11.00 Nature Watch

Amateur naturalist President Zia of Pakistan puts the anti-conservationist case. If the salmon hasn't got the guts to live in sewage and industrial waste, what bloody business has it got hanging around near our great factories? After the discussion, the Hon. Fiona Strume-Kettering will be back with some exciting new fox recipes.

11.30 Jazz On Four

The Band of the Second Battalion, the Parachute Regiment, plays more favourites, including *Tipperary, Goodbye Dolly Gray, Maggie's Tune*, etc.

12.00 Somewhere East of Suez

Programme for Asian viewers. R. D. Mukerjee, Narasimha Singh, and Ram Chaudhury recite Kipling's *Barrack-Room Ballads*, at gunpoint.

12.15 Lights Out

Roy
HATTERSLEY

"My allegation caught Mrs Thatcher in two minds, uncertain whether to brush me aside or trample me to death."

Touch of Class

IN 1972, when Margaret Thatcher had been Secretary of State for Education and Science for about three years, I became her "shadow". My task was to be ground to dust beneath her chariot wheels. Two days after I had strapped myself into the cockpit of the Zero dive-bomber (and changed the image, as perceptive readers will have noticed, from Rome circa 500 BC to Pearl Harbor 1941) I was required to tie on my rising-sun headband and dive in the general direction of her engine-room. My suicide mission was against the good ship "Education: A Framework for Expansion".

During the 48 hours between taking the kamikaze oath and shouting "Chocks away!" I consulted Professor Maurice Peston, who assisted me in the Colosseum or on the aircraft-carrier's flight-deck, depending on which metaphor you prefer. He thrust a piece of paper into my hand which would not have been more incomprehensible had it been written in Latin or Japanese. It was, he assured me, conclusive proof that the Government intended to cut the Education budget. All I had to do to secure a Parliamentary triumph was to learn the lines and repeat them with conviction.

My allegation caught Mrs Thatcher in two minds, uncertain whether to brush me aside or trample me to death. And the *Times Educational Supplement* announced to the pedagogic world that I had "miscued"—a strange allusion which, I suspected at the time, was an unpleasant reference to my misspent youth. I asked Professor Peston how I should reply. The manner of his response was part suitable for a seminar and part more appropriate to a revivalist meeting. He attempted to teach me the elements of statistical method and urged me to put my faith in him.

He also drafted a letter to Stuart Maclure, then as now the editor of the *TES*. Mr Maclure telephoned me two days later. He found my formulae persuasive. He had already consulted two acknowledged experts. If the third (one Maurice Peston by name) agreed that I was right, a fulsome apology would follow.

And so it turned out. The Department of Education and Science (though not its Secretary of State) conceded defeat. The next weekend, the *Times Educational Supplement*, pursuing its billiard hall analogy, announced that I had "potted black". I tell this tedious story so that you will understand that everything I have to say about the *TES* is warmed by the memory of an editor sufficiently self-confident to admit he was wrong, and a weekly paper so interested in accuracy that it first investigates and then corrects its errors.

But I hope that even without my rose-tinted spectacles I would recognise the *Times Educational Supplement* as a thoroughly admirable publication; essential reading for the serious and ambitious schoolteacher. It is, of course, its staff-room appeal which makes the *TES* so profitable. In a normal week it carries more than thirty pages of classified advertisements. For an assistant master or mistress who has never read Rupert Brooke on Cherry Hinton and would, therefore, like to become Deputy Head of that village's Community Junior School, or want to find oblivion in Banovallon (not a tranquilliser but a Lincolnshire secondary school) the *TES* is the indispensable Baedeker to success.

It is not, however, simply the staff-room version of *Exchange and Mart*. It manages to be funny about education—a discipline which some of its disciples treat with a glacial seriousness that freezes the interest of all but the most devoted followers of Matthew Arnold or his dad. On high days and holidays it used to publish imaginary conversations between the incumbent Secretary of State and his (or her) private secretary. It remains unrepentantly irreverent. A new Vice-Chancellor for the University of the South Pacific "conjures up the image of Mary Martin in doctoral robes". That sort of idea is supposed to pass through the heads of real people, not educational pundits.

Not that genuine pundits are lacking. "Nigel Bennett and Lynton Gray are senior lecturers in the Education Management Di-

vision of the Anglian Regional Management Centre at North East London Polytechnic," and last week they wrote a joint article on educational vouchers which was rather longer than their job description. It was also extremely interesting, driving away all thoughts concerning the possibility that the job description was wrong. Why is there an Anglian Management Centre in North-East London? Or could a Poly be doing a little mis-spelled management consultancy for the Established Church?

Of course one of the advantages enjoyed by an eighty-page educational magazine is the wealth of literary talent hanging around our colleges and universities waiting to write the odd freelance article. Which is why the *TES* is able to cover so much eclectic ground. It has four or five pages of general book reviews. And as well as providing the professional with inside information about the details of local decisions ("Powys primary school staff cuts begin to nip"), it tells its less vocational (or more dilettante) readers about the importance of education in the West German election campaign and academic freedom breaking out in Kenya.

Although it caters for a group of professionals who have not always been notable for keeping their importance in proper perspective, the *Times Educational Supplement* maintains an admirably balanced (indeed consciously sceptical) attitude towards the pomposities and pretensions of its readers. So I doubt if Mr Maclure would welcome an overstatement of his paper's appeal. I do not therefore urge educational ignoramuses to order a weekly copy.

But if you have a moment to spare in W. H. Smith (or some other admirable newsagent where browsing is allowed), at least have a free read of the back page. If you are lucky, it will be Professor Ted Wragg's week to write the "Personal" column. It is wry. It is astringent. It is entertaining and it is informative. If only it were also reactionary it would certainly replace Professor Vincent's column in *The Times* which makes no claim to be educational.

Christopher MATTHEW PROPERTY

Shop Shape

I AM not one of nature's shopkeepers. I happen to know this because twenty or so years ago my father took it into his head to buy a small shop in the village in Norfolk where we were living at the time. He sold, in roughly equal proportions, agricultural equipment and booze, for which he possessed, for some unaccountable reason, a full licence. In other words, customers could, if they so wished, not only drink on the premises but continue to do so until chucking out time.

Luckily for all of us, the village at that time enjoyed more than its fair share of pubs, and besides, the local. farmers had more pressing concerns on their minds, such as ensuring that cases of Haig appeared on the bill as "rolls of barbed wire"—a way of thinking with which this East Anglian Candide, helping out during the hols, never quite came to grips.

My main problem, though, was one of manner. Veering wildly between a Heep-like grovel and gruff off-handedness verging on downright rudeness, I never quite succeeded in striking that cheerful, helpful, confident note which distinguishes the professional sales assistant from the part-time amateur.

But then, of course, those were the days before everyone, but everyone, my dear, wanted to run a little shop, and every High Street in the land started ringing to the sound of upper middle-class accents flogging anything from second-hand books and fancy cheeses to theatrical posters, dried herbs, children's party gear and assorted Victorian tat.

This born-again enthusiasm among the gentry to conform to the Napoleonic view of English life manifests itself daily in Farrar, Stead and Glyn's commercial office in the Brompton Road, where Chris Barrow is constantly being rung up by ping-pong ball accents announcing that they wouldn't at all mind buying a nice little shop, preferably somewhere congenial like Beauchamp Place or the King's Road, where trade is likely to be brisk and their friends can pop in for a coffee and a chat.

Few, it would seem, have the foggiest notion of what is involved; many have not even gone so far as to inform their solicitor of their plans; and, luckily for Mr Barrow, who's a busy man, a lot are put off the idea straight away by the shocking news that for starters they'll be expected to stump up a healthy premium for the lease.

The amount demanded represents a combination of fixtures and fittings, location and general goodwill and can range from ten grand or so for one floor of under 300 square feet in Pimlico or World's End, to nearly a quarter of a million in that gold-paved stretch between Harrods and the top of Sloane Street.

The further out you venture, the less you'll be asked to find, until you get to somewhere like Munster Road in darkest Fulham, where you'll probably get a lease for nothing—provided, that is, you don't mind the prospect of never seeing a customer from one day's end to the next. (In Oxford Street, rents are now so astronomical that landlords will actually pay *you* to come in, but that's another story.)

The mention of a few sample rents can also prove a useful deterrent to the half-baked punter, Barrow finds. The news, for instance, that a small shop in Beauchamp Place can cost anything up to £30,000 a year, excluding rates, soon determines the seriousness of an enquiry.

"The funny thing is," he said, "no matter how high the rents go, in a good area someone will always come along to take a place over. Good properties go quickly; poor ones stick."

Hence the surprising paucity of good

"Your Honour, my client pleads guilty to the charge of attempting to defraud the Guinness Book of Records, and asks for twenty-five million fourteen thousand, two-hundred and seventeen other offences to be taken into consideration."

stuff currently on Farrar, Stead and Glyn's books.

"Occasionally you'll find one or two dotted about in the King's Road, and once in a blue moon something will come up at the better end of the Fulham Road, but honestly, I can't think of one small shop on the market in this area in the last few months that people have fought over."

Not that the chances of a beginner being accepted by a landlord in the Chelsea-Knightsbridge-Kensington *quartier* are particularly bright anyway.

It all depends on what is known in the business as strength of covenant: the more impressive your track record and the better the references you can squeeze out of your accountant, your bank manager, your solicitor and your trading partners, the healthier your chances of being picked—not by the landlord himself but by the estate agent, whose discretion in commercial matters is considerably more powerful than it is in the residential market. Indeed, in the majority of cases, the prospective purchaser never comes within a fourpenny bus ride of the freeholder.

"We consider each case on its merits," explained Chris Barrow, "and go for the strongest covenant. If two or three look about the same, we go back to them and ask for their best offers."

But if all this sounds gloomy news to would-be beginners, they should take heart from the tale of Chantal Coady, a 23-year-old ex-art student, who decided that the buying and selling of chocolates was far too exciting an activity to be left to old-fashioned firms like Bendicks and Charbonnel and Walker.

"There's something intrinsically wicked about chocolates," she told me, "and yet no one had exploited it."

So she took a ten-week business course, run by the Manpower Services Commission ("tremendously helpful but you've got to be very motivated"), worked in the chocolate department of Harrods, felt sure she was on the right track and set about finding a shop in which to put her theory to the test.

A year ago she opened the brilliantly named and perfectly placed Rococo in the King's Road, just up from Beaufort Street. It's far and away the prettiest chocolate shop in town, and in addition to gorgeous fresh cream truffles, multicoloured dragées, nests of gulls' eggs filled with praline, and chocolate rabbits with red buttonholes, she and her assistant also sell under franchise Ben's Cookies and sensational sorbets from La Maison des Sorbets in Battersea.

"It was glaringly obvious to me where the

shop should be," she said. "I earmarked this stretch and just walked up and down looking at estate agents' billboards and ringing them up. Getting them to take me seriously was a real problem, and some were really pushy about wanting to be retained. That means they can tout round on your behalf and then get a fee when they find you something: 10% of the first year's rental and 3% of the premium. In fact four shops came up, but each time I was gazumped because I had no track record. Timing was crucial. I had to get in before Easter, otherwise I'd have had to scrap the whole idea. In the end I struck up a good relationship with Jones Lang and Wootton, thanks to a good reference from a couple of kind suppliers."

Barclay's Bank were very good to her, too. She'd gone in with a detailed thirty-page document on the project, expecting to be refused, instead of which they lent her £20,000 at 3% above best.

"Mind you," she added, "they do make a lot of money out of it. One quarter I paid them £800 in charges alone."

Chantal's lease cost her £10,500, rates are £2,000 a year and the rent is £6,500, but that could be doubled next year. The custom-built glass cabinets, the marble floor and the cherubic painted ceiling cost £5,000 ("It's no good buying a cheap shop if you want to sell chocolates") and she has yet to break even. And even though her products are the best on the market and business is brisk, she still admits to finding the responsibility of it all "surprisingly stressful".

It's a feeling that is shared by Amanda Reiss, whose good-as-new children's shop, Swallows and Amazons, in Webb's Road, Battersea, is nearly four months old.

After various false starts and much time-wasting, she finally got in without a premium and at a weekly rent of £100, but not without first having done her homework and her sums.

Having been brought up to accept the idea of quite well-off people buying good second-hand clothes, and having carefully noted the enormous exodus southwards of large, middle-class families, she decided the area could stand a really good, inexpensive, second-hand children's shop. To judge by the quantity and quality of the gear that gets delivered daily by the Volvo-load, she was not alone.

Her original ambition had been to find somewhere in Northcote Road which enjoys rather brisker passing trade thanks to the big daily market, but so far she has no regrets.

"More and more people are getting to know me, and as long as I keep my prices low and tell my suppliers not to expect too much, the stuff will continue to go quickly. But even so, one is terribly tempted to panic from time to time. Soon after we opened, an Indian friend of ours came round to see how we were getting on. After a while he shook his head sadly. 'We have a saying in our country,' he said. 'Death and the customer: who knows when they will come?' That was all we needed!"

CAPTION COMPETITION
WINNERS

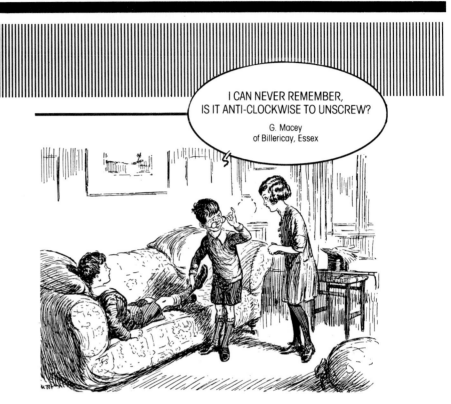

I CAN NEVER REMEMBER, IS IT ANTI-CLOCKWISE TO UNSCREW?

G. Macey
of Billericay, Essex

1924 caption—*OUR BUDDING SAWBONES.* "TUT, TUT, MADAM, IT IS JUST AS I FEARED. YOUR HUSBAND HAS BROKEN HIS LEG IN TWO PLACES AND I MUST PRESCRIBE HALF-AN-HOUR'S *COMPLETE* REST."

THE HOTEL'S ROTTEN BUT THE ROOM SERVICE IS OUT OF THIS WORLD!

M. Driscoll
of Worcester

1872 caption—AN EYE TO BUSINESS. *MILITIA GUARD ("TURNING OUT," AND IN CHORUS).* "PLEASE, SIR, R'MEMB'R THE GUARD, SIR!!!" *(EXEUNT QUEEN'S OFFICERS IN SPEECHLESS HORROR, MORE CONVINCED THAN EVER THAT "THE SERVICE IS GOING TO THE _____"* ETC.

Stanley REYNOLDS
In a Greene Wode

Gloomy Graham Greene comes to light in a new book as a regular reader of P. G. Wodehouse.

IT was one of those absolutely oojah cum spif mornings with the sky all blue and the jungle air so still you could hear a leper's nose dropping off at sixty paces.

"Good morning, Jeeves."

"Good morning, sir."

"Wizard wheeze this, eh Jeeves? I mean, up the Amazon, the jungle, nature red in tooth and whatever it is, what?"

Jeeves gave one of his little coughs of disapproval; as coughs went, Jeeves's little cough was about as subtle as an Amazonian anaconda swallowing a shoal of pigmy offspring for hors d'oeuvre before slapping on the nose-bag for the big stuff.

But hold on—hold the line a minute. I've gone off the rails. The snag I always come up against when telling a story is this dashed business of where to begin. Fool round with what they call atmosphere and all that rot and you fail to grasp the customer by the lapels. Get going like a scalded cat at the off and your reading punter is at a loss and can't make out what you're talking about.

Now this is rather a complex one, even for young Bertram. Lots of fellows seem to think there's nothing more to life than Ascot and Goodwood and hurling the old buns and bread rolls about on jolly fine evenings at Drones but, dash it all, sometimes adventure calls and a chap has just got to get away from it all, journey off the map on what I like to call the lawless roads, what! So here were Jeeves and the good self

and that absolute ass Gussie Fink-Nottle, the chappie with the pash for newts. Newts being those little sort of lizard things that charge about in ponds; what Jeeves calls, in his rummy way, the aquatic members of the family *Salamandridae* which constitute the genus *Molge*. Beats me how he thinks up these things. No—hold on. Bertram has gone off the rails again.

Right ho, the posish was this: that ass Gussie had fallen in love with a most unsuitable girl, one of those tough modern thugs, all lip-rouge, big white teeth and goo-goo eyes, called Imogen Bassington-Bassington. Now the Bass was clearly unsuitable for a newt like Gussie. The only thing was to get him a largish chunk of the globe between Gussie and the Bass. Hence, the wheeze I thought up about the giant man-eating newts of the upper Amazon. Gussie took to that like the nouveau riche take to crème de menthe.

This does not, however, explain just why Jeeves and the young master were at this moment preparing to meet the day in this seedy little banana republic where the locals eke out a modest living by overthrowing each others' governments. Aunt Agatha was the thing. You know my Aunt Agatha, the one who chews barbed wire. Yes, most decidedly, Aunt Agatha was the *point d'appui*.

Right ho, then, let me marshal the old facts.

Aunt Agatha had taken to religion the way some chaps take to drink. First thing in

the morning she'd start with a belt of St Francis of Assisi. Before even luncheon she'd be scooping up St Margaret of Scotland. In fact she'd often skip luncheon altogether for a few snorts of St Thomas Aquinas and keep right on it until dinner time, which she often skipped, and rather than tapering off with a few Blesseds and Venerables, she'd hear the chimes of midnight on the real hard stuff like St Augustine, waking up at four in the morning in a terrible state, with dog-eared copies of St Chromantius and St Chrodegang under the bed, and a thirst for Simeon of Syracuse frazzling her to absolute shedders.

All those people in Mayfair who have seen Aunt Agatha go into deep shock so they had to call in the motorcycle cops and rope off the area just because a chap walked into the Ritz wearing jazz socks—which had been all the rage, just absolutely *tout ce qu'il y a de chic* that season—will be thunderstruck when they unfold the message in the cleft stick and learn that the self same Aunt Agatha had abandoned the flesh pots of Eaton Square and was working in a Papist leper colony deep in the jungle of El San Souci.

I don't pretend to know much about religion but I know what I like and that is the jolly old C of E with the vicar playing long stop on the village XI and maybe tippling a bit with the elderberry, but all this hob-nobbing with lepers and whisky priests going round with three-day stubbles and having the DTs smack in the middle of high mass, elevating as it may be for the faithful, did raise the odd twitch to the Wooster eyebrow.

Of course, you do get the occasional trendy curate in the C of E who gets carried away teaching the Bible psycho-drama style in Sunday school and does Jacob wrestling with the Angel, joined in what looks an awful lot, to the suspicious eye, like unlawful communion, but you can always negotiate a cloud for said curate to depart under.

Now the Papes never do that. They seem to relish the seedy side where life is grey as a kulack's footcloth. And added to the whisky priest they had come up with a new twinge. There were absolute hordes of eager, young, left-wing, Marxist padres, lacing the incense with marijuana and spouting Marx and Lenin to the local goolies whose idea of sophisticated fun had previously been fornicating with the water buffalo and shrinking the head of the kid sister.

So there you have the layout—Aunt Agatha clicking the old Fortnum and Mason rosary beads in time to the leper's collapsing nostrils and falling digits, the whisky priest committing incest with the illegitimate issue, the Marxist padres fermenting revolution by giving the locals the lowdown on the 20-second fuse, Gussie languishing over Bassington-Bassington, young Bertram busily purchasing as nifty a brace of shrunken heads as ever adorned a Mayfair chimney piece, while Jeeves . . .

No—hold on tight! I must re-run the footage. Curious cove, Jeeves. It may surprise you to learn that it was his idea in the first place to follow Aunt Agatha's gum-booted tread to the leper colony.

But once here, what he did was bally nothing—nothing absolutely but while away his time in conversations with an American tourist, one Karl J. Pipesucker III of Philadelphia, Groton and Yale. We had been here for weeks, with Aunt Agatha sweeping up the lepers' spare parts and getting ready to lay the Wooster riches upon them, Gussie tramping through the foliage, young Bertram in a positive sweat, and Jeeves engrossed in nothing but the above-mentioned aforesaid plus keeping me away, for some reason, from my aunt.

In the picture, now? That just about fills it in, to the morning in question when the whole situation was crying out a warning of "Fire!"

"Jeeves."

"Sir?"

"We've been here weeks, Jeeves."

"I have been cognisant of the passage of time, sir."

"And nothing has happened, Jeeves. Aunt Agatha keeps keening over the lepers, Mr Fink-Nottle is mooning over the Bassington-Bassington, the Wooster spoils are about to be handed over to the Papal branch of the Bolsheviks and you chin-wag with young Pipesucker III. You've even kept me from going on bended to the aged relative."

"I informed your aunt this morning of your arrival."

"They are peeling her off the roof right now, eh Jeeves?"

"The new-found Christian spirit seemed to depart rather rapidly, sir. She accused the lepers in her charge of malingering, sir, emptied Father Flanagan's whisky down the sink and is even now packing her grip."

"What about the Marxist padres, Jeeves? You can buy hell's own amount of dum-dum bullets with Aunt Agatha's bullion. They won't give up without a bleat."

"Mr Pipesucker III has seen to them, sir. Like the late Mr Pipesucker II and, indeed, Mr Pipesucker I, he is, as perhaps you surmised, a member of the American Intelligence Service. He has arranged a right-wing coup. The local headhunters have been dealing with them. I believe, sir, you purchased a Father Greene and a Monsignor O'Brien at a very much reduced price only yesterday."

"Oh, rather! Rather ooja cum spif, what?"

"All very nice, I'm sure, sir, but not quite England."

"Good Lord, Jeeves! We forgot Gussie, what about Gussie, what?"

"Mr Fink-Nottle has been struck with the desirability of devoting his life to the study of the South American genus of the saurian reptile. What is vulgarly called the alligator."

"Farewell the newt, eh Jeeves?"

"Mr Fink-Nottle claims it possesses both the fascination of the giant, man-eating newt with a certain resemblance to Miss Bassington-Bassington. It is the teeth, sir, I believe, combined with the goo-goo eyes."

"E' gad, Jeeves, I mean, by Jove!"

"Precisely, sir."

So that's about the posish.

It was one of those absolutely oojah cum spif mornings with . . . ☙

"I hate Sundays."

SPRING FAIRS & FESTIVALS

A Handy Checklist

MARCH

16 **Nolesbury Pus Fair,** Nolesbury, Lincs. Marks the bursting of Edward II's neck-wen, 1318. Traditional crafts and contests: gypsy boil-letting, largest blackhead competition, Pimply Queen Parade, greasy carbuncle contest, etc. Starts 10 am, Cloth Yard.

17 **Lambert Newton Virgin Rolling,** Lambert Newton, Hunts. Dates back to pre-Christian times. Basically a form of crude football, the Virgin Rolling involves two teams of male villagers, sixty per side, who, according to rules first codified and written down in the reign of Henry III, "muste rol a Virginne of ye parisshe either to Northe Gait or to Southe Gait & not interfear wyth hir partes until one gait or other has been gayned, after ye which the wynninge teem may have thir waye wyth her, & a firkin to boote." In modern times, of course, the rules have been modified: the ·disappearance of virgins has meant that Mrs Deirdre Wentworth's standing offer is annually taken up, which has meant increasing the teams to eighty a side.

19 **Ffinchingham Stockbroker Trials,** Ffinchingham, Bucks. Village weekenders in various initiative tests: Identify-The-Cow, Fifty-Yard-Hike, Dust-The-Range-Rover, Pull-On-The-Green-Wellie, Shut-The-Bloody-Gate, Low-Beam-Head-Minding-Test, Avoid-The-Horse-Turd, Spot-The-Stream, etc. Female visitors not admitted without Hermes head-scarves. Mulled vodka.

23 **Deaf Plasterers' Rally,** Blackheath.

25 **NUM Furry Dance,** Grimethorpe. Sheep-kissing, nude grocery, Gyles Brandreth Guess-My-Smell Contest, exhibition of stuffed lemmings, Eat Something Peculiar Match (*A Cricklewood XI vs. Margaret, Duchess of Argyll*), canary race.

26 **Irish Professional Tennis Finals,** Putney to Mortlake, 4.15.

27 **Bum Sunday.** Various events nationwide: Royal Security XV *vs.* Cambridge Apostles XV, Primrose Hill; *Private Eye* Charity Mince, Greek Street to Pangbourne; Foreign Office Under-23 *vs.* Militant Tendency Water Polo Match, Chelmsford Conservative Party HQ Jacuzzi; Cruise Here Demonstration, Leicester Square; Finlay Currie Lookalike Contest, Camden Women's Co-operative.

29 **SDP Donkey Derby,** Cheam.

30 **Burley-cum-Donnington Lice-Gathering,** New Forest, Hants. Rastafarian chess marathon, bread staring (*Russell Harty Relatives vs. Eton Rabbis*), 1374 New Forest Scout Troop Suicide Bid, boil-a-dog-for-Victor-Matthews race, flea-whistling, limb sale.

31 **Christmas Eve Dance & Shinty Match,** Shamrock Ballrooms, Kilburn (*if wet, in the garden*).

LET'S PARLER FRANGLAIS!

Au Taxi Rank

Monsieur: Streatham, svp.
Cabby: Streatham? Sorry, monsieur. Pas un espoir.
Monsieur: Pourquoi pas Streatham?
Cabby: C'est le back de beyond. C'est dans le wilderness. Je ne trouverai jamais un return fare. Streatham est un non-non, cab-wise.
Monsieur: Mais je suis désespéré, et vous êtes l'unique taxi ici.
Cabby: C'est la vie, mon vieux mate.
Monsieur: OK, OK—je vais vous payer un tarif *double*. Un trip aller-et-retour à Streatham. Vous êtes satisfait?
Cabby: Non. Le samedi soir? Faîtes-nous une faveur.
Monsieur: Saturday, c'est différent?
Cabby: Blimey, vous êtes un innocent et pas d'erreur. Samedi, c'est pour les yobbos et les piss-artistes et les secrétaires qui sont malades dans mon taxi immaculé. Regardez l'heure; 11.15 pm! C'est la sortie des pubs etc.
Monsieur: Mais je ne sors pas d'un pub! Je viens de laisser un train. L'express de Bristol Parkway à Paddington. Il n'y a pas beaucoup de knees-up à Bristol Parkway, croyez-moi! Et la night-life sur le train est minimal.
Cabby: On peut très facilement se saôuler sur le train. Le mini-buffet sur BR, c'est légendaire pour les piss-ups. Surtout pour les supporteurs de football.
Monsieur: Look! Je ne suis ni supporteur de football, ni night-clubbeur, ni yobbo! Je suis un citizène modèle! Je suis totalement sobre.
Cabby: Ah—vous êtes sobre maintenant, peut-être, mais si vous avez une bouteille dans votre baggage . . . D'ici à Streatham, c'est toute une histoire.
Monsieur: Oh, mon Dieu . . . Regardez, si vous m'emmenez à Lambeth, je vais faire le reste à pied.
Cabby: À Lambeth . . . ? Non. Trop court. Lambeth est un wash-out pour un cabby.
Monsieur: Mais vous êtes impossible! Qui voulez-vous prendre comme passager? Vous êtes contre tout le monde?
Cabby: Basiquement, oui. Saturday night est no-go night. Je prendrais peut-être—*peut-être*, mind—une réligieuse d'une ordre très respectable. Une Soeur de Charité, quelque chose comme ça.
Religieuse: (*qui émerge de nowhere*) Monsieur, je suis une Soeur de L'Ordre de Saint Joseph, et je veux aller à Kilburn.
Cabby: Une féministe? Et Irlandaise? Et *une femme seule*? Pas sur votre nelly, si vous excusez mon franglais. (*Il disparaît, bien satisfait avec son night's work.*) ✿

GREASE ARNOLD ROTH

follows oil down the slippery slope
OIL 1933–1983

Simon HOGGART

ON THE HOUSE

"Dear Mr Steel, I am writing to protest about the fact that I am pregnant—don't remember what happened to me."

WHAT a strange and sometimes pitiful insight into the human condition an MP's postbag provides! It is not actually a bag; instead, each day the MP gets several bundles of letters held together by elastic bands. Around the outside are the foolscap magazines and documents: "Scum. Magazine of the Local Authority Sewage Maintenance Operatives," the report of a conference, printed on glossy paper, revealing how chemical waste actually enhances the quality of life of those who live close to it. Further in are the requests for lectures and articles, invitations to dinner at the Dorchester with the Chad Ambassador and the first loony letters—"Sir, I believe that I have discovered the cure for Britain's economic ills. If you will be so kind as to read the enclosed 250 pages and give me your opinion . . ." In the heart of the bundle, almost ready to fall unnoticed out onto the marble floor of the lobby, are the little letters from private people, abuse, pathetic cries for help scrawled on Basildon Bond.

David Steel keeps a special file of the strangest letters, some of which are funny, some bizarre, and some so weird that the smile dies upon the lips as you read. Here's a letter on child's patterned notepaper, though the writing is of an uneducated adult: "Dear Mr Steel, I am writing to protest about the fact that I am pregnant—don't remember what happened to me. Dr is lousy. Can you please help me?" What depths of despair made that woman write to a politician, a figure on a television screen? Steel wrote back suggesting a call to the British Pregnancy Advisory Service, and short of sending a cheque for £1,000, there was nothing else that he could do.

The writing and the format of a letter are no guide to the extent of its loopiness. Here's one written in old fashioned curlicued handwriting signed "British Citizen" and addressed to "Dear David and all the Alliance". It is an outpouring of hatred against the Conservative Party ("Right wing Tories are the scum of the earth. Thatcher, Tebbit, Howe etc they are worse than Hitler") though the writer's main objection seems to be that they are not keen enough on pornography. "One thing which really makes me livid is that Thatcher grovels to sexually frustrated Whitehouse. Anything to do with sexual freedom and pornography (legal other countries) then Thatcher can't act fast enough to crush these, when porn is legal in other countries and Britain should have the same sexual freedom as Germany, Denmark, Sweden . . ."

The writer's real worry seems to be that he (or she; it isn't clear) has not been getting

GREAT MOMENTS IN PUBLISHING, NO. 127 C.P. SCOTT CONCEIVES THE GUARDIAN.

enough. "Time and time again Tory MPs are mixed up in sex scandals. No laws against sex will worry them. Even if all sex were banned today Tory MPs would still wallow in porn & sex. Take the way poor Jeremy Thorpe was crucified. When anyone with brains knows House of Commons is riddled with homo-sexuals. I will name two now in Tory anti-sex Thatcher cabinet." (The writer then mentions two distinguished Conservatives, both of them happily married.) "It's written all over their *faces & actions.* These two are *obvious homosexuals.* Then they have the audacity to condemn sex and porn."

Such a letter is obviously from someone who has found life difficult to cope with and has escaped instead into writing to politicians, a fantasy quite as unreal as anything offered in the romantic pages of Mills & Boon. I suspect that the pleasure is two-layered: the politician is presumed to rely upon the votes of the public, and is therefore thought to be under a moral obligation to read anything the public sends, even if it arrives in the form of 28 pages filled with unreadable scrawl. But he is also believed to have power, and so your nostrums and your complaints might be acted upon. If they are not, then you have the delicious pleasure of righteous indignation. This too is a recurring theme of an MP's correspondence: fury that he has not awarded the merited weight to a letter.

Here's a man who got a perfectly courteous reply to a letter he had sent. He was quite correctly recommended to try his own MP. The letter, he writes in reply, "is the rudest and most arrogant letter I have ever read. I have voted Liberal for the last time." Here is a women who lives in an extremely expensive London street. She had written asking why the Liberals and the SDP did not join and form one party. Someone on Steel's staff had given a brief but informative resume of the reasons for this.

"What an *absolutely typical* politician's

non-reply to my letter," she replied, "You have told me nothing I didn't know already and your reply is exactly the sort of thing that makes the public despise and despair of politicians ... *If* you don't *know* the answer to my queries why not make a great effort to be *honest* and say so?" What people resent, I think, is not an inadequate response but the absence of a sudden conversion. The only acceptable reply would begin: "Dear Madam, when I read your letter the scales fell from my eyes. You are, I now see, entirely correct ..."

Here is another letter on expensive embossed writing paper. It is written with an electric typewriter and neatly laid out, as if by a well-trained secretary. Yet in its way it is quite as batty as the person who was obsessed by homosexual Tories. It reads: "My dear Steel, it seems you are bent upon destroying yourselves and perhaps that is the real intention of the fat fool from Rochdale. You will lose all if this continues. Thatcher must be wetting herself with delight. Yours aye ..."

Now this letter looks as if it should have been signed by Yosser Hughes. After several pages of abuse ("Your party is associated with failure and has offered the country the most pathetic policies ...") it ends: "I could use a job if you have one spare." What did the writer, a businessman from Cheshire, expect would happen? That Steel, pacing his tiny office, would cry: "This man is right! We are failures! Our policies *are* pathetic! Thank God he's willing to work for us. Get him on the phone, offer him anything ..."

A squadron-leader with seventeen letters after his name (and "Retd.") sends four pages of libel and slander from a village in Kent. "Dear Mr Steel, it has been suggested to me that the majority of Liberals are either:- (a) PUFTAS (b) PERVERTS (c) LIBERTINES or (d) BORN GAMBLERS." The missive continues with a dozen or so paragraphs of personal abuse against Steel himself, ending "I would appreciate a personal reply, for the Family Album."

Some letters begin "Dear Mr Steel," others kick off with a matey "Dear David" and some try to wheedle favour, as in "Dear Your Excellency." The saddest of all starts: "Dear Mr., I am enclosing herewith photo copies of my sworn affidavit and other documentary evidences concerning the conspirators against my life together with their backers from the big officials of the Tory government ..."

Journalists get letters like this too, often in vividly decorated envelopes which are designed to attract attention but succeed only in warning of a nutcase. But we get fewer, and the passions evoked seem, somehow, damper and more discouraged. I think if every day someone handed me so many small parcels of rage and despair I would be quite frightened, worried, like American actress Jodie Foster, about what the end result might be. Or perhaps, like most MPs, I would despatch them all with a curt reply and hope they would vanish swiftly and forever from my life.

"Not to worry, madam. This is a recurring dream in which I always wake up when we reach Cockfosters."

"I'm Daphne, Cuthbert's ex-wife. Could I just come in and abuse Cuthbert for a few minutes?"

Arthur MARSHALL

When the Roll is Called up Yonder

"Funerals, if approached in the proper spirit and provided that the deceased is, like me, sufficiently ancient, are quite agreeable."

ALTHOUGH I dare say that my score of 8 Not Out in a junior house cricket match in July 1925 at. Oundle School is still remembered and talked of with awe, I have never really cut very much of a dashing figure in the world of sport. That London Marathon was certainly something of a temptation and a challenge but I had to remind myself that I had not run anywhere competitively since 1927, unless you count that occasional sprint for a No. 19 bus, Queen of the Fleet, at those times when the queue has disintegrated and there is a general *sauve qui peut.*

Although my currently favourite and most vigorous outdoor pastime, croquet, makes heavy demands on leg, calf, wrist, eye and, most of all, temper (quite fatal to lose one's wool), the game has yet to climb into the region of popularity and familiarity enjoyed by *Pot Black* (in the days before I got my coloured TV set, the balls were indistinguishable and the programme used to reach my bemused old eyes as "Pot Gray").

But despite all these rather modest achievements and to indicate my present age (way past the allotted span of three score and ten) and therefore perilous predicament, I make use of a robust term from the rugger field and I now describe myself as "playing in injury time", with the Great Referee in the sky anxiously shaking his watch to make sure that the wretched thing hasn't stopped. Any moment now that final whistle will blow and the paragraph in a local paper headed SAD PASSING will refer to something other than the football team's inability to move the ball smoothly and unselfishly from player to player.

I am in no way depressed or distressed at the thought of my approaching departure, for, and I say it in all seriousness, funerals can be fun time and it irritates me greatly to think that I cannot be present—well at least not actively present—at my own.

Funerals, if approached in the proper spirit and provided that the deceased is, like me, sufficiently ancient, are quite agreeable. Undertakers, like furniture removers (the official ones, I mean, and not those beasts who come and pinch all the chairs while you are out of the house), are famous for their charm and efficiency, and a few fresh faces at the ceremony add variety. And undertakers, sometimes blessed with odd names—Groaner Digger, Hurry & Bussell, Goody P. Creep, The Quick-Park Funeral Home—have added to the world's ration of merriment.

As attractive social occasions, funerals have it all the time over weddings, those dreadful and wildly expensive gatherings, productive, as the long afternoon wears on and the bride has still not hoisted herself into her going-away rig and left for Babbacombe, of ill temper, wind, doubt and worry, especially when viewing the presents ("I can't see our biscuit barrel anywhere—or is that it behind that plated crumb-scoop?")

I regret that I shan't be present, not even inactively, at the aftermath of my own funeral. Whatever undignified and perhaps ignominious method is arranged for me for leaving this Vale of Tears (Vale of Tears my foot! I've had a really lovely time), and whether the Reaper gathers me in while I am reaching greedily for a further dollop of generously creamed mashed-potato, or fumbling myopically about in the cupboard under the stairs for another Haig, or falling headlong, secateurs bravely brandished aloft, into a very badly pruned Gloire de Dijon, one or other of my friends will be sure to say, "It's how Arthur would have *wished* to go."

Another popular statement is: "Arthur would have so hated to be a *burden* to anybody" (I should have enjoyed it hugely, banging on my bedroom floor with a stick and demanding difficult dishes—chicken liver risotto, lobster in aspic—at awkward hours such as 3.15 a.m.). At the post-funeral buffet lunch, with everybody munching away like mad and with glasses of sherry going down regardless, some happy eater will remember me with "*How* Arthur adored sausage-rolls! I can see him now . . . But mind you, they had to be properly *filled with sausage*. He was very particular. And the puff pastry had, bless him, to be just so!" And all these kind thoughts and comfortable clichés will eventually be followed by one of a rather more practical kind: "My dear, I *do* hope that Arthur's executors—are they here, by the way?—know that he always wanted me to have his walnut tallboy. He always called it, bless him, *your* tallboy. Go and have a peep at *your* tallboy, he would say. I can hear him now."

It also irks me to think that you can't make a neat and tidy exit from the world without having recourse to Officialdom and the Law. I know several lawyers and like them greatly but I don't care for what they get up to—the delays, the documents, the niggling little points and the total incomprehensibility of their jargon (done on purpose, of course, to baffle and make you feel small).

Wills very often go wrong and the mother of an old schoolfriend of mine, a delightful comical lady, distrusted Wills and those who operate them. Instead of a Will, she wanted to leave an Instruction that, immediately after her death, all her possessions were to be competed for by her relations, the competitions to be athletic ones and in the form of races run on the lawn. "Line up for the hundred yards for Dorothy's fur coat. And after that it's the three-legged race for her grand piano."

I have recently had to cope with the departure of my dear old Cousin Madge at the splendid age of 91 and, after a very happy life, she would have been the last to complain. She would also have been the first to chuckle, for she wanted her cremated ashes to be strewn on her mother's grave in a cemetery on an exposed hillside above Ilfracombe. So the ashes were transferred from an urn into what I have probably misremembered as being a Bellamy's EESIFLO Scatter-pot (patent applied for), kindly supplied by the funeral authorities. Despite this wise precaution, not even a patented Bellamy's could cope with the violent hurricane of wind that sprang up and which caused Madge, hard as I tried to direct her at her mother, to distribute herself all over Devon. I feel no guilt in writing thus lightly of the episode for she would have much enjoyed the whole occasion. I can hear her laughing yet.

As for me, pray scatter me anywhere you like. That badly pruned Gloire de Dijon might be glad of me, pioneer as I would be of human recycling. And in this connection, have you ever heard about the famous actress who, somewhat plagued in life by a very demanding and grasping theatrical agent, gave instructions that on her death she was to be cremated and 10% of her ashes were to be thrown in her agent's face?

"The cat got it."

"Bloody hell, Mavis! The bus leaves in ten minutes."

"He's not completely tame yet."

The KRUM CORRESPONDENCE

Comrade Dimitrov:

I am writing to inform you of a most serious development here. It first came to light yesterday morning as I was making my routine weekly check of the staff's private quarters. They don't know I do this, of course, so I have to wait until they're all busy with their respective duties before slipping upstairs to go through their rooms and belongings. I am motivated simply by a sense of duty; the procedure rarely yields anything of interest. In the drawer of Stambouliski's bedside table, for example, there are only two objects—a faded photograph of a wild-eyed, bare-footed woman wearing wolfskins who appears to be cooking a hedgehog in a cave (it is signed "Mummy") and an antique volume issued by a Bombay publishing house entitled "The Thuggees' Handbook & Compendium—An Illustrated Guide to Throttling Pilgrims" by Dr Ollie Singh PhD (Darwin).

Beside Big Rosa's bed, on the other hand, I find magazine pictures of Warren Beatty and endless boxes of rahat lakoum, for which she has a notorious weakness (give her a pound of the mixed rose and lemon, comrade, and she'll beat you through your bedroom door and hit the quilt running) while Excellency Blok's private drawers contain all the usual stuff required by a man of his age and station: there are Zumbo energising tablets, an oxygen bottle and a variety of expensive Oriental sex-aids, including one curious device with bells and a quick-release harness and another, bullet-shaped, which seems to work on the principle of the whistling kettle.

Yesterday I wandered into the room of little Basil, his hulking, monosyllabic fourteen-year-old son, and, riffling idly through the clutter of Polo wrappers, old calculator batteries, conkers, girlie mags and scrawled notes placing a succession of voodoo curses on a boy called Hepplethwaite, I suddenly came upon a piece of white pasteboard. It was printed with the words YOUNG CONSERVATIVES ASSOCIATION WILLESDEN BRANCH and contained the typewritten name—and childish signature—of Basil Blok. I chuckled, assuming that it was a joke played on him by one of his schoolfellows (perhaps the unfortunate Hepplethwaite,

having survived the lightning strikes and asp bites Basil had ordained for him, was getting his own back). But then, tucked away beneath an abandoned Airfix Messerschmitt with a Smurf wedged in its cockpit, I suddenly came across a photograph of Mrs Thatcher. She was wearing her Falklands face, eyes trying to cause a meltdown in the camera, lips slightly parted as though preparing to catch an Exocet between her teeth. My blood froze, but worse was to come. Nearby I found a letter headed Number Ten Downing Street and written by a female assistant. "Dear Basil," it said. "The Prime Minister thanks you warmly for your interest and good wishes, and has great pleasure in sending you the recent portrait you asked for. There are no pictures available of her in suspenders and black stockings, but I hope the enclosed will do instead."

So! We had a little revisionist in our

> "She was wearing her Falklands face, lips slightly parted as though preparing to catch an Exocet between her teeth."

midst! It was the fault of his wretched English school, of course, with its emphasis on traditional Tory virtues and aspirations. Play the game! Bite on the bullet! Beware the sticky wicket! Under the weight of this barrage of claptrap the poor chap had, like a worn pouf, come apart at the seams. Picking up the evidence, I descended the stairs to his father's study, interrupting him in conference with Big Rosa. "Ahem!" I said from the door, noting that the nature of their business was so confidential that he was transacting it while sitting on her lap.

"What is it, Krum?" he asked, looking up with some annoyance. "I am very, very busy indeed. We are engaged in urgent discussions regarding the state of the embassy drinks cupboard. It is empty, and our month's liquor allocation has already been spent. You comprehend the scale of

the problem? I was up on my feet, pondering the wisdom of getting Grigoriev to break into the Augustus Barnett shop in Pugh Road late tonight when, quite suddenly, I lost consciousness and fell heavily in the position in which you see me now. I was overcome by the cares of office and could have broken my neck. Rosa probably saved my life. Anyway, I am still in a very shaky state, too weak to move, so perhaps you would do me a favour and come back later."

I crossed the room and wordlessly handed him the Thatcher picture. He looked at it and grunted. "Yes," he said vaguely. "A good likeness." Then, all at once, I showed him the Downing Street letter and the YC membership card and he went as white as a sheet. "Aaarrgh," he said, running a trembling hand through his hair. He clutched my wrist, his eyes wild and feverish. "My dear fellow," he said, hoarsely. "You will of course say nothing of this little, um, jape, to Comrade Dimitrov, that fearful man in State Security you send your weekly report to. Young Basil is a Marxist through and through. Why, when Comrade Andropov appeared on television the other week without leaning on his Armenians, the little chap jumped up and cheered."

I gave him a thin smile and stalked from the room. At lunch he was gloomy and preoccupied, sprinkling parsley on his junket, avoiding my eye, saying nothing. The others knew what had transpired and looked uneasy. Only Stambouliski, who has absolutely no interest in political dogma, seemed unaffected, humming some old gypsy air as, with his thumb, he made a series of excavations in his mashed potato.

At 4.30 little Basil arrived home.

His father and I got to him together. Excellency Blok made frantic signals to the boy who, not comprehending, made for his room, his laden schoolbag crashing up the stairs as he towed it behind him. He sat down, tipped a tube of Smarties down his throat, placed his huge feet on the desk and lit a Silk Cut.

"Basil!" his father wailed. "Why do you smoke? It is so bad for the wind."

"Everyone in the scrum smokes," said Basil, who plays rugby for one of his school teams. "Norman Goatley gets through ten

Birkett

slim panatellas a day."

"I'd like a word with you," I said.

"Goatley can blow smoke rings," Basil added.

I held out the offending photograph and documents. "I found these on your desk." I said.

Excellency Blok gave the lad an anguished look. "Sweetheart, you are in big trouble," he croaked.

Basil was looking at me quizzically, head on one side. "Did you go through my things, Krum?" he asked.

"*Mister* Krum," I said, my voice icy.

"Yes, darling," said Excellency Blok, anxiously, "he is always Mr Krum when he is speaking to us in his capacity as an arresting officer."

What little Basil did next surprised me. As you know, he is a big lad and unusually strong with it; some years ago when his pony refused a jump at the Plovdiv Gymkhana he dismounted, picked the beast up bodily and threw it over the fence in question. Now, to my astonishment, he adopted the same kind of tactics with me. He stood slowly, abruptly seized my lapels and held me up against the wall with my feet several inches above the ground. "I have joined the Tory Party," he said, "because when I grow up I want to make a million pounds, have a house in Chelsea, be a member of the MCC, win the Derby, get into Parliament, know the Queen and marry someone who looks like Joanna Lumley."

Then he dropped me and I hit the ground so hard that I may have fractured my ankles. I now have shooting pains and a very pronounced limp. Excellency Blok, I think, was deeply impressed by his son's declaration of intent and has been looking upon him with a mixture of fear and pride ever since. My problem, comrade, is that I am uncertain how to proceed. Instinct tells me that I should send him home, shackled, for a spell at a Young Pioneers' Camp. But what if he infects the other susceptible malcontents with the same kind of wild thinking? We could finish up with a stock exchange in Sofia and the triumphant re-emergence of all the old money in Wonk. Advice, please!

Fraternal salutations,

Simeon Krum
Fifth Secretary

*"And **again** the early ball through the middle, and **again** the defence is caught square—and this time it's Dalglish—the shot, though, was always going high over Corrigan's bar. **But**—no doubt at **all**—that this City defence is in all **kinds** of trouble, and right now it's Liverpool who are asking all the questions!"*

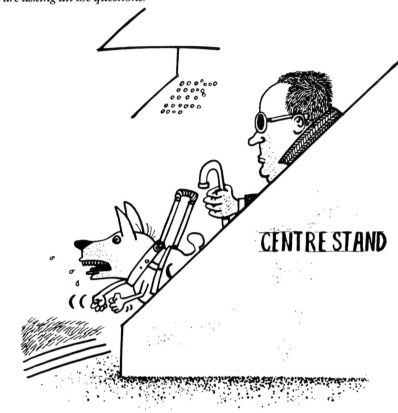

CENTRE STAND

*"I keep telling you, Mr Olmroyd—an injury resulting from a late tackle in the 1914 Christmas Day football match does **not** qualify as a war wound."*

Hunter DAVIES

FATHER'S DAY

The Goodbye Man

"People were very surprised when they got the invitation to my farewell party, presuming I had left years ago."

I HAD a farewell party last week. It was an unnecessary gesture, purely symbolic, but I thought to hell, I've given the best part of my life to this particular company, all the way back to 1958, and now that my association has finally come to an end, I'll go out with a few laughs, bit of fun. Anyway, I happen to like office parties.

My wife thought it was potty, but then she can't understand offices or farewells, never having worked in an office or been given a farewell. I like farewells, and reunions. That's what working with people is all about. The camaraderie. The office jokes. It does help to cut down on the time actually spent working.

She gets furious if her old college even dares to send her notification of an Old Girls' do. Straight in the dustbin. Ooh, she's a hard woman. I got one last week from my old college, as Old Castlemen the world over meet up every April in Durham. I drool over all the details, read every word of what people are doing, almost all of whom I've never heard of. Hmm, so old Nutter-Philpot

is teaching in Dar-es-Salaam and invites any old Old Castleman who finds himself in that neck of the woods to pop in as his Oak will still be Sporting! They love exclamations, do the Old Boys. Well, I might be stuck there some day. And Podges, that drunk, is now a Canon in the West Country, who would have thought it.

I don't actually *go* to any of these reunions, haven't for over ten years, but I think about it and get very nostalgic. I like reunions best when you've just recently parted, such as half an hour ago. That way you still have so much in common. Once the years pile up, it's pretty hopeless trying to establish any rapport once again.

When I was full-time with this particular company, I changed departments several times, and on each occasion I gave a farewell party, then an arrival party for the new department, then a reunion every few weeks with the old gang. Even though the departments were next door. Ah, those were the days.

Jake denies it strongly now, but when he

left primary school for secondary it was all sobs on his last day as they had buns in the classroom and made vows always to keep in touch. Even at five years old, when he went up from the Nursery to the Infants, he was in tears. He had moaned all the time he had been in the Nursery, but once it came to an end, the tears came out. No more Hop, hop, one, two. That was some dopey little game they played.

This is Jake's last year at secondary school, and I know that come July, it will be fond farewells, despite the fact that for the first five years at this school he moaned all the time. Flora, in her turn, leaves primary this summer. She's looking forward to a good cry.

I can't remember Caitlin crying, but she goes through life having reunions. When she went with Fig and Sophe to Geneva for a week when they were fifteen, they had reunions every month for years afterwards, sitting round the fondue in our kitchen, swapping memories and hysterics. A stranger could never have believed that they were all in the same class in the same school and lived just 100 yards apart.

I can see Caitlin going through life having reunions. She does have a capacity for keeping in touch with her old friends, almost all of whom are still her present friends. I've lost all of mine from my childhood and there is only one college friend I keep in touch with, and he lives in California.

But I have so many work friends, people I have been in the same office with over the last 26 years, that I plan to keep in touch with many of them for ever. Hence my farewell party.

The office which I formally left last week was *The Sunday Times*. People were very surprised when they got my invitation, presuming I had left years ago. I had, really, in spirit, but by a sequence of events I was still on a small part-time contract, though, God knows, I haven't done much.

For so many years I was on the full-time staff, and those were the years I wanted to remember. I decided it would be champagne all round. My wife was then convinced I was potty. All those freeloaders and drunks, half of whom you spent most of your time moaning about, what do you want to see them again for. Ah, my petal, you don't understand these things.

I sent out brilliant invitations, run off on one of the *ST*'s duplicating machines, yes, I'll never be able to use them again, or nick free typing paper. Offices do have their uses.

I did a little montage of all the notices and

"Parables! We're sick of parables—don't you know any Irish jokes?"

letters I have saved, right back to that amazingly exciting letter I got from Kemsley House on May 15, 1958, saying yes, they were going to take me on as a graduate trainee. I'd also kept the note which went on the noticeboard, in December 1960, appointing me to the *Sunday Times* staff— at a salary of £1,350 a year. Half the people invited said how strange, imagine having kept those boring notes all these years. The other half said yup, they did exactly the same.

I joined as the assistant on the Atticus column, with Robert Robinson in charge, and for the next five years I wrote millions of scintillating words, and never once got my name in the paper. At that time, you didn't. They rarely threw by-lines around.

Naturally, I made a few notes before my farewell party, memories to regale everyone with, stories about Ian Fleming, my days with Nick Tomalin, the arrival of the awful Insight gang. I hated them. They worked so bloody hard and completely revolutionised the office. I'd been the bright young eager-beaver, till they appeared. Do you know, they sometimes used to work all night long in the office, if they were on a big story. My definition of a good story, throughout all my *Sunday Times* days, was one that got me home in time for tea.

I eventually wrote the Atticus column, in the late Sixties, deliberately interviewing Northern, uneducated, hooligans, just to annoy the old guard on the paper, though of course by that time they were not hooligans but trend-setting and terribly exciting young persons.

I then did the women's pages, the beginning of the so-called Look section, and that was my happiest time on the paper, along with Jilly Cooper and Molly Parkin. God, the lunches we had. It was so new, doing those sorts of pages at that time.

I wrote profiles for ages, worked in several other departments, then edited the Colour Magazine for a couple of years, but that wasn't very happy. There were too many battles trying to change things. But I invited them all, those people I had worked with,

and almost all of them came, even Bob Robinson, all the way from Chelsea. My boasts about having been first appointed to the *ST* staff in 1960 were rather ruined by Dilys Powell. She joined the paper in 1924.

All I had said on the invitation was: join me for a glass of champagne at 6 in the Look offices, which they kindly said I could use. I invited sixty and bought two dozen bottles of champagne. From Waitrose, of course, as they're my new love-hearts. I left a crate in the car, thinking only half would turn up, plus some large bottles of cheap wine, in reserve. I also took along my tape recorder and two old Beatle tapes. You really are mad, she said, no one wants to hear all that rubbish.

We were still drinking at ten, by which time every drop had gone, which was neat, then a gang of us staggered for dinner to a place called the Zanzibar where Molly Parkin's daughter works. Daughter. Gee whiz, I can remember her in a pram. She's now the manager.

I didn't get home till after two o'clock. I did try to creep into the bedroom, as quietly as possible, but I made a noise, apparently, trying to get my shirt off. I just couldn't undo the buttons. No, I wasn't drunk. When one is the host one has to keep relatively sober. It was the fault of an old Sixties badge, a Sergeant Pepper one, which I had pinned on my shirt, just for old times, and had forgotten about.

I think it went well, but then hosts always like to think it went well. Only two things went wrong. I came home without my tape recorder and tapes. I lost them somehow between the *Sunday Times* and the Zanzibar. See, she said, I told you it was all stupid.

And then despite making a few little impromptu notes in my head, all about the gooden olden days in Grays Inn Road, just in case, you know, no one asked me to make a speech. Rotten lot.

So now you've heard it. Sorry there's no champagne left. But come early to my next farewell party. I'm bound to have a few more. Or perhaps a reunion, to celebrate the last farewell.

St Valentin, Leap Year Etc

Femme: Tu as reçu des cartes de St Valentin?
Mari: Non. Et toi?
Femme: Oui. Cinq.
Mari: *Cinq?* C'est beaucoup, à ton âge. Qui sont tes Casanovas?
Femme: Le plumber, le 24-heure cab firm, la milkpersonne et Barclaycard.
Mari: Ah, bon? Les St Valentins sont maintenant commercials? Et ils ont des rimes, et tout ca?
Femme: Oui. Par exemple, la milkpersonne dit:

Vous êtes mon pint de golden top,
Vous êtes la crème de la crème;
Ne changez pas votre daily order
Et restez always the same.

Mari: Charmant. Et l'autre?
Femme: L'autre quoi?
Mari: Cinq Valentins, tu dis. Je compte seulement quatre.
Femme: Ah, oui. L'autre est de mon secret lover.
Mari: Bon.
Femme: Qu'y a-t-il dans *The Times* ce matin?
Mari: 20 pages de Valentins. C'est ridicule. Le headline est "Andropov donne des greetings à Reagan". Je suis sûr que cela aussi, c'est un Valentin. Comme:

Bonjour, Ronnie, macho man,
Vous êtes my kind of homme.
Soyez toujours mon Valentin
Et ne droppez pas votre bomb.

Femme: Peut-être. Tiens, c'est Leap Year en 1984, n'est-ce pas?
Mari: Tu ne vas pas proposer encore une fois, non?
Femme: Non, mais, c'est curieux. Feb 29, cet extra jour—qui est le saint patron?
Mari: C'est vrai. Tous les jours possèdent un on-duty saint. Mais Feb 29 est différent. Le saint de Feb 29 travaille *une* fois dans *quatre* ans.
Femme: Peut-être est-il patron saint de l'overtime ban.
Mari: Curieux. Dans Heaven, il y a une porte marquée: "CETTE POSITION FERMEE. BACK EN 1988." C'est un job avec des perks.
Femme: Ou St Valentin, qui fait un peu d'overtime. Eternité and a half.
Mari: Incidentelement, c'est qui, ton secret lover?
Femme: Je ne sais pas. Il n'est pas signé.
Mari: Mais c'est moi, espèce de dolt! Donnez-moi un kiss... (*Musique, credits, etc...*)

"Son—you're big enough now to be told that we're not in fact your real parents. Also, Mother would like to boogie!"

TOM CRABTREE

LIST
Departments.

Dresses, Silks.
Mantles, Furs.
Made-up Costumes.
Gloves, Haberdashery.
Laces &c Ribbons.
Trimmings, Outfittings.
Family Mournings.
Brussels, Tapestry and
Scotch Carpets, Rugs.
Floorcloths &c Linoleums.
Iron Beds &c Bedding.
Bed &c Table Napery.
Flannels, Blankets, &c.
Printed Cretonnes.
Millinery.

INDOOR MARKETS

DURING my National Service I learned two vital lessons. One was to put down smoke and go left. The other was that it pays to buy the best. One of my pals—Sandhurst chap—in his one good suit, leather-elbowed sports jacket, blazer with lots of silver buttons, *always* looked smart.

I, in my made-to-measure forty-shilling suit, looked like a crofter or somebody who had wandered into the mess from Rowton House. Though I had, in fact, come from the wrong side of the river, there was no good reason to appear as though I'd actually come out of the river.

My mother, of course, was to blame. She had a thing about markets. She was always hopping on a bus to get the latest bargains: towels that wouldn't dry you, shirts with sleeves that ended at the elbow, pullovers that would—after a first wash—hardly have covered Action Man, not to mention top quality toothbrushes at rock bottom prices with bristles that came away in your mouth.

I once asked her why she didn't go to shops. "It's company, isn't it?" said my mother. The oracle at Delphi was lucidity itself compared to the old girl. She just liked the hustle and the bustle, the idea that you could get quality, cheap. She was on the edge of Life's Roundabout, flung from stall to stall. Only in Moss Bros, I wanted to tell her, do the seams hold together. I never did. When things fell apart, as her purchases invariably did, it gave her another excuse to go to the market.

That brings us circuitously to indoor markets: the posh and the tatty, those that are purpose-built and those that have sprung up where old cinemas, department stores and supermarkets used to be. The supermarkets have moved to the shopping centres, to make even more money.

In the north IM's have been going for about five years; around here they're fairly new (about a year old). Some of them are like deserted aerodromes, have very few customers, still-empty stalls. I like that. I can't bear people to touch me when I'm shopping, not without my permission.

The good thing about IM's is that you don't get wet if it rains and the goods are cheap. My brother, up north, bought four digital watches (£1.90 each. Is this a record?) for his family, and my nephew, aged six, now goes about the house announcing: "The time is 43.17." At that sort of price it's worth buying one for the baby.

A somewhat manic chap I know has recently purchased a cement cat (for porch or garden, black or white, £2.45), a rubber tree plant (£5), a basket of fruit with a yellow ribbon on the handle (£1) and a wok (£4). These are all going to be Christmas presents. The problem is what to give to whom: would his mother like a wok? Anyway, I'm all for friends buying their presents early. I can't stand people who leave their Christmas shopping to the last minute when I'm trying to do mine.

I've had a few bargains myself: a large bag of dolly mixtures (35p) a packet of 50 wafer biscuits (20p), a melon (15p) and a 78rpm record (second-hand, slightly scratched) of Dean Martin singing *That's Amore* (10p). Not on the same day, of course. I'm not made of money.

Around here, being *nouveaux arrivés*, the stall-holders have to contend with the problem of customer loyalty. Some of our senior citizens have been shopping at Debenhams (or Dingle's) for sixty years, at least. Will the prospect of glitter leg-warmers (£1.50) lure those elderly ladies away from their regular haunts (and lisle stockings)? It takes time for new ideas to catch on, especially in Bournemouth.

Will the elderly gentlemen one sees in Beale's and the Pleasure Gardens be tempted by embossed leather belts (£1.50), coarse-cut pork pies (large size, 55p) and white shoelaces with lots of little red hearts on them? I'm not sure that these sort of laces go terribly well with brown boots.

Despite this, the man who owns the tea-stall at our local IM tells me he's managing to build up quite a nice little clientele. He's an ex-college lecturer and speaks very nicely. I'm sure that will help in these parts. I've told him about my mother and her cake-queue outings (that's one shop she did go to). The tea man is thinking of a coach outing to Longleat, if he can get the support.

Anybody can hire a stall, providing one has the money and, I suppose, something to sell. A stall will cost you from £7–£15 per day. A pal of mine was thinking of selling books. "Dirty books?" asked the market manager, eagerly. That put him off. My daughter had a plan to sell cakes. Good idea except that you have to sell an enormous amount of chocolate crunch to make a profit, even on a £7 outlay.

One meets a nice class of people amongst the stall-holders (more than can be said for some shop assistants). The young lady on the wool stall (odd balls, 15p) told me that she had a degree and just liked anything to do with wool. Oxford, I'd guess. Philosophy. Or Classics. Indoor markets, I gather, are more a way of life than a means of making money.

I like the people, am not all that excited about furry snake draft excluders (£1.45), turtle poofs (£2) or the quality of Christmas cards at 15p per dozen. Quality counts. I was talking to the man on soft toys (large black and gold teddy bear, £3.50) when I noticed his sports jacket. Beautifully cut. He told me he bought it at Austin Reed. New. Not even in the sales. Must ask him what regiment he was with.

KEATING

Robson's Choice

"The Ipswich president was asked if she'd like to meet Mrs Thatcher.
'Frankly, I'd much rather a gin and tonic,' she replied."

THIS week marks the end of Bobby Robson's beginnings as the England soccer manager. The manner as well as the result of the European Championship match against Hungary at Wembley will determine whether the throng in the amphitheatre is prepared to give the thumbs up to the first phase of Robson's stewardship. He has been in the job for six months, during which time, once or twice, England have looked very, very good. But when they've been bad, they've been horrid.

The game against Hungary could not have been a more evocative fixture for Robson. Thirty years ago this year, on November 25, 1953, the insular, arrogant English were trounced by the Hungarians, by 6–3. It was the first time in history that England had been beaten at home. Next morning, Geoffrey Green wrote in *The Times* of Hungary's "rich, overflowing and, to English patriots, unbelievable victory over an England side that was cut to ribbons for most of an astonishing afternoon. Here, indeed, did we attend the twilight of the gods."

When he settles into one of those moulded plastic bucket seats that serve as the Wembley "bench" this week, Robson will fix a nostalgic, watery eye, and wink a remembrance to the very spot over there on the terraces where he stood on the day that England's ponderous WM formation withered in the face of the MM line-up. The Magyar Marvels, indeed.

Robson was a Fulham reserve then. He and his mates caught an omnibus from Craven Cottage at 11 am. They'd heard these Hungarians were pretty nifty. "They might even give us a good game," we were all saying. The bus went through Hammersmith and up the Harrow Road. For the scrawny Robson the route might have been marked "Damascus Road". They queued at the turnstiles. "Once we were in, the Hungarians came out to warm up. Nobody in Britain had ever heard of warming up, and all around us people were thinking 'this is a rum do,' and they were all laughing and saying 'they'll be knackered· before the game.' But then they kicked off and it was obvious from the very beginning that England would be thrashed."

England, says Robson, worked in little triangles in those days, "but the Hungarians had every player involved in the team unit. When England were ripped apart that day it had a profound effect that has never left me." Soon afterwards he started attending

FA coaching courses at Paddington Street, just off Baker Street, and gave up his part-time apprenticeship with an electrician. He was on his way. And now, thirty years on, the Hungarians are back. And Bobby's on the bench.

That seat under the Royal Box at England's musty, dusty, ancient "national" stadium has become part of the legend. Remember how Alf Ramsey would hunch there, stone-faced whatever the score. "Sit down, Shepherdson, and pull yourself together!" he muttered to his magic sponge-man when Hurst scored England's whooping fourth on that golden summer's day in 1966. For Leeds and England, Don Readies, er, I mean *Revie*, stared out, tortured, from that bench for a decade. More often than not he would lose unloseable Cup finals and, for England, have to endure that exit around the greyhound track perimeter, hands deep in Gannex pockets, collar turned up as if to muffle the baying melody, "What a load of rubbish!"

Then Uncle Ron: he had to march off in time to those anthems more than a few

times. Dear old Greenwood would look permanently glum, kneading his Granny Giles lips thoughout the game, then would mope off with a world-weary sigh to over-enunciate such homilies to the nation as "bein' given chances and not takin' them, that's what life's all about, isn't it, Barry?"

Benched, Robson is more restless than his predecessors. He tries to be nonchalant, attempts in turn the carefree look, or that of the impassive tactician. Then an involuntary twitch takes a grip on the expressive, rubbery, pale face and it gives the game away. His eyes get oystery at whichever end of the emotional scale his heart may be. For most of the time he tries to sit calm—then suddenly he's not there, but up at the back chatting to a substitute or trainer. But always with a haunted, anguished glance at the patterns on the pitch.

So far, the most triumphant concert Robson has conducted from this Wembley bench was five years ago when his club side, Ipswich Town, laid waste the Arsenal in a beautifully paced, exuberant show in the 1978 Cup final. That was the day the

Ipswich president, Lady Blanche Cobbold, was asked in the Royal retiring room if she'd like to meet Mrs Thatcher. "Frankly, I'd much rather a gin and tonic," she replied. That was also the day, after the match, that Mrs Thatcher was asked by Radio 2 who she thought was Man of the Match. "Unquestionably", she trilled, "it was Whymark, the man in the No 10 blue shirt!" She was probably trying to be funny. But her advisers had been too clever-clogs. The injured Whymark had pulled out on the eve of the match. Her nation chortled.

Robson's spaniel dog is called Roger—after Osborne, the boy who scored the winning goal for Ipswich that afternoon. Last autumn I popped in to have a drink with England's new manager at his handsome Ipswich home. It was a lovely, soft, East Anglian day. We sat on the patio and the buzz was from the birds and the bees and the sycamore trees, . . . and Robson rabbiting on about gardening. You want to get the griff on the England footballers, but here he was rhubarbing on about his vegetable patch . . . or that serene weeping willow by the potting shed, or the chestnut, or the purply brightness of that clematis blue over there. Bright Ipswich blue.

Okay, gardening's one thing, but what about this drink, then? He comes back from the kitchen. Sorry, not even a Double Diamond. His rugby playing sons must have polished off the last one the day before. Well, fancy that; soccer managers in England aren't meant to keep a dry fridge. They are meant to be pretty free with the fizz, the real McMoet. And, come to think of it, where were all the gold necklaces, the six inch Havanas, the rings and the ringlets, the Gucci pumps with gold buckles? No offence to your Atkinsons, Allisons and Bonds, but "Gerraway with you!" says Robson. His brown slip-on shoes cost just a few quid—"this is the second year they've done me; nice, aren't they?" The most expensive suit he has ever bought cost exactly £100—for the Cup final in 1978. Where from, Savile Row? "Don't be daft—from Ridleys, the Ipswich outfitters."

Robson's feet are plonked, firm, on the ground. His first half-year as England's manager has hinted at boldness, intelligence, courage and consistency. We shall see what we shall see. Certainly, this week the honeymoon is over.

His only passion is football—learned in the north-east, at Langley Park, by kicking around a lump of coal all day if there wasn't a tennis ball handy. And every other Saturday his coalmining dad would take his son the 17 mile journey to Newcastle—"regular as clockwork, from the bus station we'd walk to Fenwicks for a cup of tea, then on to St James's Park. As often as not we were first in the queue." And then his Magpies of United would sing for him . . . Wayman and Cowell, Stubbins, McMichael and Milburn!

His eyes moist up at the memory. Just as they will this week when he thinks of Hungary and thirty years ago. 🐦

"Pull yourself together man—we're all disappointed!"

NED SHERRIN

There Is Nothing Like A Dame

PUTTING politics into pantomime, as Peter Nichols has done again this Christmas in *Poppy* at the Adelphi, is the latest load to be laid on an ancient, beloved, bewildered, cobweb-clad art form. Mind you, I like my pantomimes to come with cobwebs and would as soon visit one unfestooned in such a manner as I would call on Miss Havisham after her drawing-room had had a brisk going over with a Hoover. (At the Adelphi I was glad to see that some of the worst excesses of last year's Barbican production had been eliminated and David Firth, Ken Wynne and Alfred Marks brought new strength to the cast, although I missed Geraldine Gardner's legs and Geoffrey Hutchings as the Dame seemed to be resting on last year's laughs rather than going out and getting them all over again.)

I suppose the pineapple of perfection was the first pantomime I saw—*Cinderella*—at the Playhouse Cinema, Street, Somerset in the late Thirties. Hindsight tells me that this was not the most lavish I have attended; but, possessing already a cumbersome toy proscenium, shakily constructed according to the instructions on Kelloggs cornflake packets (while my older brother was neatly assembling balsa-wood aeroplanes) I was keenly interested in the grown-up stagecraft on display at Street.

There was a certain disappointment in being able to see mice and pumpkins picked up and manhandled peremptorily away in the half-light so that curtains could part and reveal a straggle of moulting Shetland ponies and a minute rococo coach; but Dandini offered ample compensation when, in spangled black tights, he/she emerged through the same tabs, redrawn to accommodate the construction of the Ball scene, and prefaced that spectacle with a paper-tearing act, transforming a large white sheet of paper into an elaborately laced doily before our astonished eyes while the thin band played *Red Sails in the Sunset*.

The next year I nagged my parents ceaselessly to buy tickets for the two-week season, fearful that it would be sold out. I would guess the story was *Red Riding Hood*. Finally we set out to make the reservations in AYA 422, an Austin Seven, with my mother at the wheel. Unfortunately, AYA 422 was unceremoniously overturned in a collision with a neighbour's car on the outskirts of the town, leaving us upside-down and my mother in bed for a week. We had no tickets against the day and when Hitler marched into Poland, *Red Riding Hood* was one of the first casualties.

I had to wait impatiently until 1945 when hostilities ceased and I could see a much more sumptuous pantomime at the Bristol Hippodrome.

Bristol had two main pantomimes—one at the Hippodrome and one at the Empire in Old Market Street. This latter was considered a somewhat shady house, the home of touring nudes outside the Christmas season, and for us it had to be the Hippodrome and *Jack and the Beanstalk*. Again, it was a family outing and the drama of the journey is a more vivid recollection than the actual performance. I do remember the strapping, blonde principal boy, Nita Croft, and the comic, "Monsewer" Eddie Gray. I recall being impressed by the mechanics of the Giant and the Beanstalk up which Miss Croft clambered at the end of Act One; but much more vividly comes back the neurosis of my father, who drove at a snail's pace in the country and hated to drive at all in towns.

Just past the Hippodrome he saw a reassuring "Car Park" sign. Suddenly he found himself having his first experience of the spiral ascent of an indoor garage. He drove up faster and faster, arriving at the top in a frenzied sweat and stopping just short of the concrete wall in front of him. I don't think he enjoyed the performance at all because of the prospect of driving back down. In fact, that wasn't so bad but, having negotiated it and breathed a sigh of relief, he turned right into the oncoming traffic in the newly created one-way system.

In vain, my brother and I chorused him to stop. One-way traffic was another first for my father and he was not keen to go along with it.

There are a few things more irritating than cocky adolescents who think they know better than their betters. As he got angrier and angrier the crescendo of car horns grew and grew. I don't remember how he extricated himself but I do recall not getting the expected celebratory tea at The Little Thatch on the way out of Bristol, so it can't have ended happily.

This was the period when the wireless schedules were peppered with live outside broadcasts of thirty-minute excerpts from pantos around the country and the impresarios who seemed to have a monopoly of these entertainments were Prince and Emile Littler, Francis Laidler, Tom Arnold and George and Alfred Black.

These broadcasts my father considered "a waste of time—if you can't see it"; but if I could get the portable Bush radio into an icy room far enough away I was only too happy to go along with the hushed tones of the commentators—"... as the boys and girls leave the village green/market square/centre of Old Peking, here comes Alderman Fitzwarren/Sarah the Cook/Widow Twankey/Simple Simon, in the familiar person of Frankie Howerd/Tommy Trinder/Norman Evans/Cyril Fletcher/Clarkson Rose/Arthur Askey/Jimmy Wheeler and the scene changes to the kitchen/the laundry/the haunted bedroom..."

One feature of these broadcasts was the panto song of the year—be it *Love and Marriage, I Like a Nice Cup of Tea in the Morning*—plugged unmercifully in *Aladdin* at Taunton—or that most suitable anthem, *Tiuoo Diff'rent Worlds, we live in tiuoo diff'rent worlds* which won hands down in the critical business of stating baldly the central dilemma of class distinction which lies at the heart of every pantomime. The phrase is embedded in the big duet of Peter Nichols and Monty Norman in Act Two at the Adelphi; but it perfectly sums up the gulf between Charming and Cinderella, Aladdin and his Princess Baldrabadour, Dick Whittington and his Alderman Fitzwarren's daughter, Alice, until the final curtain cuts out class and the walk-down sees both sides dazzlingly accoutred.

The Forties was still the period of the last legendary Principal Boys—Adele Dixon still striding—bridging the gap between the Old Vic and the Palladium—Evelyn Laye concentrating on elegant classy lads, like

"It took time but we finally got him house-trained."

Prince Charming—no gamins or urchins for her, no Aladdins or Sinbads. However, there were also Pat Kirkwood, Noele Gordon and Hy Hazell from a younger generation.

And there was still the radiantly optimistic Dorothy Ward reigning unchallenged as the greatest survivor. I have never forgiven myself for not going to Liverpool at Christmas in the mid-Fifties when three theatres featured a revival of *Finian's Rainbow*, Dorothy doing her last pantomime and Tommy Steele doing his first. (I also decided against going to Paris to catch Piaf in what turned out to be her last throw—but I always live in hope—you can't lose 'em all).

Miss Ward, happily still with us, had her own sincere approach. She had seen a Sinbad or a Crusoe who needed the assistance of a microphone: "What," she intoned, "can the kiddies have thought when this thing came up through the waves?" Her favourite role was Jack (of Beanstalk fame). It was "a role I can get my teeth into—not like that silly Colin in *Mother Goose*, nothing to act!" Her partner was invariably her husband, Shaun Glenville, "This is my husband who plays my mother," and she approached her big scenes with a proper sense of their importance.

In *Jack and the Beanstalk* one of the big moments comes when Jack strips his only asset—the family cow—for a mere bag of beans. Dorothy, relishing the drama inherent in the situation, always asked, when told of other new Jacks, "How did she sell her cow?" with the same eagerness that a definitive Ophelia might enquire of a rival debutante's mad scene. She brought so much conviction to her own interpretation that, legend has it, when her son, Peter Glenville, then aged three or four, now a celebrated director, was taken to see her performance he could not contain his anxiety. From a stage box at a matinee he yelled through his tears, "Mummy, Mummy, don't sell Jessie!"

Curious people crop up in pantomimes nowadays. I have before me a bill for the Theatre Royal, Bath, this Christmas, scattered with telly names. The story is *Aladdin*, the cast includes John Nettles (*Bergerac*), Henry Kelly (*Game for a Laugh*), Lucie Skeaping (*Take 2*), Mark Curry (*Get Set for Summer*) and Julie Dorne Brown (*Crackerjack*). I preferred the old bill matter, "Method in his Madness", "A Smile, a Song and an Ocarina", etc. But each pantomime cast throws up its own oddities.

I remember in the Fifties seeing Eric Porter as a fruity Norman Evans as Dame and Peter O'Toole improbably cast as a eunuch in *Robinson Crusoe* at the Bristol Old Vic. Caryl Brahms and I achieved some sort of record when Cleo Laine played Cindy Ella for us in *I Gotta Shoe* at the Garrick, finishing the run eight months pregnant—surely the least virginal Cinderella ever to get to that Ball.

This year the only West End pantomime is *Aladdin* at the Shaftesbury. It opens on December 16th. I'll be there. ●

The Visit

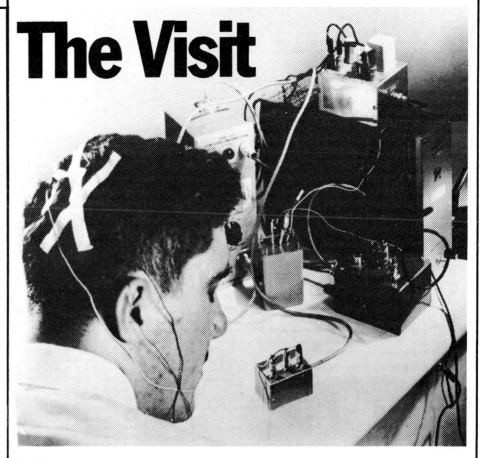

BBC1 Desmond, 59, is a very honest man with his own suit. He suffers from eye-trouble; glycerine keeps getting in them. He also has some appalling voice-affliction, which makes him sound as if he is rubbing his hands; it has had the awful social effect on his life of making people edge away from him, in case he is going to touch them for a tenner.

His wife Esther, 43, is a big fertile woman who terrifies pedestrians for money. She has not had any plastic surgery, and gets along as best she can. They are both very very brave.

Life, and smart accountancy, has kept them apart for long periods, making television programmes. Desmond has recently been away, and Esther has not seen him for some time. Now he is coming home. No one can say quite how the reunion will turn out, but these two remarkably courageous people agreed to be interviewed because they felt that a television audience should share everything with them, except the fee.

Here is a transcript of part of that interview. The rest may be seen over the next sixteen weeks on BBC1.

Interviewer: Esther, for some time now you have been without the wheedling whine of Desmond. How do you, in your innermost heart of hearts, feel about having it back?

Esther: At first I thought: how can I adjust? Most womanpersons have a normal human being around the house, rather than something which creeps along the wall, murmuring to itself. Most of the time you can't hear what it says, so it makes it quite hard to guess what it wants.

Interviewer: And what sort of things *does* it want?

Esther: It varies. Sometimes it wants to know what it's like to have projecting teeth. Sometimes it wants to know if I have the address of anyone with a terminal illness, who would like to co-operate in a book. Sometimes it wants to be taken to Hyde Park Corner to wait for accidents.

Desmond: Mumble, mumble, wheedle, mumble, sniff.

Interviewer: What does it, I mean, he, want now?

Esther: He seems to be looking at your leg. I should think he wants to know if you have a limp he can look at.

Interviewer: I see. I wonder if I might turn to him, and ask him what I am sure everyone watching at home will want to know? Desmond, you really are sickening to look at, as I'm sure you realise, and I know that you would not want me to mince words, there is far too much hypocrisy in this world and I am certain that you would be the first to agree that stripping the afflicted soul naked is absolutely essential if one is to make a bob or two, so tell me, when ordinary decent human beings see you or Esther bearing down on them with a microphone or camera and they begin shrieking and trying to run and throwing up, what do you, in your innermost heart of ... ●

HANDELSMAN

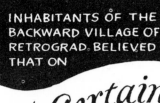

INHABITANTS OF THE BACKWARD VILLAGE OF RETROGRAD BELIEVED THAT ON

A Certain Night in Spring

WATER NYMPHS APPEARED IN THE LAKE ADJOINING A DESERTED CASTLE.

Why should we believe these old wives' tales, Vasya?

Old wives are Russia's greatest resource, Varya.

Allow me to relate to you the tragic legend associated with the castle...

"THE WIDOWED COUNT SAMOVARSKY LIVED THERE WITH HIS DEVOTED DAUGHTER. ONE DAY THE COUNT BROUGHT HOME A WIFE.

Valya, dear, this is your stepmother.

But she is looking at me with jealous hatred.

Ah, well, you will soon grow used to it.

"THAT NIGHT, AS THE GIRL SAT WEEPING IN HER CHAMBER, A FIERCE BLACK CAT ENTERED AND ATTACKED HER.

Meow!

Me eye!

"VALYA MANAGED TO LAND A HAYMAKER ON THE BEAST'S EYE.

"AT BREAKFAST THE NEXT MORNING, THE NOBLEMAN'S BRIDE WAS SPORTING A TERRIFIC SHINER.

How did you get **that**?

As if **you** didn't know, Vanya, you naughty raging bull!

You mean, in my reckless passion I —? Well, tee hee.

"BUT VALYA UNDERSTOOD! HER STEPMOTHER WAS A WICKED WITCH.

As she will soon turn my father against me, I can save time by committing suicide now.

"LATER THE STEPMOTHER ALSO JUMPED IN, AND NOW THEY ARE BOTH WATER NYMPHS."

So poor Valya is still not free, Varya.

Enough already, Vasya! Next time remind me not to ask... Let us join the carefree young people dancing to welcome the spring.

What a girl you are, Varya, really smashinskaya! I wish my father the mayor would let me marry you.

I wish he would too, for I believe I am ever so faintly pregnant.

Everyone stop dancing and go home, by order of His Honour Mayor Paranoyev!

We just want to enjoy ourselves.

Enjoy? Have you forgotten what country this is?

130

FABLES (MUSIC by RIMSKY-KORSAKOV)

WHEN THE YOUNG PEOPLE HAD BEEN DISPERSED, THE MAYOR OF RETROGRAD HIMSELF APPEARED AND KNOCKED AT VARYA'S DOOR.

Varya, my darling, take pity on an old swine— I mean swain...

Go away, Mayor, or I will report you to your son!

Vasya? That callow boy?

Energy! That is all these young fellows have! Dancing and jumping about... What do they know of mature, fatigued love?

I forbid you to slam the door.

SLAM

Pompous hypocrite!

Now I see why the old paskudnyak withholds permission! I shall play the mournful "Elegy to Spring" by our great composer, Mendelssohnov.

STRUM STRUM

Noble youth, so true and good, Every lovely nymph Rises from the lake (knock wood) To thank you for your symph.

My God, the old wives were right!

Stalwart youth, I am the late Valya— and my evil stepmother is one of the other nymphs, but I know not which!

Her presence somehow interferes with my sidestroke. Help me!

Very well. Hey! Can any of you nymphs do witchcraft?

I can.

That is the one.

THE NYMPHS PROMPTLY GOT RID OF THE WITCH (NO DETAILS, OUT OF CONSIDERATION FOR THE SQUEAMISH).

Here is your reward, exemplary youth: a forged letter from the Tsar, ordering your father to consent to your marriage. Farewell!

Who would have expected His Despotism to take an interest in our humble village? I now pronounce you boy and wife. Have a nice equinox.

Too fat for me anyway.

MORAL: Better vernal than venal.

131

200 YEARS OF INFLATION

FIRST CUT-PRICE TRANSATLANTIC BUCKET SHOP OPERATION began on 1 April 1791 and went bankrupt the following Tuesday. Balloonists were offered a no-frills, walk-on, jump-off service between Vauxhall Gardens and New York, or possibly only Cork, Tunbridge Wells, Delhi, Madagascar or the Isle of Man, depending on the winds. Provided bookings were confirmed 21 days prior to inflation, Super Anthrax Stretcherbearer fares offered a 50 per cent discount on alternate Thursdays via Eastbourne OR Rangoon during the off-peak shoulder season.

FIRST CHOICE OF MAIN DISH AND COMPLIMENTARY DRINKS FROM THE TROLLEY were offered to Business Basket passengers in a roped-off section of Trans World Balloons' Clipper Class dirigibles plying the busy London to Croydon service. Shrink-wrapped chicken in the basket was soon established as a firm favourite with busy ballooning executives but was deductible from the statutory personal allowances if ballooning from within the EEC or purchasing more than 5.75ml of Mamsel Jouclas atomiser or Mister Pastry after-shave, inclusive of $3\frac{5}{8}$oz flagons of tax-deductible gaseous sherries OR miniatures of 70° proof brandy balloon substitutes.

FIRST IN-BALLOON MAGAZINE was *Hot Air*, published and edited by Wilhelm Davis The Elder in 1783 and subsequently re-published as *The Best of Hot Air*, *The Hot Air Balloonist's Executive Diary*, *It's No Sin To Re-Print Hot Air*, *The Balloonside Book of Hot Air* and *Hot Air Talks*, the monthly digest of the Balloonists' Building Society.

The first edition, and indeed most subsequent editions of *Hot Air*, featured an article by best-selling author, broadcaster, explorer, wit, gourmet and ballooning critic Malvolio Morley on Oscar Wilde's first trip by balloon and a feature on how baskets were maintained, entitled Wicker's World.

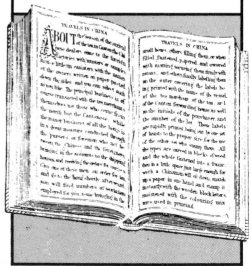

FIRST BALLOON TRAFFIC CONTROLLERS STRIKE over payments for blowing-up time and holding wetted fingers up to the wind during unsocial hours brought balloon movements over Europe to a standstill in the summer peak period of 1882.

This party of British package balloonists were sandbagged for more than 2 months awaiting a fortnight of their dreams on the Costa Hispaniola or other fine field including free use of unlimited-mileage barouche. On the night of September 3rd, after more than half had perished from exposure, the captain finally explained the cause of the delay over the cabin megaphone and the other half of the passengers were helped back to the departures lounge for a pot of tea at the balloon company's expense.

FIRST GAY CABIN STEWARDS were Clive Mont-golfier (left) and Sebastian Saunders-Roe (who played in-basket mandolin for a modest extra charge). Together they manned the duty-free perfumes trolley on a coke-fired de Havilland Herpes flying an 1881 excursion to the Club Aphrodite, Rhodes, chartered by the 2nd Battalion, The Coldstream Guards.

Clive, who was obliged by illiberal IATA regulations of the time to dress up as the first balloon stewardess, was mortified at being totally and completely ignored, quite honestly to the point where he might just as well have risked his all clambering into the basket and attempted suicide by slapping his wrist. He was finally brought round after more than 200 attempts at mouth-to-mouth resuscitation and went on to found BOAC—Ballooning Overseas Alternative Cabin Crew.

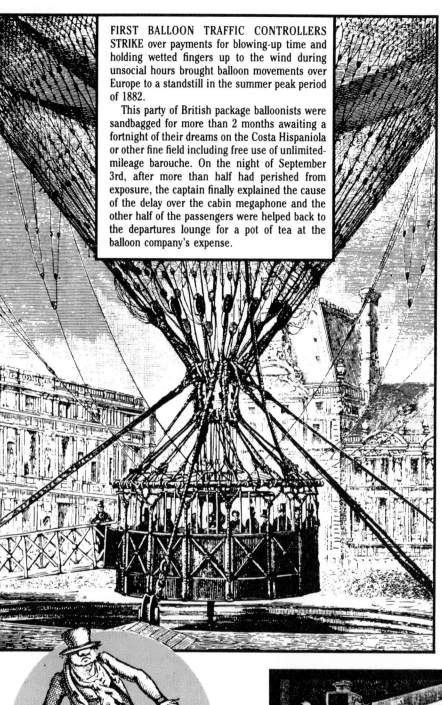

FIRST VICTIM OF BALLOON-LAG was Jeremiah Frost, a breakfast magic lantern displays executive and best-selling author of penny dreadfuls who, after completing more than 300 balloon flights on business during 1890, found that by 1892 he was unable to stagger out of El Vino's without assistance.

In a celebrated lawsuit, Frost then sued the balloon company for more than 20 million dollars compensation but the case was dismissed after it was disclosed that Frost had neglected to read the small-print of the Warsaw Balloon Convention printed on the inside of his ticket.

FIRST IN-BALLOON MOVIE consisted of a cunningly composed compilation of crudely animated, X-rated etchings by the controversial German Escapologist, snake-charmer, fireworks technician and precocious cinéaste, the Phantasmagorical Herr Fassbinder, entitled *Balloon Wars*.

This sci-fi melodrama anticipated the day when balloons might be fitted with weird wings and preposterous propellers and their controllers would fight savage battles for the lucrative London to Edinburgh Shuttle franchise. It went on to smash all balloon basket records but many passengers complained that they were seated behind ropes and sandbags and could not get a decent look at the canvas screen. Since the only copy of *Balloon Wars* broke down during a thunderstorm off Brighton and was badly snagged, no one after 1880 ever got to see the dramatic ending.

Keith
WATERHOUSE

Mists of Time

SMOG, the impenetrable mixture of fog and smoke that cloaked cities in 1953, provided Ministers with an impossible problem, as Harold Macmillan, then Housing Minister, pointed out in a memo to the Cabinet.

There was little they could do. "But we can seem to be very busy—and that is half the battle nowadays," he advised. "Ridiculous as it appears at first sight, I would suggest that we form a committee."

—*Daily Mail*

1. The 144th meeting of the Standing Committee on Smog took place in London. The minutes of the 143rd meeting as circulated were confirmed and signed, subject to the excision of paragraphs 9 i–v, where on the evidence of minute traces of hops and malt finings having been reported in a Smog sample, the Committee forcibly expressed its concern at pollution of the atmosphere by breweries. The Secretary has noted the Public Analyst's request for future samples to be stored in clear glass containers rather than brown ale bottles.

Apologies for absence

2. Apologies for absence were received from the Baroness Harrogate, who was detained in Cheltenham for a meeting of the Standing Committee on the Shocking Price of Everything; and from Lord Cheltenham, detained in Harrogate for a meeting of the Standing Committee on the Awful Weather We've Been Having.

Matters Arising

3. i. Brigadier Puce said that after some delay he had now heard from his brother in Capetown, from whom the Committee might recall he had undertaken to obtain details of how the Smog problem was being tackled in that part of the world. The answer in short was that there was no Smog problem in that part of the world. Brigadier Puce now proposed to make it his business to ask his brother if this had always been the case thanks to climatic conditions, or whether there was anything the South Africans could teach us about the elimination of Smog.

ii. Lady Noggs reiterated her contention, expressed at the previous 143 meetings, that Smog was being wafted into this country from the Soviet Union as part of their cold war strategy. What Brig. Puce had heard from his brother only went to confirm this. The South Africans, being made of sterner stuff, would have sent the Russian Smog packing.

Chairman's Remarks

4. i. The Chairman welcomed two newly co-opted members to the Committee: Canon Flute, sometime chairman of the Churches Commission on Bell-ringing, and Dr Linctus, noted for his work among agricultural workers with bad backs and a member of the Truss Export Council. Both would bring an open mind to the subject of Smog.

ii. The Chairman said that he had been thinking long and hard about cigar smoke, which despite its agreeable aroma was without doubt one of the thousand and one elements of which Smog was composed. The Chairman wondered if notices put up in the smoking-rooms of Clubs, asking members to extinguish their cigars when visibility fell below a certain point, would be regarded as an infringement of the liberty of the individual. Perhaps male Committee Members would care to carry out a discreet canvass in their Clubs, and report back.

Giant Fans Working Party

5. i. Sir Oswald Snout's Working Party on Giant Fans reported. The Working Party was set up to explore the possibilities of dispersing Smog by a system of giant electric fans mounted on the roofs of office buildings and department stores.

ii. Expert evidence taken by the Working Party indicated that such a system would run into the same snags as encountered in the pilot scheme for Very Big Vacuum Cleaners, ie, it would place too great a strain on the National Grid. Even were this difficulty to be ameliorated by the requisitioning of private generators, a considerable co-ordination exercise would be necessary to ensure that all the giant fans so harnessed were facing the same way, otherwise they would simply be blowing Smog back and forth across London, instead of out to sea. Further, tests carried out on the Air Ministry roof with a simulated giant fan—in reality, an autogyro mounted on a stick—had proved disappointing. The Working Party, in the circumstances, could

"Now you're in big trouble. Here comes my solicitor."

not at this juncture recommend heavy capital investment on giant fans, and certainly did not feel justified in following up Lady Noggs' suggestion of asking the Foreign Office to part-fund the cost of blowing the Smog back to Russia.

iii. After discussion, it was agreed that the Working Party on Giant Fans should be re-empanelled as a Working Party on Urban Windmills, with authority to apply to the Ministry of Agriculture and Fisheries for grant-aid to construct a test windmill on Derry and Toms' roof garden.

Hand-clapping Scheme

6. i. Lord Port's discussion paper on Hand-clapping as a Means of Smog Dispersal was circulated. In his brief preparatory remarks Lord Port said that he had been greatly impressed, on a visit to China, by the sight of the citizens of Peking turning out en masse to clap their hands at a given hour, in order to keep down the starling population by preventing the birds from landing until they dropped from exhaustion. What could be done with starlings could be done with Smog. It could be kept on the move. Lord Port had it in mind that schoolchildren could be pressed into service, with thousands of them clapping in unison at Smog black spots, to which they would be transported in special buses as and when the need arose. Their health would not suffer, as they would wear masks. It was all in the discussion document.

ii. Lady Noggs said that while the children's health might not suffer, their education certainly would. The discussion paper was a Magna Carta for truants. Lady Noggs could envisage lessons and examinations being disrupted or abandoned while whole classes went on "Smog patrol." Then there was the question of holidays: how were the children to be assembled for hand-clapping duties when the schools were closed? They would have to be summoned by announcements on the wireless, which could result in them rushing out into the Smog and getting run over. Lady Noggs did not wish to prejudge the issue, but she wondered if the scheme had been properly thought out. She also had grave reservations about emulating any scheme, cruel to bird life, that had its origins in Red China. Supposing, after an

afternoon standing about in the Smog clapping their hands parrot-fashion, the children were to be brained by dead starlings falling out of the sky? It would be just what the Communists wanted.

iii. Lord Port said he was content to leave the merits or otherwise of his discussion document to the Committee, which he was confident would find it at least as worthy of consideration as Lady Noggs' recent most interesting paper on the feasibility of ladling the Smog into large drums which would then be shipped to Leningrad with HMG's compliments.

Broadcasting Policy

7. Mrs Amelia Throat JP believed the Smog nuisance was exacerbated by overexposure on the BBC, where it was given wide coverage in news bulletins and weather forecasts. Mrs Throat was not asking the broadcasting authorities to suppress or distort the seriousness of the Smog menace, but there was such a thing as a sense of proportion. Mrs Throat had noted that since the Committee's last meeting, London had enjoyed seventeen completely Smog-free days as against only fourteen days of Smog and two with Smoggy patches; yet on not one occasion had the BBC interrupted its programmes to announce that there was no Smog today. What was wrong with giving prominence to the good news for a change? Mrs Throat would go further. Why not, as an experiment, when there was Smog, announce that there was no Smog? It would be constructive, it would raise morale, and it would encourage tourism.

Any Other Business

8. i. Dr Linctus asked if as a "new boy" he could be forgiven an obvious question—had the Committee ever considered the idea of a Clean Air Act?

ii. The Chairman said that the suggestion was a novel one: perhaps Dr Linctus had in mind putting the air through a kind of carwash apparatus in order to drive out the impurities? Or was he proposing sending Smog to the laundry? Perhaps Dr Linctus would care to consider the practical difficulties involved before putting himself to the trouble of committing his excellent idea to paper.

LET'S PARLER FRANGLAIS!

Dans le Travel Bookshop

Monsieur: Buenos dias.

Bookman: Pardon?

Monsieur: Bonjour. Je pratiquais mon Espagnol. Je vais en Paraguay.

Bookman: Ah. Bon.

Monsieur: Avez-vous un phrasebook pour Paraguay?

Bookman: Non.

Monsieur: Vous êtes très défini.

Bookman: Oui, well, je sais straight off. Un phrasebook pour Paraguay n'existe pas. En Paraguay, on parle Espagnol. Donc, il faut acheter un Spanish phrasebook.

Monsieur: Mais en Paraguay il y a sans doute des phrases locales. Des idiomes natives. Le rhyming slang Latin, peut-être. "Donnez-moi un kilo d'Oscars, s'il vous plâit."

Bookman: Oscars?

Monsieur: Mangos. C'est rhyming slang en Paraguay. Oscar Tango. Mango.

Bookman: C'est vrai?

Monsieur: Je ne sais pas. C'est une spéculation. Mais il est possible que ça existe. C'est pour ça que je demande un phrasebook de Paraguay.

Bookman: Nous sommes plutôt un bookshop antiquaire. Nous stockons les classiques de travel. Par exemple, nous avons "J'ai traversé Paraguay sur un vieux Raleigh 3-Speed en 1932", par Lt-Col Fawkes.

Monsieur: Non, merci.

Bookman: Nous avons "48 Heures en Paraguay" par Evelyn Waugh. "Egon Ronay Guide de l'Amérique de Sud, 1948". "Des Impressions Personelles de Paraguay par un Gentleman", 1748, seulement £400.

Monsieur: Non, merci. Quelque chose par Paul Theroux?

Bookman: M. Theroux a payé une visite volante en Paraguay mais il était violemment malade tout le temps.

Monsieur: Hmm. Avez-vous un livre par le bloke de Paraguay qui a gagné la Prix Nobel?

Bookman: Prix Nobel? De Paraguay? Qui est-ce?

Monsieur: Je ne sais pas. Mais il y a toujours un bloke d'un Third World pays qui a gagné le Prix Nobel.

Bookman: Si vous suivez mon advice, les phrasebooks sont un waste d'argent. Pour apprendre les phrases de Paraguay, il faut passer le soir avec une belle fille de Paraguay. Un peu de romance—et un peu d'expérience!

Monsieur: Et où vais-je trouver une belle fille etc?

Bookman: Ici, monsieur! Rosita, dites bonjour au gentleman et donnez-lui un good time.

Rosita: Buenos dias, señor. Vd me gusta mucho.

Bookman: Au revoir, monsieur. Je vais vous donner le bill quand vous revenez avec Rosita.

DUNCAN COMIC CUTS

Hospitals hire 'MASH' theatres

By DAVID FLETCHER
Health Service Correspondent

CASH-STARVED health authorities are renting mobile operating theatres as a cheap way of clearing long lists of patients waiting for operations, it is disclosed today.

"For God's sake hurry, man, before the Chancellor introduces new cuts."

"All he said was, 'Hand me the scalpel, Hotlips!'"

"In this game you have to have a sense of humour or else you go under."

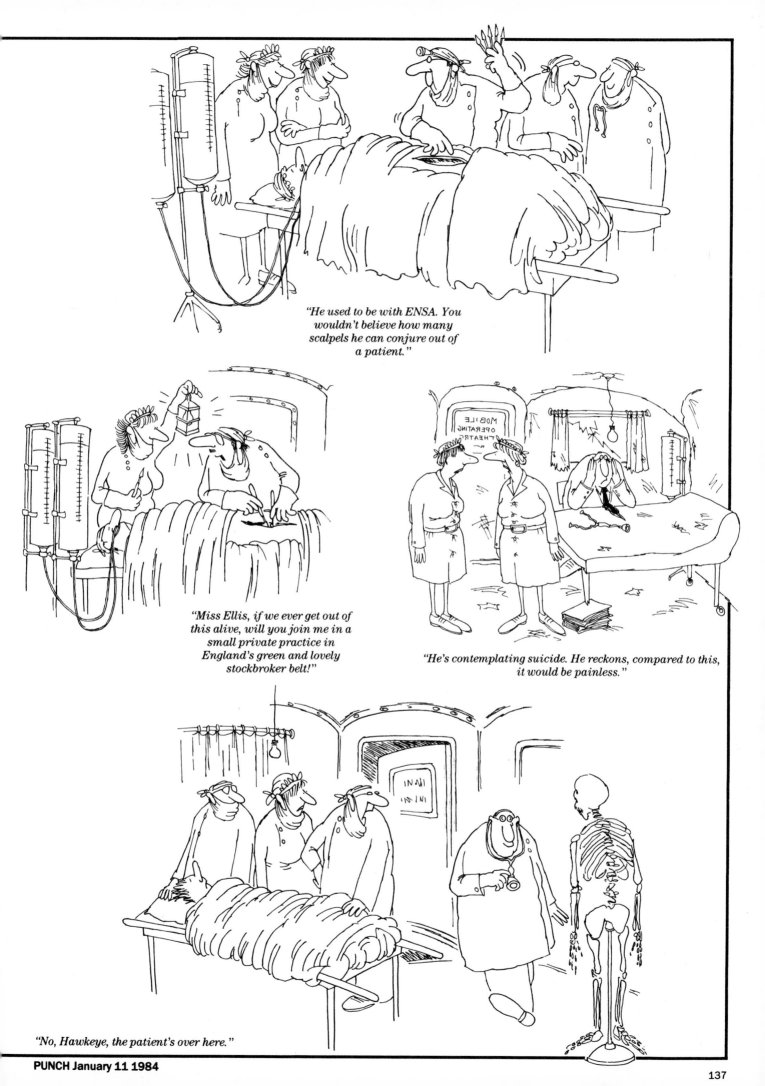

"He used to be with ENSA. You wouldn't believe how many scalpels he can conjure out of a patient."

"Miss Ellis, if we ever get out of this alive, will you join me in a small private practice in England's green and lovely stockbroker belt!"

"He's contemplating suicide. He reckons, compared to this, it would be painless."

"No, Hawkeye, the patient's over here."

Valerie GROVE

Sons and Mothers

WHEN Mrs Thatcher waved goodbye to Mark, the Lupin Pooter *de nos jours*, motherhood gained another martyr. In the view of Peregrine Worsthorne, Paul Johnson and co, Mrs Thatcher was right not to try to explain. "It is an act of maternal loyalty," wrote Worsthorne (Mum's the Word, *Spectator*). "In this matter she can only come clean by landing Mark in the dirt. Her vindication would be his indictment. And mothers, unless they are monsters, do not betray their sons."

Indeed not. At a stroke Mrs Thatcher is lined up with all the dear old Mrs Rippers who stand by their Jack: "He was always such a good boy at home ... so gentle and polite." What remains inviolate long after the hoo-hah dies down, is the apple-like status of the boy in the mother's eye.

I never saw myself as likely to follow Mrs Thatcher's personal code of behaviour but here I am: have you met my son, the baby? I am now the mother of a boy and the way is clear: it's him and me vs the world.

Until last August 4 (a birthday shared by the Queen Mother, for those who are connoisseurs of auguries) I had specialised in daughters. In the current climate few dared express sympathy except Barbara Cartland, whom I happened to be interviewing just after the third daughter was born, and who shrilled, "My-dear-how-*gharstly*—you *poor thing*! *All* men want sons, to teach them to shoot and fish!" In turn I began to deploy a similar reaction if any friend of mine produced a son. "A boy—how dreadful!" I would remark. Everyone knew, didn't they, that boys were more dull-witted, incontinent, slow to speak, demolishers of orderly homes, and likely to be soccer hooligans.

I didn't even want to try one, thanks. All that is now changed. He may be only two foot six in his "Toddle-pod" bootees, and he has not so much hair on his head as dandelion-clocks, but he is (as all can see) born to lead, or at least to be doted upon. I will not go on about his looks or the sick-bag will have to be passed round. But I do now realise that there is something peculiarly unassailable about mothers with sons. It brings about unsisterly sentiments. Lock up your daughters in the year 2001: not for their protection but for that of my boy. Already I see the girls lining up as vamps, scheming temptresses, succubi. And me keeping them at bay on his behalf.

No wonder the Denises of the world begin to look enfeebled. In *Sons and Lovers* Mrs Morel takes one look at baby Paul's deep unblinking blue eyes and "She no longer loved her husband." Keith Waterhouse, in his *Mrs Pooter's Diary*, knows exactly how Carrie feels about her dear boy Willie, who is doing very well in the bank at Oldham ("he has all the 'drive' that his father lacks"): "Last night Lupin came in very late from a concert at the Assembly Rooms, full of the new comic songs," she writes. "I thought they were highly amusing but Charlie, who seems to resent the boy enjoying himself, began grumbling and picking fault ..."

Mark's Lupin-like attributes were coolly appraised by Penny Junor, Mrs Thatcher's latest biographer, long before the Oman thing blew up. She described an insufferably pompous little boy who would bark "Thatchah!" when answering the telephone, in imitation of his father.

She said Mrs Thatcher would have preferred a "strong, handsome, independent" son like Cecil Parkinson. But for someone who failed his accountancy exams three times, Mark got by OK. Mrs Thatcher was able to marvel, "People are offering him jobs right and left!" Penny Junor described Mark Thatcher's management consultancy job as "a little woolly". He was loath to talk about it, she said. But when interviewed by *Honey* magazine he gave his opinion that the British ought to get off their arses and do a day's work. "Mrs Thatcher," said Penny Junor, "won't have a word said against him." A mother, as the Yiddish saying puts it, has glass eyes.

Daughters-in-law know this pattern well. My mother-in-law has three fine sons and not a morsel of food will she take until their plates are laden with man-size portions. She may want coffee; I may want coffee; but unless her son wants coffee, we don't have coffee.

People tell me the mother–son bond is

'Oh Lord, I left my worries on the doorstep!'

138

fundamentally sexual and I am sure this must be disgustingly true. The nappy-changing, for instance: goodness how he enjoys it and, frankly, so do I. His three sisters are not so much envious as obsessively interested and I don't blame them; it is a thrilling new department for us all. For at least two days at first I couldn't even bring myself to look. "How are you managing the infant willie?" my friend Margaret wrote breezily. Apparently, when her son was born her daughter, then two and a half, said: "What a good job it's not on his face, Mum."

The women's movement would say pshaw to all that, but one of the results of feminist inroads into patriarchy is that the guidelines for bringing up daughters are now more clearly defined than for sons.

A comprehensive schoolteacher I know tells me her girls grow more confident, ambitious and self-possessed daily but the boys are pathetic, spending most of their time showing off to one another. What with whole lessons devoted to Women's Studies (sandwiched between Peace Studies and Parentcraft) a schoolboy needs his mother more than ever.

A mixed-up mother wrote in the *Guardian* women's page recently. She had brought up her son to do as much housework as his four sisters did, she said. So when he married, "I congratulated myself on what a good husband he would make." He washes, he irons, he baths babies. And his mother feels dreadful. "I resent the fact that his wife can take for granted all the perks of living with a domesticated man while her friends look on in envy . . . I feel that my son is being put upon in some way."

That's the *Guardian* woman for you. Even when she's in the right she is convinced she's in the wrong.

This is not the kind of anguish that is likely to beset Mrs Thatcher but she is now established as the kind of mother a boy can rely on through thick and thin. It is usually fathers who go in for Lord Chesterfield/Old Polonius advice (never break your word, do not laugh too immoderately) or write Open Letters like that of William Rees-Mogg (life is like a great cathedral on a northern hill, etc.) Now Mrs Thatcher has proved that mother love stretches beyond keeping the cricket whites white and not forgetting the fruit gums. At the moment I cannot imagine Oliver beyond the Babygro stage but if one day he needs a little assistance with a £300m building contract . . . what's a mother for?

"We have until sundown to accept the double-glazing."

Pie in the Sky

PEOPLE keep telling me about meals. Not directly. They are telling other people, waiting their turn to tell. I just get scooped in for a comprehending nod or the amazed exclamation.

They leave me out after an hour or so, sensing a minimum response. I am thinking of other things. Norman Tebbit flying me somewhere, it could have happened. Synonyms for feet.

I like food. I eat it. I am often curious enough to ask what it is, particularly meats. There aren't many meats, but I can still guess wrong, even after scraping off the gravy. Seeing mustard helps. Then it isn't mutton. If no mustard, it could be. If mint sauce, it is, sometimes coming on a curved bone, and not amounting to much when it's been got off it.

Beef used to be clued by horse-radish. But this has now started coming with a cold fish, throwing me. Game is a problem unless I find a shot in it. Is quail, are quails, game? I would say I had never eaten them or it, but may have done when my curiosity was low. Pork is signalled by pineapple rings, though I wouldn't put a goose past it. Poultry are

puzzling, though fortunately few. I class them as chickens.

Venison could rank as a meat, but you have to know a haunch when you see one.

Fish are legion. I easily identify sardines, but things with k's in them confuse me. Haddock and mackerel. One is easier than the other to get the spinal column out of, but I can never remember which. Is salmon trout more salmon than trout or the other way round? Both often prove easier to eat the other way round, but I usually find that too late, when I have jerked a lot of it on to the table cloth if worn.

People think I am not interested in meals because I don't talk about them, and it's true that if I talked about them more, I might be more interested. There isn't a lot of opportunity for this, because the other people are talking about them all the time. Or I could look at pictures of them in full colour.

Many do, though I don't see what they get out of them. Photographs of a table laid for eight, and a big lump of something in the middle, surrounded by brilliantly-hued vegetables, with frills on it and stuck all over with nuts, leave my tastebuds dormant

and dry, compared with two fried eggs in real life, which I can eat and understand.

Those whose mouths water at photographs have a mysterious affinity with people who glide their eyes in silence down a musical score and hear trombones. But there are more of them. As there are more of them talking about food than handing round photographs of it that they have seen in the hairdresser's and torn out to bring round in their handbag: and me standing there saying, "What do you want to drink, love?" six times, and not a hope of an order until all present have done their oo's and lip-smacking and said wonderful, they would never have thought of roast oysters with turbot and lychee fritters, and wasn't it rather like something we had in Exeter, Bob, but without the blobs of *bündnerschinken* on the how's-your-father?

Past nosh-ups figure plenty. Never mind photographs, how about photographic memories. We have people in who can recite the forty-two meals they ate in Provence in 1976, though with the occasional clash, as between reminiscing spouses, on whether it was Roquevaire or Draguignan where they had the goat's

140

brains in rook soup. Still, someone else has shouted them down by then. Has anyone tried the new place at—? No, well, yes, but just a minute, they're Swiss, you can have Swiss restaurants in Greenwich, can't you? Well, you should try it, shouldn't they, Clive?

Clive is hardly off about thistle-heart salads and lobster butter before the room is crackling with crayfish. Wild parsley hangs from the ceiling. Powdered nutmeg settles on the sofa, the air cloys with burnt creams. Snouts of brandy-basted piglets snuffle for trufflles in the skirtings. You could move a leg and stand on a strudel. Camemberts coagulate widely.

Cheeses are hell.

Pistol my head with a choice of wine buff or cheese buff and I'll pick the man with the inside cork-knowledge every time. Food talk is no longer confined to the little women. Big men talk it.

We had a big man in yesterday evening who mimed a cheese. This takes space. I had to move furniture to give him a centre-stage. He caused nods of comprehension and exclamations of amazement, if not from me. I was being left out by then, in any case not fully comprehending. This cheese, it seemed, as he pulled his cuffs back for realism, had to be poured at an exact angle of pour. It was a pouring cheese. Moreover, he warned, manifesting before our very eyes a loaf-shaped cooking-foil container almost too hot to handle, the minutest drop on temperature caused lumps. You had to keep shuttling back and forth to the hot-plate.

He used the piano for this. We could see, some of us, steam misting the keyboard lid. Many dashed moisture from their mouth corners. When he sat down, sated, my wife said, "And no lumps?" He said he felt pretty confident.

Betty Hooton, who had half-mimed a held-out platter, said she thought they'd once had it in Geneva. So had the Goughs, in Souillac, thought George, with mountain-spider pâté and sliced salmonella if I have that right. The Crick-Bartons, courageous about losing face, said they had heard about it, but never seen it done before.

Conversation then became general. Within today's limits, that is. Calves' kidneys in duck-stock. Marrow-bones glacés. Wipe with a faintly damp cloth. First pierce your stuffed chub with a larding-needle. That new place run by Danes near Godalming, who avoided the common trap of over-marinating their Swordfish à la Tebbit, under-spicing their *Petits Pieds Synonymes* . . . I was getting confused.

As they were only with us for drinks, and now breaking up to go off and eat God knows what, we had to skip the afters. Lucky. I could have had to choose from the trolley.

My wife said, as we clashed the glasses into the sink, what about some quick beans? Delia Smith was on in ten minutes.

I'd wait, I said. I felt my indigestion playing up. 🐌

"*You're absolutely right—the top one suffers from vertigo.*"

"*Now I see why you have to own a Porsche!*"

"*You've got to hand it to Harding—he was an anthropologist's anthropologist!*"

Noel Ford:
OFFICE FOREPLAY

143

PAUL JENNINGS

"Indians are the only people who giggle; the Swiss may laugh but they never giggle."

Memsahib Monika

NTIL I saw the ads in the *Neue Züricher Zeitung*, I would have said, as unthinkingly as anyone else, that India was the *opposite* of Switzerland. I mean, we all think we know about Switzerland, the compensatory neatness of those towns with the shops of jewellers and antique dealers selling sixteenth- and seventeenth-century wooden altar-pieces under the wild, demon-haunted, untidy glaciers and crevasses, the Calvinist chapels and French Gothic gradually giving way to south-eastern onion domes. "... Nor let us be too hard," wrote Belloc, "upon the just but anxious fellow that sat down dutifully to paint the soul of Switzerland upon a fan."

Indians are the only people left in the world who giggle; the Swiss may laugh at some fairly obvious joke but they never giggle. The Swiss (at least until the digital-quartz revolution) are almost identified with the measurement of time, the Indians don't know how it is divided up, they only know about sunrise and sunset. Indians use cow-dung as fuel, Switzerland has the only cows in the world that don't produce any dung. From the milk they make rich, rather sickly chocolate. There is no such thing as Indian chocolate. And obviously, the Swiss are rich, Indians are poor.

They are also always advertising for marriage partners. Pick up almost any Indian paper and there are columns of Slim B.A.s, high caste, wanting to meet Slim English-speaking girl with good eyesight under 30, no dowry, etc. (Somehow you never see one, in any country, where it says Fat illiterate merchant-class male seeks bride, doesn't matter if she wears glasses so long as she can cook and has kind heart.)

Switzerland is the last country in the world where you can imagine anything so chancy as marriage-advertising, and even if there was any it surely wouldn't be in the gnomes' daily? Well then, look at these:

Indian resident boy, 28, slim, decent, working class, willing to settel abroad, seeks early marriage with sincere effectionate English speaking peasant lady. Please write with details and recent returnable photograph to Mr Pradeep, Box ... Bombay ...

and

Ich bin 46/168/56, dunkel, vewitmet, ohne Anhang. ...

At first I thought it meant that this lady, whose name I shall keep to myself as closely as Mr Pradeep's box number, was without hang-ups, as well as being dark, widowed and (it seems to me the only possible interpretation of those statistics) practically globular, unless the Swiss order these things differently and the middle figure is her height ... yes, it must be, if it's centimetres at 2.54 to the inch that makes her 5 feet 6 inches, they obviously don't bother about the waist, or at any rate hope no one else will bother. But on looking up *Anhang* I see it means she is without appendix, supplement, addition, codicil or party.

As always with marriage advertisements, any reader with the slightest imagination must be led into a spot of matchmaking, if only because of the challenge in such an unlikely pairing. How does Mr Pradeep expect *any* peasant lady to know English? If she does, she will surely be working in one of those neat banks or jeweller's or florist's in Zurich or Berne or even just Winterthur or St Gall.

Aha, but suppose it's the other way round, suppose she is a highly sophisticated urban lady who, like many of them (and unlike practically any of us) is perfectly fluent in German, French *and* English and, at this crisis in her life when her first husband has died, decides that she would like to break all the rules and *become* a peasant. She met Bruno when they were both students in Lausanne, idealistic, fond of poetry. But it is hard to make a living by poetry anywhere ... especially perhaps in Switzerland; and, like Roy Fuller, he is compelled to enter the legal side of a huge building society. But (unlike Roy Fuller) he finds this impossible to combine with a literary career. The ruthless pressures of commercial life in Zurich (the only city where I have seen people stop in the street to look in shop windows where they show minute-by-minute fluctuations in the rate of exchange) are too much for him, and he dies at the youthful age of 31.

We see this only in flashback in what I

"Something's gone radically wrong, Beveridge. I'm cold and hungry."

now perceive to be obviously one of those Channel 4 films. It is called *Monika*, after the eponymous heroine. And it starts 6000 miles away, say on Juhu beach, Bombay. Mr Pradeep, one of those handsome Aryan types with a pencil-line moustache, his dark hair blown by the sea breeze, is being argued with by his friend, the intellectual Mr Motilal, (they have both been laid off by a local Bata shoe factory). Mr Motilal has been to Europe, indeed he had a year at the Sorbonne, became a communist and is now trying (hopeless, glorious task!) to organise the workers of Bombay. He is the kind of Indian Sir Richard Attenborough has never heard of.

"Goodness gracious me, Pradeep, I am telling you that you are not finding a peasant lady at *all*, least of all in Switzerland. It is contradiction in terms. Perhaps it could be like Hindu *maya*; if king dreams he is peasant for twelve hours out of twenty-four, and peasant dreams he is king for same period, which is king and which is peasant? But it is not real life, you understand . . ."

Nevertheless, Mr Pradeep persists in spending an enormous number of his precious remaining rupees on this advertisement. Meanwhile Monika, who has bought seven cows and a crumbling farmhouse (or as near to crumbling as anything in Switzerland can get) in the Alpine village of Hupt, still regarded with deep suspicion by the real peasants, old men with drooping white moustaches and shapeless women with lined, weatherbeaten faces, is seen calling in for her *Neue Züricher Zeitung* (to which she is the only subscriber in this village; she is also the only person with hips of 14 inches, if that is what the 46 is, in the world . . . indeed if I've got it wrong and the 56 is the waist, that is still a mere 22 inches, pretty enviable for anyone, let alone a widow).

You can imagine the kind of music that accompanies the scene when, in her already nicely faded blue denim dress and broad-brimmed straw hat, she reads Mr Pradeep's ad in the sloping field of the high summer pasture, with the great innocent unattainable pure snow peaks behind. You may imagine him, shivering in thin clothes, having disregarded Mr Motilal's advice, arriving in winter at the tiny Hupt station, kept in touch with metropolitan Switzerland by efficient snow-ploughs . . .

A great deal of the latter part of *Monika* in fact has, as sound track, a voice-over reading of Mr Pradeep's letters back to Mr Motilal. The ending very much depends on the director. If it is one of these gloomy Germans like Fassbinder or Wim Wenders it will end with a mass attack on and burning of the Pradeep farm by rabid, xenophobic villagers. If it is Godard or one of the lyrical French producers it will end with a beautiful Eurasian child toddling into the village shop of Hupt (in summer again, of course) and greeted with smiles by all the old villagers. I needn't tell you, I hope, which one I pray it will be. 🌀

"Just think—twenty years ago we'd both have been stuck in the kitchen."

"What I can't stand is those yobbos drinking my particular brand of beer."

Haldane: WHO'S UP, DOC?

DOCTORS who are members of America's astronaut corps are to be added to two Space Shuttle flights this year.

Daily Telegraph

"For God's sake, Doc, we take off in five minutes!"

"The next time round perhaps you could say Ah!"

"I'm sorry, Dr Rogers is busy at the moment!"

"I've done all I can but I think he's getting too old for this game."

"Oops. For a moment I thought I was back in Maternity."

"Here comes your second opinion."

"Actually, we're not weightless. He's on Valium."

"I said I'm sorry, Mrs Guthrie—you'll have to make an appointment!"

"Talk to the doctor? That **is** the doctor."

CHINA
SYNDROME

Robert MORLEY on the Long March to Peking

Hong Kong to Kunmin by way of Sydney and a shortage of jam

"HERE, Desmond," remarked our hostess, "are the hard-boiled eggs. Don't forget to take them with you."

Desmond was our tour leader: we had just finished a buffet-style supper at the luxurious flat overlooking Hong Kong harbour and retained by the travel firm whose name is famous in the Far East for organising improbable package tours to China and Tibet. Not that our lot was going as far as Lhasa. This was to be a strictly blue-rinse tour, or so I imagined: nevertheless, the eggs worried me somewhat. For one thing there was just the right number, eight, in the paper bag. There were seven of us and Desmond. "Explain about the eggs," I urged.

"They will supplement the lunch China Airways provide on tomorrow's flight to Kunmin. Indeed, it may be the only thing you care to eat."

"In that case," I told him, "we should have at least two eggs apiece. I do hope there is to be no cheeseparing during our fortnight's once-in-a-lifetime excursion."

"I'll buy some biscuits," he assured me, "and chocolate perhaps. It's a pity these tours start from the Mandarin Hotel; people so often expect the same sort of comfort in Xian for instance."

We had met in the Bamboo Room at the Mandarin for our pre-tour briefing. Des introduced me to the others. There was a splendid but not particularly sprightly old lady of 87 who wished to climb the Great Wall and was a collector of ancient monuments besides herself and me. Last summer she had inspected Stonehenge. She had brought two grandchildren, a boy and a girl who should have been at Cornell University, and an all-purpose shooting stick. My senior by a dozen years, she proved uncomplaining of the trial ahead and as yet unaware of the hundreds of stairs she would have to climb during the next fortnight. I, too, was travelling with my younger son but when the briefing commenced he was still en route from Australia.

Completing our group was a splendidly co-operative couple, retired from the scholastic profession, who regularly toured the world: an example to the rest of us of how a package tourist should behave on all occasions and game not to miss a single pagoda or Friendship Store.

Des grouped us around the table and explained the rules of the game: never to be last on the bus; always to make sure our luggage was outside our doors in plenty of time; only to drink boiled water, of which apparently there would be a limitless supply in jumbo vacuum flasks in the bedrooms. Payment in China was to be made in funny money available by travellers cheques in the hotels. When we arrived anywhere the Chinese Government would decide where we would stay and what we were to see: tours of the Stone Forest, a visit to the circus, a river picnic, possibly a school, certainly a commune and always time to shop at the Friendship Store. Des kept glancing at his watch while he awaited the arrival of an American professor from the Hong Kong University who was to put us in the picture and give a short lecture entitled "China Past and Present".

When teacher arrived and started marking up his blackboard I was immediately reassured. His talk was witty and wise. He knew the history of the West's hopeless and unreasoning attitude to the country which presently contains almost exactly half the entire population of the world, and has consistently disappointed generations of the other half by refusing to be conned into buying what they neither needed nor could afford to pay for. The Americans at first hoped to sell them a billion pairs of boots a year; at the turn of the century the British believed that by providing a slightly larger shirt than Chinese peasants wore, the cotton mills of Lancashire need never close.

They were, of course, hopelessly frustrated on both counts, and like the Japanese resorted inevitably to violence and opium looting. If the Chinese persisted in going barefoot and inadequately clothed, they could surely use opium. Indeed, they were required to do so by the British. The Americans at present have switched to more sophisticated hardware, but he doubted that the Chinese would prove any more eager customers for tanks and missiles. After all, as he pointed out, they already tie up a million Soviet forces on their borders and seem to believe enough is enough. "I fear," he told us, "the pendulum between hope and disenchantment is about to swing once more."

He considered the political climate in China was by no means stable. The army, as always, was a powerful factor which he thought might at any time attempt to destabilise the present regime. We would see for ourselves how the majority of the farmers (the word "peasant" was now frowned upon) lived. The Government had successfully removed the fear of famine: if the peasant worked overtime these days it was to procure a television set.

As if on cue, my younger son Wilton arrived. These days he is a not inconsiderable force on the Australian entertainment scene where he was presenting then three plays simultaneously. He confided to Des that he proposed to leave the tour halfway through, when we reached Shanghai. Not for him the terracotta figures of Xian or the Forbidden City of Peking; he was obliged to return to Sydney for yet another first night.

Des opined this would create enormous problems. Once you are on the manifest the Chinese require not only orderly behaviour but an orderly departure. No one, Des opined, ever left the group except in the case of severe indisposition or death. In the latter case the corpse was immediately cremated; as for the indisposition, that only happened in Lhasa where both the food and the altitude sometimes raised problems.

Always a seeker after the morbid truth, I pressed him to expatiate on sudden death. In his one experience, he had discovered an unexpected Chinese efficiency and indeed briskness. Although not allowed to attend the ceremony, the husband of the deceased received the ashes of his late wife back the same morning and was in time to join the rest of the party for luncheon and the afternoon excursion. On another occasion, when one of the group had become heart-stricken in Tibet, Des had stayed until a complete recovery had been effected but had been obliged to send the rest of the party forward with only a local Sherpa in attendance.

If there was one thing that struck me about Des at this early stage, it was that he had a very low anxiety threshold. I was to find out later that this was not entirely an advantage. He was also, in my opinion, rather too ready to allow the local authorities to pronounce any deviation from their own plans as "impossible". It used to be the same in the early days of Intourist when visiting Russia.

"We shall have to try to get Wilton off the manifesto in Shanghai, but by the time we arrive there it will be the Chinese New Year and everything will be closed," Des affirmed.

"Including the frontier?" asked Wilton.

"No, not the frontier, but the offices. At the Chinese New Year everyone, but everyone, will be letting off fireworks."

We left the conference chamber and were sent upstairs to brush and wash up and met later in the hotel lobby for transport to the inaugural reception. Presumably because we were such a very small group, our hostess had invited, besides ourselves and the American professor, some prominent residents of the European garrison to leaven the proceedings. Having once performed a cabaret session at the Mandarin for three weeks, I was prepared for the inevitable covey of bankers, consultant engineers and investment brokers and their by no means uncomplaining wives. There is a good deal of money still to be made in the Colony but even more to be spent. English public school fees, not to mention the air fares at holiday time and frantic attempts by the Government to reduce a formidable deficit in the annual budget, send the prices rocketing and make Hong Kong one of the most expensive places in the world. Then, of course, there is the ever-present terror of what the Chinese intend to do when the lease expires.

"I imagine," I opined, "any final settlement will be linked with the problem of Taiwan?" I had cribbed this from my American professor.

"In no way," asserted a high British Government official. If there is one thing I have learned, it is that when an expert tells one it can't happen it almost invariably does.

On more certain ground, I questioned Des on what people most wanted to see in China. "The Wall," he told me, "although this time of the year it is bitterly cold because of the wind. It's a three-hour journey from Peking and only the Ming tombs to visit on the way back. There is nothing in them, of course."

I decided to avoid the Wall. "What else?" I asked.

"On my last trip," he told me, "it was the abattoirs. One of our guests insisted on seeing as many slaughter houses as possible. Of course they are not always easy to find. There isn't a lot of meat and the peasants kill their own pigs, usually by the roadside. Why, I can't imagine. It tends to upset the tourists."

Did everyone have to go? "No, although normally we like to keep the group together."

"Do you suppose he was a butcher?" I queried.

"More likely a salesman for humane killers," Des thought.

We senior citizens left the party early but the younger ones stayed up most of the night in Kowloon where, stopped and questioned by the ever-watchful Hong Kong Constabulary, they had ended up in a Police Club drinking till the ferries restarted. For me it

Photograph by Wilton Morley

was time to repack. It's extraordinary, the amount of time one spends rearranging the contents of one's suitcase and deciding which of one's possessions to include in the overnight bag provided by our hosts. There is nothing that pleases tour operators more than to see each member of their party sporting an identical bag. Like school caps, they advertise the success of the establishment, ensure that no one breaks ranks but do tend to add to the confusion when claimed in error by other pupils.

I HAD a good deal of packing to accomplish, having arrived in Hong Kong via Sydney and Penang. Sports shirts were out from now on, winter woollies were in. Nearly everyone at the party had enquired whether I had brought thermal underwear. On our first evening in Kunmin, when the luggage had been delayed somewhat, I realised how unprepared I was in that department. The corridor of the hotel was filled with Japanese, who for some reason had stripped down to their long johns and were separating their suitcases from ours and humping them to the bedrooms.

I had found Australia much as usual. The front pages were filled with pictures of the stupendous Miss Sutherland about to give her annual concert in the Domain, and then to belt it out in the Opera House with the famed Pavarotti in a selection of arias and duets later in the week. Every seat had been sold at roughly £75 a time, and only then was it announced that the whole concert would be televised live that evening. Dining out with friends, I contrived to keep the party grouped round the dining-table as long as possible but eventually we retreated to the parlour and then heard what was, I suppose, the last hour of encores. I have always resented the way the public carries on when listening to opera or watching ballet. Enough is enough, in my opinion. But at last it was over, the stage covered in squashed

roses, the participants dripping with perspiration.

One thing, however, has radically altered the Australian scene: the police have been given a new toy. Not on this occasion the plastic bullet but the breathalyser. They play with it, and the citizens, long past bedtime. Now, at a party in his home, only the host gets drunk and in restaurants the consumption of Perrier water has quadrupled. Only a very small amount of alcohol changes the colour of the bags, one's licence is then sequestered and without a car the citizen is immobilised. Luncheon parties end nowadays as early as they do in Kent. "Three o'clock," as my sister who lives there once told me; "After all, we are all busy people."

It is our custom these days, after the hurly-burly of recording television advertisements in Australia, to repair to Penang and its extravagantly elegant hotels and beaches. Lying in the shade under the lilac trees, we were only foolish enough on one occasion to leave the environment of pool and sea and venture into the town itself on a rather warm afternoon to witness a Hindu ceremony at which the men fastened themselves with hooks through the back and dragged carts along dusty streets, the more devout or dotty among them having driven large silver skewers through both cheeks.

We left precipitately to drink iced lemonade at the Eastern and Oriental Hotel, the Malaysian equivalent of Raffles in Singapore, where the only other guests were two English girls being entertained to a late luncheon by what, in my opinion, were palpably a couple of white slavers. My instant recognition of these dangerous traders was confirmed when after the third lemonade the two girls approached and thanked me profusely for putting in an appearance. "You saved us," they told me, "in the nick of time." On thinking things over, I suppose I constructed the scenario after they had expressed their gratitude. Never mind, for I was in the right place at the right time.

▶

UT all that was now behind me and the plane for Kunmin was to leave at noon, which gave me plenty of time for last-minute shopping. If I'd known what I know now, I would have bought gin, biscuits, chocolate, jam and instant coffee. As it was, I contented myself with a notebook, on the cover of which was inscribed: "This notebook is well bound with automatic excellentic machine, makes you demonstrate your youth and pride. Get acquainted with it and you'll start a relationship that will last a lifetime."

Des was awaiting us in the hall of the Mandarin. I was to learn that he was the one who, on all occasions when the troupe was in motion, supervised the closing of the minibus door having satisfied himself we were all present and fairly correct. Once we had moved off, the guide took over and Des retreated, to my mind, a shade too hurriedly. His constant surrender to local pressure irritated me again and again. "Can't we see the Zoo?", "I'm told there is a very good duck restaurant in Huai Hai Road, why don't we try that and cut out the Gateway of Longevity and Eternal Happiness?"—all such suggestions were over-ruled by our dual escorts. My sole success was in stopping the bus one morning for an urgently needed pee.

Des's interest was mainly in antiques; I don't mean the 87-year-old and myself but fragments of discarded pipes or pieces of wood carving, for which he bargained fiercely with the local peasantry. He sought the crock of gold at the end of the rainbow and so, I suppose, did the rest of us.

As we filed down the staircase to board the bus to take us out to the plane, we were presented with plastic mackintoshes. Later, on the flight itself, we were given key rings and small packets of boiled sweets. On every succeeding flight the same gifts were proffered and on one occasion a whole bar of chocolate and an embroidered handkerchief. Luncheon was not as bad as Des had foretold but we were grateful for the hard-boiled eggs and the whiskies and soda with which he armed himself and us.

We arrived at Kunmin at the evening rush-hour; the streets were crowded with seated cyclists, all identically clothed and most masked. The Chinese are particularly fond of a clinical pad which is worn over the nose and mouth, especially by children. Its purpose is to exclude the dust, of which there seemed very little evidence. No doubt it was according to a government directive given at one time, possibly while plague was raging, and the custom has lingered in the consciousness of a nation which is deeply hypocondriacal. The Government attaches great importance to a get-fit programme they recently put into operation. Enthusiastic members of the Party are for ever organising physical jerks on any spare bit of waste ground, and many office workers carry dumb-bells slung round their handlebars.

Because we were only a small group, we never rated a national guide and were at the mercy of local talent. Dinner on the first evening gave a foretaste of what was to come. China keeps institutional hours, at least for her visitors. Every meal is advanced at least one and often two hours. We rose at seven for breakfast, took lunch sometimes as early as eleven and dinner never later than seven and often at six-thirty. Bowls of soup, and rice, floating vegetables, small portions of pork gristle, the occasional meticulously sliced duck, boiled meat and a large number of stews were dumped on the table before us and scrambled for with chopsticks or, in my case, a fork. I found myself able to cope only with the stewed eels and steamed pike, with the aid of hot sauces which eventually took their toll of my digestive tract, and I succumbed fairly soon to what in my youth was described as the universal complaint.

With the exception of Shanghai and Peking, the food is not of the kind one can get one's teeth into. When one does so it is usually gristle. I formed the theory that local kitchens are given a quota of food for each guest and most of the choice cuts are disposed of elsewhere. This was certainly true of the jam in Guilim. I took a stand at breakfast on the first morning, failed to obtain any and ventured out later in the day to buy some, returning with a jar of mixed pickles. I explained my frustration to a professor from Canada temporarily teaching at the University; he disappeared briefly, then returned with a large pot of marmalade which he presented to me. "But where did you find it?" I asked.

"I bought it from the kitchen," he told me. "In China you must know the ropes." I would not wish to convey to the reader that corruption is rife. The Chinese are undoubtedly a good deal more honest than the rest of us, although they do have to pay the occasional night watchman to ensure their bikes are still there on the morrow. ✧

"He watched his first unrecorded programme today."

SCOUTS in London will have to let gays join their ranks if they want cash grants, it was revealed today.

The Standard

Dickinson's
Scouting for boys

"Now this is what I call a camp fire."

"I'd like to be a Queen's Scout, but my dad won't let me take the test."

"That's my GLC badge for helping old dykes on to the Greenham Common bus."

"Surely you know what to rub together to make a fire at your age?"

"Thank God Bob-a-Job week's over for another year."

Michael BYWATER

DOLEDRUMS

"My sympathies are with the man who, on emerging into the daylight with his maundy money, stole my car to get down to Piccadilly Circus to buy drugs."

OCKSIDE weather today, redolent of cranes, and mournful hooters, and rust, suitably for the matter in hand. Broke around lunch-time, nothing dramatic, just a hint of frigidity in the sky, a touch of imminent displeasure, like a maiden aunt ignored at dinner, followed by restrained weeping. Nothing loud or common, but making her feelings clear.

Her, of course, being the great goddess Ceres, probably, a.k.a. Demeter or Mother Earth, though I dislike the last appellation, rather, laden as it is, no longer with fructifying images of sheaf, churn and flitch, but of dungaree, tent and pamphlet, and a hierophantic clutch of grubby acolytes called things like Freda People (real) and Ayma Druid (made up by me but probably soon to be adopted).

"The Last Great Adventure," they witter in the small-ads, "And Only A Woman Can Be Part Of It," which I suppose should fill me with excitement but merely succeeds in depressing, given the weather, two-thirty pee em and I've got the big light on, grey and damp outside, tyres hissing on the tarmac, rain on the windows, footsteps on the wet pavement, the whole thing disgustingly full of atmosphere; soon it will be dark, and I have no doubt whatsoever that the street lights, true to stereotype, will cast thin yellowish pools of light on the glistening street, and a man in a trenchcoat and trilby will walk past, deep in thought, pause in one of the pools of light, q.v., and light a Strand, and look over his shoulder, and, with an expressionless face, walk on out of sight as, in the distance, a siren wails and the full orchestra takes up the second subject, *molto pesante*, roll final credits and fade out, meteorology courtesy of MGM, all rights reserved.

Probably something to do with getting old. Three decades, rich in experience, have drifted past and suddenly I find my mind has snapped shut like a leathery cerebral sphincter, Pok!, and everything's changed.

I used to wallow in the advent of autumn, peripatetic and yearning in places like Nottingham and Sheffield and Cardiff, in love invariably and unsuitably, a mental gramophone ready to start buttering Gershwin into my inner ear the moment the festival shutters came swishing down with a drizzly hiss, a moment identifiable not only by the soundtrack but also by lettuce suddenly starting to look rather pointless, and pubs welcoming, and people like people rather than like raw food for some gargantuan carnivores browsing around the stratosphere.

That bit was rather nice, particularly with the girls wrapped up nice and snug like parcels, and rosy and clear from the soft English weather, so that one could take them home, and warm them up before the gas fire, and give them cocoa and rum-and-warm-water, and then . . .

All changed, now. Particular love of individual humanity has transmuted to general sympathy, on the assumption that if I nowadays find it dreary, everyone else must, too. Compassion for all men is my autumnal portion, and when I say "men" I mean precisely that, *men*, male, X and Y chromosomes, stubble, don't touch it or it will drop off, or, in short, gender. Excluded from my empathetic communality are women, who, on the whole, can take it; the lunatic Wicca/Wimmin fringe, huddled wetly in tent or protest, and good enough for them, too; and those strange, piping, indeterminate creatures who muck around with quangoes and Islington council, or wear Brut Hairspray For "Men" (A. Scargill, prop.).

Put it this way. At the end of the street in which I drag out my apportioned lot, there stands an Unemployment Office and "Job-Centre", presumably so designated by the same chirpy wit who christened those banking machines "Servicetills" on the grounds that under normal circumstances no service whatsoever is obtainable from them.

This place does a lot of business. In the summer, it is relatively cheerful, not what you'd call a riot but then being abused by a bunch of spotty halfwits bent on asserting their superiority and only getting enough

"I think you should know I'm an expert in passive resistance."

cash to keep a ferret in dogfood is not conducive to elaborate gaiety, and all things considered, they do their best; the clients, that is, as opposed to the staff, who generally speaking do their worst.

Come autumn, however, as it did today, things change. Everything gets wet and gritty and dreary, with a lot of mooching and shuffling, as if Ken Loach has suddenly taken over in the middle of an Ealing comedy. I noticed it instantly this morning when I went up to the shop for an egg-and-tomato roll (no lettuce, incidentally, the nifty little pineal gland, or Third Eye, having spotted the seasonal drift several hours before the other two) and became aware of a lot of gloomy men hanging around across the road, all looking like George Orwell except for the ones who looked like Harry Belafonte.

I felt the urge to join them, there's nothing I like better than a nice hang around at this time of year, but duty called, so I went back and hung around my office for a bit, wondering what they all did. I mean, you must go bananas after a bit, talking to the furniture and so forth; I do that myself, my inmates are not in the least surprised to burst in and find me with my snout buried in the bowels of an amusing little applewood escritoire, drivelling eighteenth-century inconsequentialities at the dovetails. Can't stop, m'dear, just *yahrning* fer a plaguey great dish o' tay . . .

. . . But you wouldn't get much in the way of stimulation from an MFI knock-down laminated coffee-table, ballet dancer on the top or no ballet dancer on the top, particularly since the largesse of the Government is such that the bailiffs are probably waiting for the gimcrack front door to fall off its rusting hinges before shambling in and carting it off, there being nothing in County Court rules about not distraining on alleged close personal friends if the sheriff's man has reasonable grounds for believing said friends to be made of plywood with four lacquered spruce legs with little brass feet.

This needs work, does this one, otherwise with things going the way they are (and never mind Arthur Scargill) there's not going to be a single *dweadfully* entertaining little *Antiquerie* from The Shambles to The Lanes safe from marauding gangs of the unemployed—Scum! Filth! Wasters!— driven mad with accidie and the overriding urge to bust in through the Georgina-style bottle-glass bow window and get the head down for a nice chat with a classy bit of Sheraton.

As usual, the Bywater Advisory Bureau has arrived at a solution, and, also as usual, the solution has been tried and found wanting, not due to inherent defects but to the stupidity of the others. (What do you mean, what others? The two classes of humanity, dear—people like us, and people who purse their lips.) The solution was a bold and dramatic one, brought on by my own brief sojourn within the charitable bosom of the Department of Stealth and Total Obscurity, and subsequent observation of the plight of others in its bleak clutch.

If you've never been in a dole office, perhaps I ought to advise you that, at their best, they have all the grace and welcoming charm of those public lavatories that even the perverts avoid, except for the major distinction that one has too much bumph, and I'll leave you to work out which. Long queues, dim light, dirty paint, scrubby notices, ugly ill-humoured staff and cack-stained flooring all combine to give the overriding impression that the DHSS is a sort of overstuffed commissionaire exerting his authority.

Beastly, in short (though good enough for the unemployed—Scum! Filth! Wasters!— of course), and my sympathies are wholly with the man who, on emerging into the daylight with his maundy money, immediately stole my car in order to get down to Piccadilly Circus to buy drugs as soon as possible. (The police found him later that day, sitting in the passenger seat with the engine running, wondering mildly why he wasn't getting anywhere but not really too concerned; then they lost the car, having told me where it ought to be, so that I reported it stolen again; and, when it turned up in the garage of Holborn nick, and I drove it away, a vigilant copper immediately tried to arrest me for driving a stolen vehicle. But that's another story. Actually it isn't, because I've just told it. Oh to hell with it; I'll sort it out with the sofa-table, later.)

So what I thought was, why not tart up the dole offices a bit, shove in a bar, open up a little cafe, install some pleasant chatty furniture and so forth, somewhere to sit and chew the fat, drink a cappuccino or a pint of beer, get rid of the stigma of being on the dole (what stigma, anyway? Bloody thing's getting almost compulsory, these days).

Somebody might even make a bit of money out of it, given some enterprise and so forth.

But of course it's been tried, somewhere down South, I can't remember where, but I read about it in the newspaper so it may perhaps be true. And guess what happened? The *staff* complained, on grounds which were a specious disguise for their obvious belief that their clients—Scum! Filth! Wasters!—didn't need that sort of treatment, and that the money could be better spent on *them*. And loony extremists from Polperro to the Wash complained, on grounds which admit of no rational penetration, but which spring from minds which regard it as more useful to pay for e.g., a crowd of ugly women to ride around London in a gaudy bus containing a video camera and a photocopier, or to start a newspaper which nobody will buy, so you give it away and support it by getting your local loony council to put advertisements in for jobs telling people what the council is up to, notwithstanding rats in the streets, rubbish piling up, threat of plague etcetera, this being called Camden's Going Local and expressed in the sort of jolly Idiot Pioneer Corps language which makes one feel that catatonic schizophrenia has something to be said for it after all . . .

. . . And nobody asked the punters— Scum! *etcetera*—what *they* thought at all. Daft, eh? But, there: it may have been a bad summer down south, it may have been an early autumn, perhaps there was a duff lettuce crop so that their pineal glands, or Third Eyes, were collectively fooled, and misty autumnal gloom fell too early. The idea, anyway, is still there, but my own feeling is you might as well talk to the wall.

Which is a good thing, since that's all there is anyway. 🌑

"I think everybody's filling up before the Budget."

TELEVISION: JENSEN

EUBIE!

THE JEWEL IN THE CROWN SUSAN WOOLDRIDGE *as Daphne Manners* ART MALIK *as Hari Kumar*
TIM PIGOTT-SMITH *as Merrick*

IT'LL BE ALRIGHT ON THE NIGHT   DENIS NORDEN

THE WINDS OF WAR   JAN-MICHAEL VINCENT *as Byron Henry*   ROBERT MITCHUM *as Pug Henry*
GUNTER MEISNER *as Hitler*

SPECIAL RELATIONSHIP

Exactly two hundred years ago, the American War of Independence ended, thus making it impossible for the two countries ever to be independent of one another again. To celebrate, we have chosen a few random examples of close co-operation from the past couple of centuries.

THE RUNAWAY SUCCESS

of his efficient but cheap motor cars quickly persuaded Henry Ford to set up an operation on this side of the Atlantic, relying on British management and labour. Soon, models like this were rolling off the assembly lines at the rate of nearly one a week.

GUMMO WRIGHT (1879–1958),

who, though by far the dumbest of the three aeronautical brothers, was the only one to master the secret of flight. The secret was not to invent anything that could actually get off the ground; that way you lived longer. Unable to make a living in America, he eventually emigrated to Britain in 1920 where he received enormous Government subsidies to work on his two major projects, the Saunders Roe Princess flying boat, and the Brabazon.

DURING the nineteenth century, the hunt for Moby Dick became ever more frantic by American sailors. Moby Dick was nautical slang for the infection introduced into the Pitcairn Islands by Fletcher Christian and other English sailors following the mutiny on the *Bounty*, and fear of contracting it on the South Seas run ran like wildfire, and indeed like Moby Dick itself, through America's fleets, particularly since women were often carried, as we now know from several hundred Hollywood movies of the 1940s. Female surgeons, in fact, like Gloria Steinem and Bella Abzug *(shown here)* were employed to operate on any men found to be suffering from the complaint. Many historians now feel that it was out of such innocent beginnings that the women's movement grew and subsequently flourished.

IN THE INFANCY

of the cinema, many young English actors emigrated to Hollywood to seek their fortune. Can you guess the identity of this famous figure, whose original name was Henry F. Breene? Here is a clue: the thing he is standing in front of is not a movie camera, although he thought it was. It was in fact a fraud set up by the notorious Rigatoni brothers in a cellar on W. 89th Street, New York, to which they would lure arriving Britons on the pretext of a screen test for Mack Sennett. They would then steal their possessions and throw their corpses in the East River. Henry F. Breene is better known as The Headless Limey.

BRITAIN

has always been ready not only to cater for the fantasies of the distinguished American cousins, but also to protect their reputations: take, for example, Wallis Simpson, Roman Polanski, Dwight D. Eisenhower, Larry Adler, Walter Annenberg, and many more, including Ernest Hemingway, who was, of course, terrified of anything free-range larger than a hedgehog. He is shown here in 1935 on a secret visit he made to Britain to collect okapi heads for his den, shooting at Whipsnade.

AN EARLY PHOTOGRAPH,

taken from Ellis Island, c. 1883, showing two fugitives from European persecution excitedly pointing out the Statue of Liberty to one another. They are both British rainwear manufacturers, driven out of their native land by unfair competition from the newly-formed Marks & Spencer. The man on the left is Mr Hyman Burberry, while on the right stands Mr Nat Mackintosh. Both subsequently made fortunes in the United States, where they became bywords for "the English look" and plenty of room under the arms. Their wooden waistcoats, however, never caught on.

WORLD WAR TWO

was of course a period of incredibly close co-operation and mutual assistance between Britain and America. During the Blitz, for example, it is doubtful whether Londoners could have held up against Hitler alone, had it not been for the enormous contribution made by Bing Crosby and Bob Hope in lifting their spirits with films like *The Road to Singapore* (1940), while Hope and Crosby, in their turn, were able to get enormously rich. ▶

THE HISTORIC MEETING

of the Utah Committee of Enquiry in 1869 at which British emigré pioneers Casey Buckton, of the Union Pacific Teamsters, and Pete "Iron Horse" Parker of the go-ahead Atchison, Topeka and Santa Monica Whopperburgers-To-Go Company, finally hammered out an agreement on flexible rostering in the caboose and thus opened up the way for Golden West Awayday Dollarsnatcher Vacations.

But the triumphant co-operation was short-lived. Iron Horse Parker's dream of electrifying the line coast-to-coast was thwarted when the Chief Engineer, Dwight Edison, sold out his interest to his brother, Con, and Casey Buckton joined Ford Motor Company to mastermind production of the Edsel. This early Daguerrotype was taken by Eastman Ilford Jr, who later went bust.

SIR ALGERNON OTIS,

the Victorian Staffordshire dwarf, made his fortune out of elevator shoes but tried unsuccessfully to interest gadget-mad America in his invention of the elevator chair, borne aloft by Hispanic houseboys. A later electrically-powered version unfortunately short-circuited and killed him, but was patented by the US Federal Penitentiary, Otis's daughter, Chloe, inherited her father's inventive flair and went on to make a second family fortune in the lift business. She was invited to the White House in recognition of her services to the nation in helping to combat cardiac arrest in persons taking the staircase up skyscrapers but refused to attend, sending her regrets. A grandson of one of the original Hispanic houseboys went on to have a walk-on part in *West Side Story* whilst another is now second-in-command of the Argentinian Navy.

ERROL FLEMING,

an ancillary worker at St Mary's Paddington, who, after refusing to clear up a pile of evil-smelling cultures left on a window-sill, discovered next day that the accumulated overnight mould had caused a nearby rubber plant to shrivel.

Fleming caught the next plane out to America and was subsequently awarded the Purple Heart in Da-Nang for his discovery of Defoliant-X.

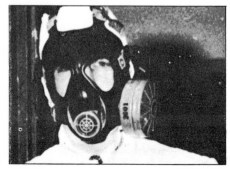

MINDFUL

of the furore which ten years earlier had attended Earl Grey's ill-fated export drive with finest English teas for Bostonian society, Clerkenwell grocery sundriesman Bert Maxwell bided his time until 1783 before berthing his cutter, the *Hermesetas*, in Coney Island harbour and setting up as a coffee shop on 17th and 21st called Maxwell House.

Maxwell faced stiff competition, however, from his fellow-European neighbours Kurt Budweiser and Enrico Martini and was cruelly disenchanted to discover that his dream of nationwide prohibition was more than a century ahead of its time. Custom fell off and, in desperation, Maxwell's wife, Betsy, began bottling the cold coffee dregs as a novelty soft drinks she called Betsy-Cola. That, too, was a flop and so the Maxwells sold both their patents to American friends for 5 bucks apiece and sailed home again to Clerkenwell to set up a blueberry pie business. They died in penury.

AS FEARS

of American warmongering in Europe rose to fever pitch during the winter of 1898, a determined group from the Berkshire Women's Peace Movement mounted a vivid demonstration of European public opinion by holding hands around Cuba and demanding that the US keep its forces and armaments out. President McKinley appeared to be unimpressed by such actions, but in due course the Americans did pull out of Cuba, which has been very little trouble ever since.

IT WAS AS THE 19th CENTURY

drew to its close that the dawn of 20th-century Anglo-American co-operation in the telecommunications explosion was vividly anticipated during an epoch-making visit to the lavish Camden Lock home of the Rev Jedediah Frost by the Massachussetts inventor, Samuel Morse. Before an incredulous audience of 7, from the cream of London's intelligentsia, including Abraham Parkinson and Dame Emily Rippon, Morse tapped out his historic message, "Good Morning, Britain". Before a century had passed, that same message was to be re-transmitted to an audience almost double the size.

MORE THAN HALF A CENTURY

before the Beatles took America by storm, housewife Mrs Glenda Miller and Her Paramount All-Stars undertook an exhibition tour of Georgia and the deep South to introduce the Birkenhead Palm Court Sound to the uproarious 1920s society. The tour was not a success and the entire ensemble was put on the first boat down the Mississippi. Frustrated managers with cancelled bookings to fill seized on the first boatload of musicians coming up-river. The fact they turned out to be black and unable to stick to the melody didn't seem to matter at the time. 🦜

Sheridan MORLEY

California Here I've Come

"IT'S no use trying to explain to people why one lives here," said Christopher Isherwood when I once asked him why he chose to live by a Californian beach instead of somewhere sensible like Earl's Court, "either they understand it's the only place or they don't." Me, I've never understood California at all. Boston I can manage, largely because I once got married there and the in-laws still do Sunday lunch and somewhere nice to stay. New York I can survive in, just so long as I stay two blocks east of Broadway in a hotel where they get the London papers by lunchtime and the liftman can still tell the difference between me and Clive Barnes, which is now only about a stone. But California is something else entirely, and though I have been coming here faithfully once a decade ever since 1947, I still don't much care for it.

Back in the late 1940s, of course, Los Angeles and I were both a lot smaller: those were the days when there was still a Hollywood Raj, that community of ageing English actors who had found a place in the sun and a pool and had to sacrifice nothing more crucial than their talent in order to play a succession of crumbling butlers and housekeepers and old colonels in the movies of Kipling and Victorian Empire that were still being churned out by MGM in double-featured dozens. Many of the Metro studios executives indeed solemnly believed that if ever they got to London (then still a ten-day journey by train and boat) they might well get to meet Prince Albert waltzing with Greer Garson in thick fog down a cobbled street linking Windsor Castle to the House of Commons.

Nowadays, of course, English princes come rather differently cast: where once they were Ronald Colman or David Niven (if good) and Basil Rathbone (if treacherous), now they are more likely to be Prince Andrew himself who, during a singularly unfortunate royal visit here last month to promote the Olympics, managed instead to turn a paint sprayer on a lot of understandably indignant American press photographers, a gesture for which the local press sensibly billed the embassy a total of twelve hundred dollars for damaged cameras.

It therefore occurred to me, while introducing the first Mrs Gregory Peck to the Maharajah of Jaipur (the kind of thing one gets to do all too seldom elsewhere nowadays) that things must have changed a bit since the time when I first made the discovery of sunshine and ice cream and bananas and swimming out here almost forty years ago. Being a journalist in California now is much like being the night-watchman at Madame Tussaud's. For the authorised David Niven biography (out next year, place orders now at all good booksellers), I have been back here interviewing some of the oldest film stars in the world, all of whom shall remain nameless until their often widely differing views of Niven appear in the book. Some were in a quite remarkable state of preservation, living high in the Hollywood canyons surrounded by minders and sixth wives and telephone-answering machines all of fantastic inefficiency. In theory, Californian telephone-answering machines can now tell you the time of day, apologise for the absence of their owners and forward your call to some totally new destination where your friend may or may not be visiting his analyst. In practice, once you have heard the tell-tale click of the machine grinding into action, you'd be better off talking to your toenails.

My college friend in California is one of the great gays of our time, a man my wife and I first encountered twenty years ago at the University of Hawaii when she was sharing a room with Bette Midler and I had to have someone else to talk to during the long summer evenings. He now survives as a film editor of immense talent in Hollywood, living largely on a diet of chocolate milk laced with low-calorie Pepsi. When I arrived to stay with him this time there was, he told me, one new problem: in order to protect his numerous dogs and the supplies of chocolate milk in the freezer he had installed a new burglar alarm of a complexity rivalled only by his telephone-answering machine which now plays *Brigadoon*.

The burglar alarm has to be set on a series of time switches whenever one leaves the house: get one of them wrong, he told me, the bell will instantly sound and within seconds squads of police marksmen, firing from the navel and asking questions later, would descend from all sides, surround the house and kill anything that moved, probably including the dogs.

I need hardly tell you that the first morning I was there alone I inadvertently set off the alarm, which rang loudly for several minutes. I then waited for the police to arrive, having rehearsed my explanation of the problem and timed it so that I would have been able to shout it through the window before being kneecapped. Needless to say, the bell rang for several hours in all. People walked by the house, delivered mail, exercised poodles, told me to have a nice day now. Of policemen descending from the hills I saw no sign. California is like that: the ideas are wonderful, offices hum with computers, but try to post a letter or hail a taxi or make a phone call or buy a bottle of milk and you'll be there until long after the Olympics that the locals are now dreading as much as a twenty on the Richter scale. Judged as an efficient society, Los Angeles is resoundingly beaten by London Transport.

Some of its stars, as I was saying just before that last detour, are in a quite remarkable state of preservation, and if you look very closely they even breathe. Others, the ones who failed to invest in 1950s real estate or do the right television soap operas or make the right money marriages, are living further out toward the ocean in what the road signs so graphically describe as the Slide Area, where houses and careers tumble into the sea at Malibu whenever the weather turns rough. But what all my interviewees, the legends and the rich and the failed and the still hopeful, had in common, was a kind of tenacious survival: bleached by years of Californian sun, preserved forever on late-night cable TV reruns of their worst movies, undisturbed by the fall of even a leaf (since the leaves here stay on the trees until the trees are cut down to make way for yet another Mexican restaurant)

"Out with it, woman—you've been seeing that Gulliver chap, haven't you?"

they hang on like veterans in some tropical Folkestone.

Journalists here still tell you about the night Robert Newton turned up for an interview in his pyjamas, and that would have been about 1949: not a lot has happened since, and the only paper really worth writing for out here is the showbiz journal *Variety*, since that seems to be the only one the local residents can read without moving their lips. In New York now it takes about an hour to hear by radio or television of anything that has happened in Europe or the rest of the world: in California it still takes about a month.

Liberace can still sell eighty thousand tickets in a fortnight here, beating Boy George and Michael Jackson combined, and they've just barred *Gone With The Wind* from the official Olympic film festival because they think it may give a bad impression of race relations in the US. Not Perelman, not Heller, not even Thurber or Buchwald could ever begin to make America as funny as it seems when you get to California. Where else in the world do you get signs welcoming you to the Mexican Fruitfly Quarantine Area? Where else would they advertise a 100 per cent brushless car-wash (presumably naked go-go dancers come out and run their wet hair over the windscreen)? Where else would a television journalist, accidentally beaten up by local police during an Oscar night brawl, manage to get revenge by having his entire television company investigate on air the morality of the local Beverly Hills police?

Oh yes, I knew there was something else. In my gay friend's refrigerator, just beside the chocolate milk and the diet Pepsi, he keeps cans of household air freshener. These he inhales in bed to improve his sex life if the overnight guests are, like me, less than ideal. Now he seems to have burst a blood vessel in his eye. There may well be no connection: I just thought you'd like to know. There is nothing else in his refrigerator. I have moved to a neighbouring hotel.

But my oldest and most reclusive and most beloved friend in California is now also, I think, the happiest of the local residents I met this time: an eighty-year-old character actor and fish mimic and movie director of immense distinction and charm with whom I once spent an entire and blissful 1963 Christmas Day at the cinema watching nothing but old musicals. Now, with only about ten per cent vision, he seems to have discovered the secret of perfect West Coast joy: "The great thing about blindness, dear boy, is that you no longer have to see how the Californians dress to go shopping." There is undoubtedly a lot to be said for his life, especially now that the Braille Institute sends him the whole of English Literature to listen to on tape by his pool. I think that if I could choose to die anywhere, it would probably be in California: it's just the living there I can't stand.

"We're seven dwarfs, but not *The Seven Dwarfs.*"

"Know what really chokes me? That £50,000 computer I stole now sells for £69.95."

DAVID IS ASKING THE ADVICE OF GRACE WHEATEAR, DAILY HELP AND NECROMANCER, ON THE CONDITION OF THE LAWN....

There are these great patches of weed in the grass, you see, Grace.

No honest grass will ever grow there, David— those are The Devil's Footprints! Didn't you know? The Devil jumped on to Dream Topping, took seven strides, and leaped on to the Great Mynd....

...And as he went he tossed away his punchbowl, and the punch flowed out and became the river Blather....

.... and the punchbowl became Wheatear's Ironmongery in the High Street; and then in a rage he swung down his tosspot, and that became The Devil's Punchbowl, and the punch flowed out and became Druscilla's goldfish pond....

...Then he tossed his head and with a terrible clap of thunder it took root and became mysterious Dicky Heart Wood, except for a few beard combings which became this dense mass of brambles that you call your herbaceous border!

My God! Why have I not been told this before? So much for the solicitor who conducted our search!

The garden is doomed — we must move immediately — but where?

Grace, did the Devil ever throw his lawnmower down and it turned into a length of perfect sward, never more than ¾" high? If so, where?

No need! Wheatear's Ironmongery will see you right! We're throwing away lawnmowers for only £69.99 in our sale.

53

NEXT WEEK: STRIPPING THE WILLOW.

Alan COREN A Stalag Christmas

WEDNESDAY 30 NOVEMBER

They brought a new intake in this morning, must have been fifty blokes in all, more dead than alive. They'd been on the truck for three days after they'd been caught, hardly any food, hardly any water, you could practically see their ribs.

Brought the number in our compound up to near enough three hundred, at a guess. I said, bloody hell, you can't hardly see the ground for feet, no proper ablutions, I said, it's hardly surprising there's doings in the food, is there, Nob? My mate Nobby, I call him Nobby, God knows what his real name is, it don't seem to matter in here, we're all Nobby, Chalky, Smudger etcetera etcetera, no names, no pack drill, all muckers together, anyway, my mate Nobby said yes, he said, there was definitely sunnink hanging over breakfast not a million miles from widdle, but what can you do, who can you bloody complain to, and don't talk to me about sleep, I can't remember when I last had a decent night's kip, I got six blokes sharing, I was practically away last night for the first time in I don't know how long when the bloke at the end suddenly shrugged and I was on the floor, I could have done myself a serious mischief if I'd fallen wrong, break a leg in this place and they shoot you.

Or strangle, put in Chalky.

Gerroff, I said, you been listening to rumours again.

Straight up, retorts Chalky, I was talking to this bloke who knew a bloke who'd been there when they actually *done* it, this other bloke was just ambling about minding his own business when a couple of sadistic bastards grabbed hold of him and wrung his neck.

There's laws, I said, there's international regulations.

Ho yes, says Chalky, ho yes, laws in *here*, pull this one, and while we're on the subject, there's another thing, pulling this one is another of their little games, I have heard where they have pulled legs off blokes, there is no end to it.

I was just about to give Chalky a mouthful for spreading alarm and despondency, me being a Senior Man etcetera, when one of the new blokes stuck his two penn'orth in, that is not the half of it, he said, place we passed yesterday they take your insides out.

We all looked at him.

Ask anyone, he said.

Go on, said Nobby.

They do you in, one way or another, electrocution, gas, piano wire, what's the odds I say, and then, while you're still warm, they take your bloody liver out.

God Almighty, muttered Chalky, what do they want to do a thing like that for?

They collect 'em, says this new bloke, they take everybody's livers and they put 'em in a big kind of a vat effort, don't ask me why, they're all bleeding mad.

I put my head on one side and gave him one of my sharper looks.

Anything else, I said, while you're about it?

Yes, he said.

Well? I said.

They pluck you, he said.

THURSDAY 1 DECEMBER

Smudger made a break for it this morning, but the bastard guards got him before he was halfway over the wire. They brought him back with his feet tied together, he was trussed up like a, what's the word, anyway they just slung him in a corner.

I am amazed they never done you in, Smudge, I said, having a bit of a peck at his bonds, but no good, the cunning swine use this plastic stuff now, you are up against the top technology, what chance have we got?

They never done me in, says Smudger, on account of they are going to use us for these experiments, and before you say anything, no I have not been talking to no one, this is on the level, they inject you.

Inject you, exclaimed Nobby, what do they want to inject you again for, we had all that up our first place, you get a bumful of sunnink against foul pest, I thought that was all over and done with.

It is no good asking *me* why they want to inject you, replied Smudger, who knows why they do anything, I do not even bloody know why they took us prisoner, I was hopping about a bloody farmyard, it is not as if I blew up trains or anything, it is not as if I had a go at any of 'em, one minute I was

ambling about round behind the cow-shed, the next I was on the truck, who knows why these loonies do anything, if you want my opinion they are after world domination, they will have the livers out of everything before you know it, they are driven on by maniacal passions we wot not of.

I think we ought to dig a tunnel, said Chalky, you organise it, you're Senior Man, I think we ought to have an escape committee, we could all get to Switzerland, I remember hearing that's what you have to do.

Tunnel? I said, how can we dig a tunnel, we are not bloody moles, we are not ferrets, you got to have four legs to build a tunnel, a couple to stand on and then you have a couple up front to dig with, I watched a dog do it once up our farm, it is not turkey's work, a tunnel.

Apart from that, put in Nobby, you don't want to go to Switzerland, you would not credit what they do to people like us up Switzerland, they stick you in clocks and fire you out on the end of a bloody spring, I would rather have the injection.

You wouldn't say that, remarked one of the new lot who had just hobbled over, if you'd seen what I've seen. They give you an injection, and you blow up like a bloody balloon.

I wonder why they do that, I said.

FRIDAY 2 DECEMBER

Things are definitely looking up. Just shows you how wrong you can be, even the new intake are perking up a bit, and I'll tell you for why.

There's been this terrific improvement in the grub. I mean, there we were one minute, they brung us in from all over, so weak we could hardly stand, and all of a sudden (a) they've cleaned the place out, (b) they've turned on some kind of a central heating effort, and (c) they've, here's the best bit, they've started filling our troughs with this really top-class grain etcetera, and soon as it's gobbled up, bang, they only come round and fill it up again, don't they?

Stone me, said Chalky, it is like the bleeding Waldorf, there must've been someone down from the Red Turkey, or whatever they call it, I told you they couldn't go on treating us like that, it don't take long for word to get out, I even saw one of the guards shovelling up doings.

Also, there is the remarkable business with Smudger.

Early this morning, they come round and untied Smudger's feet. He is a game little bugger, and no sooner had the circulation come back than he announced he was going to make another break, central heating etcetera was all very well but it was a prisoner's duty to escape, anyway the question of the injections had not been resolved, and he was off, he had found this guard's uniform behind a bale of straw, it's a sort of a blue striped apron they wear with a straw hat, they are very hot on that kind of thing, it is their wossname, code, it probably accounts for the way they have overrun Norfolk in nought seconds flat, you ought to see their trucks, spotless, you can see your face in the aluminium, anyhow Smudger had found this uniform and his plan was to put it on and just walk out of the gate whistling, all right, gobbling.

So we got the apron round him eventually—it is not easy, beaking a knot—and we stuck this hat over his little head, and we pointed him in the right direction, and off he waddled.

He was out of luck. So happened they must've had a particularly sharp-eyed bastard on the gate who probably caught sight of Smudger's bare feet and put two and two together. Or three and three, these being the number of Smudger's toes.

But here's the peculiar thing. We was all poised for a quick shot in the back and goodbye Smudger, but stone me, they just wheeled him around, brought him back to our compound, felt him all over, tut-tutted,

and stuck a big meal in front of him.

You know what I reckon, says Chalky, I reckon we are going to be liberated, could be the Americans, could be the Russians, and the guards is all scared witless. It is our birthday, says Chalky, collect ten pounds from each player, har-har.

MONDAY 5 DECEMBER

Chalky was not wrong.

They give us our injections Saturday morning, but no problems, that new bloke was dead wrong. True, we have swolled up, but it is all good stuff, no fluid, no fat, I look like Rocky IV, you can see my chest bursting through the feathers, also legs like bloody champagne bottles, it is a good job we never started that tunnel, we would never get down it.

Not to mention where it is all Mister Nice Guy with the guards. They do not let us lift a wing. They just feed us, carry us over to the weighing machines, smile, carry us back, and sling another bucket of top grade millet in front of us.

The Americans must be blooming close, says Nobby, I'm surprised we can't hear the guns.

I wonder where Chalky's got to, says Smudger, he was here a minute ago.

TUESDAY 6 DECEMBER

It is with a heavy heart that I report these words. In the midst of life we are in death, and no mistake, poor old Chalky, just when it is nearly over, just when he had nearly made it, the grim reaper got him by the short and curlies and would not be denied.

He didn't come back into the hut last night.

The next time we saw him was this morning. He was outside the compound, where he had always dreamed of being, much good it did him when it came. He was on this kind of conveyor-belt effort. He still had his head on at that point, but we would have recognised him anyway, he was a good five pounds heavier than the rest of us, he had been putting away the grub like there was no tomorrow, which in his case, as it turned out, there wasn't.

He must've overate hisself, murmured Smudger, as Chalky went slowly past.

The guards'll be very upset, said Nobby, he was one of their favourites, I noticed how they was all smiling and nodding when they had him on the scales, dear me, was it only yesterday?

I wonder why they've got him on that belt, I said.

Oh, said Nobby, they will be sending his remains home, I have seen them do it before when someone inadvertently snuffs it, they remove your head so as not to distress dear ones and they sort of fold your wings over your chest, it is all very decorous, then they bung you in a freezer so that you do not decompose, and after that they send you home.

No expense is spared, murmured Smudger, it is like them posh funeral parlours, they do not just shove you in a hole. It only goes to prove they are worried, we shall all be out of here very soon, they are taking great care to play it by the book. It would not surprise me, said Smudger, if the Americans was just down the road.

Yes, I said, it certainly looks that way. At this rate, it will all be over by Christmas. 🦃

"I'm beginning to wonder if McDermot and his dog were quite as close as we were led to believe."

"Well, so much for the conga!"

MAHOOD's Antiques Fair

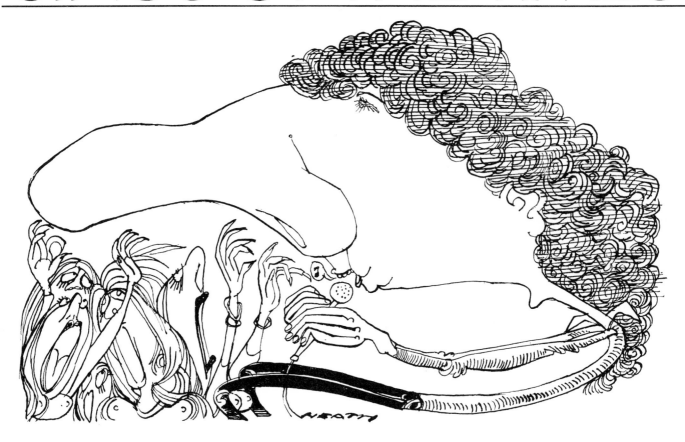

From our Hollywood Correspondent

When the great Jimmy Durante died somebody just had to take over. It could have been Richard Nixon, but his agents let him down. It was Barry Manilow who took the title. Manilow now has the most famous nose in the world. Wherever he may travel, bringing the solace of song to the huddled millions, Manilow's nose precedes him. His nose is news. Yes, nose news is big news where Manilow is concerned. And make no mistake, he is concerned. He watches that nose like a hawk. It is the first thing he sees when he wakes in the morning. It is the last thing left upright at night. What he does with it in the meantime is everybody's business. I ask you, if you saw the headline "Manilow Blows It", would you read on? Of course you would. We all want the latest nasal appraisal. It's only human nature.

Manilow doesn't flaunt the nose. A lesser artist would come onstage in a yashmak, or a balaclava helmet with the hole darned over. Ba-boom ba-boom would go the drums, and to the strains of *The Stripper*, by David Rose, the nose would be teasingly revealed . . . a flash of septum here, a flaring nostril there, till with a cry the garment would be cast aside and the limelight would splash onto that legendary organ, a tassel adorning its end. Manilow disdains such show. It would have been easy for him to pull string beads or tinsel out of the nose, to impress the crowds. But he has never

done so. The nose could have been dipped at any time in fluorescent gold paint. But no, if Manilow has tried this, it has been in private. For his is an essentially private nose. What we see is only the tip of the iceberg.

Photographers agree that Manilow is one of the most difficult of stars to get completely in focus. Gossip-writers are frustrated too. Half of Manilow, they claim, lives in perpetual shadow. Which half depends where the light is coming from. But in performance this is a boon to Barry. He can create exciting effects of lighting just by moving his head from side to side. In fact, for fear of being plunged into darkness by the shadow of the nose, Manilow's onstage musicians tend to learn their parts by heart. It all helps dispel that stuffed-up feeling that the concert situation can produce.

Audiences from Gnome to Nova Huta know that Manilow is a clean-living boy. He has to be. Can you imagine what the nose would look like if Barry drank? Why, if he were a cocaine-sniffer he would have blown his head off years ago. So he is clean and reliable. His act is always up to snuff. Sure, you will hear rumours—that the nose is a silicone job, that it plans a solo career, that Manilow has been closeted for weeks with the big men from Kleenex. But somehow nobody ever hangs a thing on Manilow, however tempting it may be to try.

And what about those audiences of his? Looking among them, you will see big fat girls of every conceivable shape, size and sex, and many shy-looking men with strange noses. They cry, they call, they squeal, they hug, as Barry struts the stage hoovering the air with his savage proboscis. He teases them. "You know what they say about people with big noses!" he shouts. Peals of speculation from the ladies. "They have *big hearts*!" hollers Barry. "HEARTS!" he repeats, in case anybody thought he said harps. But everyone knows what he meant. He meant big hankies. And they're going to be out pretty soon, for the nose is nuzzling the microphone and it's ballad time . . .

Barry's repertoire is admired the world over. He writes much of it himself, difficult though it is for him to see the manuscript-paper with both eyes at once. He never refers to his nose in his songs. Yet it is the forefront of his experience, and the audience feels it. It is a silent presence in all he does.

In his concerts, as he approaches the piano stool for the first time, many in the enraptured stalls below are thinking of a story dear to all Manilow fans—the one that tells how the little Brooklyn boy, prematurely stooping under the weight of his fully-matured beak, collided with his uncle's pianola, nosedived into the keyboard, and produced his first crashing discord. Till that moment he had always assumed that pianos were storage-racks for ceremonial Jewish dominoes. But since that day he has never looked back. Not while sitting on a piano stool, anyway.

What is it like when the world revolves around one's nose? Few of us have had that experience except when too drunk to remember it. For Manilow it is a permanent condition of life. Entering Sardi's in New York or London's Ecu de France, he must sometimes wonder which it is that people see first, the nose or the person. Indeed, if he comes in round a corner they have no choice. But you will seldom hear Manilow complain. He simply concentrates on keeping as low a profile as nature permits. And that's not easy when perfect strangers are liable to come up to you in the street and present you with a bouquet. Especially when they insist on calling it a nosegay.

So what is the secret of Barry's rapport with his public? Well, for all the freneticism of his new dance numbers, a sense of tragedy hangs about Manilow, a feeling that amid all his success he is deprived and endangered. Like many of his devoted fans, he has found some of life's broadest avenues closed to him. He could never be a welder. He might literally become too attached to the job. As a tango-dancer, his career could only have been brief and expensive. One snap of his head and he might have clouted his partner off the dance-floor and straight into a court of law. He is vulnerable to gas attack, for no mask-manufacturer can guarantee to cover him. Sneezes cost him thousands of dollars in breakages every year. His many Eskimo fans would love to greet him in the traditional way, but their Health Minister warns against it. And so it goes on: an imprisoning web of disqual-ifications and disabilities, trapping Manilow in the loneliness of success. No wonder his favourite reading is said to be George Eliot's sombre "Sinus Marner".

Sitting in his Hollywood office, Manilow knows that he is envied, and then again not. Given the choice between his and ours, let's face it, most of us would pick our own noses. But Barry, to his credit, has never hidden behind his famous feature. Nor has he tried to balance up his image by pretending to have huge feet or exceptionally knobbly knees. A nose is a nose is a nose is his motto. For is it not written in the *Song of Solomon,* "Thy neck is as a tower of ivory; thine eyes like the fishpools in Heshbon, by the gate of Bath-rabbim; thy nose is as the tower of Lebanon which looketh towards Damascus." Manilow's nose actually looketh towards Sunset Boulevard most days but who counteth? Lebanon is no place for a singer at this moment in history.

Time is on Barry's side. Cheeks may wither and hair fall. The voice may sink to the basement. But a nose, with care goes on for ever. It does not depreciate. If anything, it grows. And it is this conviction that Barry Manilow surely brings to his shaving mirror—the biggest in Beverly Hills—every morning. "Wow," he must whisper as his razor skirts the most expensive exhaust system in the world today, "this one will run for ever."

"If you've got it, flaunt it."

"Trouble is, once he gets going they can't stop him."

"I can't stand it any more, Sidney—I'm going back to your mistress."

Guy PIERCE

Cat Fever

TO resist total assimilation into the American mainstream without resorting to the reviled persona of the Professional Englishman Abroad is no easy task. For example, the grim novelty of American television proves fascinating for a while. When, however, you find yourself dashing home in the mid-afternoon to catch the ninth re-run of *Gilligan's Island,* that's the time to nip the nascent addiction in the bud—fast.

It is surprising how trifling a token gesture can restore some degree of sanity, always assuming you started off with some (sanity) in the first place. I always make a point of placing the day before the month when writing out cheques, contrary to common practice here. It irritates cashiers but acts as a valuable placebo for me.

It is a losing battle though, in which even the Wodehouse canon proves an ineffectual weapon. Immediately after completing *Psmith Journalist* (his finest creation) in one absorbed sitting I rose from my chair to announce that I was just popping out to get some "stuff".

Horrors!

"Stuff" is a much-used term this side of the Atlantic, defining a number or amount of unspecified items or material. It has its own

collective noun, "a bunch of . . . "

Should you require an inordinate amount of this peculiar "stuff", you are advised to search out a "*whole* bunch . . ." of the matter before stocks are exhausted.

It's at distressing moments such as these (becoming more frequent) that I hurriedly board the N Judah tram and head for a darkened water-hole in San Francisco's Financial District, safe in the knowledge that friends and acquaintances will never discover me amongst the moneylenders of this iniquitous sector of the town.

There I place elbows upon bar, summon a Tanquerary and tonic, and once again give myself up to *Six Men, Talk About America* or any other works of Alistair Cooke that I can beg, borrow or panhandle.

For an hour or so I cluck contentedly to

myself as America's Greatest Living Englishman (albeit a now cosmetically naturalised Yank) pares the nation to the bone.

Invariably his observations, many of them well past their silver jubilee, stand as true today as they did when first set to script. This is due not only to Cooke's undoubted perception but also to the great lie that America is in a state of continual progression.

It is not. The great sprawl that lies between the west end of New York's Lincoln Tunnel and the exit of the Oakland Bay Bridge is parochial to a fault. It is wary of innovation; wary of strangers. If it welcomes either it is with suspicion, reluctance, and little or no benefit of doubt.

It is a rare moment indeed when I beg to differ then with one of the timeless recipes from a Cooke book but this week, while wearing out my jacket elbows in the Iron Duke, one point of his struck me as decidedly archaic.

In an otherwise telling profile of common American man he quoted a French essayist (a dubious source albeit) as citing the nation's central problem of loneliness as the total lack of cats. Tongue in cheek, Cooke begged to differ. "This is not strictly true," he commented, "I have spotted at least a

"I am not so crude as to attempt wholesale assault. I prefer individual assassination, and time is on my side."

dozen in the past ten years."

Prudence Kitten, thou should'st be living at this hour.

Cat fever has gripped America for the past few years, and, with only the minor distraction of *ET*-mania to interrupt it last summer, continues to do so. There are cat beauty contests in which the contestants strut their stuff and doubtless inform the judges that they want to catch mice in Third World countries.

America's favourite comic character is not the hapless Dagwood, nor the resiliant Viking Hagar the Horrible. Loyal followers of the *Wizard of Id* and *Bloom County* must step aside for Garfield, a saucer-eyed cat whose daily pronouncements on life are taken as shards from the pot of eternal wisdom. If they weren't espoused by a singularly effete feline I doubt that his creator would have got further than the art department door of *Dandy*. Unfunny they most certainly are but America laps it up like the cream the dreadful Garfield is constantly pursuing.

Garfield isn't just cult. Garfield is big bucks. Garfield is pillows, calendars, T-shirts, cartoon anthologies, dolls and other assorted marketing detritus.

Snoopy should look to his laurels.

It is all the fault of the British, I suppose. Or one in particular. Cartoonist Simon Bond let his fevered imagination loose and the end result was *101 Things to Do with a Dead Cat*. America took it to heart. Unfortunately like so many similar ventures, while the original was witty and clever, it led to an avalanche of spin-offs with the result that cat-consciousness spread like wildfire.

Across the Golden Gate bridge in marvellous, moronic Marin, realtors and Porsche salespersons were nothing in the eyes of their neighbours if they failed to provide accommodation for a Persian Blue or Siamese at least. Needless to say, with the brilliant imagination so characteristic of the Marin community, nine out of ten were christened Kat Vonnegut Junior.

When calling upon friends I always make a point of asking whether a cat is in residence. This is not to ensure that the luckless creature doesn't fall under my feet. Quite the reverse. If I can add a little suffering, a smidgeon of pain, to a cat as I travel down life's highway, I feel that much better.

The moggy has not escaped the notice of the White House either. The Democrats may be courting the gay minority for all they're worth, the Republicans, however, are canvassing a wider source of support. Recently a Birmingham, Alabama, resident, Omar Katz, received a letter from the Grand Old Party, pleading for him to support them in the forthcoming congressional and senate elections. It was a signed by no less (and no more) a person than President Ron.

Omar is a five-year-old Persian cat. Or rather, Iranian cat. To add insult to injury his owner, one Jan Lewis, was overlooked in the 50,000 mail-shot. Like all good Americans, Jan promised to register Omar as a voting citizen.

You can be sure that the first question that spun through Omar's mind was, "What's in it for me?" In the cat world there is no "fellow American". Self-centred and selfish the cat has always been, and just because he's been enfranchised that's no reason to change.

But still America takes the appalling animals to its heart.

And while Medicaid and Medicare are being drastically pruned for homo sapiens by the current administration, no such drastic cuts are planned for the cat who has everything, be it leukaemia, halitosis or even feline fluke.

Thanks to Dr Lee Prutton, the Feline Veterinary Clinic is at constant red alert; a single phone call will have the pussy-medics at your door anywhere in the Bay Area ready to put pussy to rights.

Just try and get *your* local doctor to make a house call. Your only chance appears to be to tell him you're constantly chasing after strands of wool and choking on fur-balls.

My neighbour Julie called upon me last week, inquiring whether I could help her out with some trigonometry she had to have ready for a college test the next day. She might as well ask Arafat to run a bar mitzvah. We fell to chatting, and after ten minutes or so she invited me into her apartment to "meet the guys". Visions of baseball-shirted, blow-dried young things crouched over mathematical conundrums flashed through my mind. Nonetheless, I agreed, but to my amazement found myself being introduced to, I think, Ahab, Hepzibah, Crippen and Titania—four felines.

Actually I counted about twenty as with cartoon-like speed the quartet recognised the vengeful grin that flickered across my lips for a moment and set them off flying around the room, colliding with each other and wearing down claws to stumps in an attempt to secure safety atop cupboards, wardrobes and the fridge.

Foolish things: I am not so crude as to attempt wholesale assault, particularly with my hostess looking on. I prefer individual assassination, and time is on my side.

Television commercials for such things as cat litters (which I first took to be a mode of transport for the more pampered puss) and cat food match anything the British can conjure up in the bile-rising stakes, but that, I suppose, is the same the whole world over, except in those regions where they sensibly eat the cat.

Animal-associated advertising has long been one of the more nauseating facets of western culture, though one in particular has endeared itself to me recently. A cartoon beagle, on being proffered a low-quality dog-food, loudly retches into his bowl. The human face of Snoopy at last.

So just why are Americans such cat-people? Contrary to popular opinion I believe it is because in their heart of hearts they *don't* wish to be loved. The American is never happier than when bemoaning that after all his country has done for the rest of the world we ungrateful shower pour scorn down upon Ole Betsy. To receive thanks from a thankful planet for America's gracious bounty would upset the natural process.

The cat merely confirms his view. He wouldn't have it any other way.

"OK, she can keep the ring and the runcible spoon but the pea-green boat is mine!"

Melvyn BRAGG

Beauty and the Beast

UNTIL that big shift in attitude in the eighteenth century, we thought of animals as inferior; to be beaten or eaten. There are those—there always are—lagging behind in the march of time, who still believe that: oddly enough, I know some farmers who would be shocked to think of their "beasts" in any other way—and yet they will ascribe to them an intelligence and range of feelings which quite contradict their domineering behaviour. Christianity for centuries reinforced the Aristotelian idea that man's soul gave him superiority over all other living things on the planet. Animals were mortal and therefore made solely for man's use: there could be no abuse.

Once again it is difficult to conceive of the size of the change of feeling and apprehension which has occurred. It is not

"Most of us are no more than sedentary farmers or horseless huntsmen."

as great, perhaps, as the change in ideas about the causes of death. Three centuries ago, for example, in the register of a parish near my cottage in the Lakes, several deaths are accounted for as "taken by fairies (3), frightened to death by witches (2)." The point is that people intelligent enough to be part of a culture already appreciating Shakespeare and understanding Bacon were quite prepared to find such explanations of death sufficient. Similarly, it is hard for us to understand that, in the same period, most people believed that animals

had no feelings at all, so that when they were thrashed or whipped the cries they made were not sorrowful, merely mechanical.

Since then, the emergence of the landscape as the subject and object of so many aspirations and aspects of our view of ourselves and the world has coincided with a profound alteration in our attitude to animals. Vegetarians stand at one end of a spectrum, which also includes a huge variety of people up to and including those who hunt, all of whom—especially the huntsman/woman—see in animals evidence of intelligence, personality and feeling. Militant vegetarians are only expressing in extreme form a general feeling when they declare that butchery for meat is no less than the murder of a being. D. H. Lawrence is again only the extreme expression of a

"Five minutes, everybody!"

172

widespread and kindred belief that somehow animals, far from being inferior, are superior: they seem—increasingly—better adapted to the planet, harming it less, helping it more, teaching us, should we learn to attend, how properly to live.

Between the vegetarian and the Lawrentian view, most of us now fudge around, carving the joint but respecting the beast. Eastern philosophies long since granted individuality and holiness to animals. At the moment we stand midway between the two: or, put another way, we want to enjoy the best of both worlds: to slice the meat but still ruminate on the implications. Most of us are no more than sedentary farmers or horseless huntsmen; we want to catch, kill and eat the animals and also we grant them qualities which we would swear we wish to preserve. Between nut cutlets and St Mawr.

The plants and vegetables we grow, those too, have found a new place in the ecology of our perception. Looting the land is no longer viable: but before that—as part of that same movement which led to Wordsworth—it was already being considered undesirable. When Arthur Young, the agriculturalist—yet another British gentleman of the Enlightenment whose scientific investigations led him out to the country and into a new philosophy which involved changes in feeling as well as thought—came to the Lakes, he discovered it to be the most backward part of the Kingdom. He found that the local farmers were still ploughing with the rowan plough and bullocks, still following methods known to Joseph and his Brethren. Young, Townsend and in Cumbria (as elsewhere) several of the local gentry and aristocracy determined to cease the hapless scrabbling for bare pickings and introduced new systems; they wanted to nourish the soil, spread the feeding seasons; quantify resources—in short, bring a different order to bear.

What is significant, though, is that the order they wanted was to do with a new appreciation of Nature. They thought it ought to be a place for continuous fertility and it ought to be capable of improvement: just like man. Young and his brilliantly educated peers saw Nature as a companion and sustaining force at a time when for most people it was where you hacked wood, drew water, fed up beasts for slaughter and were on your guard against its tricks.

It was not that Young mastered Nature. For all general purposes that had been done time and again. Forests were toppled by the men with the first porcellanite axes; grain was cultivated often—in previous civilisations such as the Egyptian—with awesome industry and ingenuity; animals were bred and cross-bred—hunting hound with prize bitch, the canary with the finch; but Young and his men introduced the idea of association. Better husbandry, yes; more effective looting, if you put it that way; but, most importantly, the idea was introduced that we have to preserve the land not only because it could yield more but because neglect would consign us to stagnation and,

"Here's my card. It has an area that you can scratch and sniff."

eventually, extinction. Because we ourselves are part of Nature. The great eighteenth-century push towards cultivation preceded but with extraordinary foresight, the time—now on us—when the balance between the population, pollution and the planet is such that treating Nature as an associate is not so much a sensible as an essential measure.

In the nineteenth century it was rapidly taken further. Not only did we need to treat Nature itself well; we needed Nature to treat us well. Indeed, to make us well. That is the single goal aimed at—in however many different ways—by those who come to the Lakes: they want to "be", to "feel" better. There is no doubt that they do; but it is due as much to the ideas we now have about landscape and its multiple benefits as to the pleasures of fresh air and exercise. We feel better in the landscape because it is now the place which most comprehensively satisfies our needs and our imagination.

"Rex! What are you doing here? Didn't you get my memo?"

LARRY'S
SCAFFOLDERS

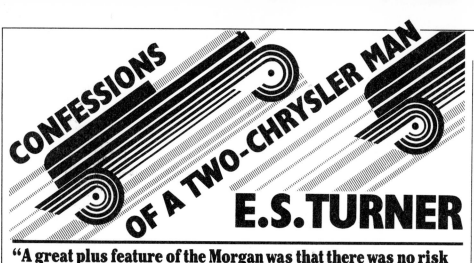

CONFESSIONS OF A TWO-CHRYSLER MAN

E.S. TURNER

"A great plus feature of the Morgan was that there was no risk of backing into anything, since it had no reverse gear."

I NEVER had to pass a driving test. In those happier days Englishmen were born with the ability to control engines, horses, women and empires. It was called Innate Knack. Gradually the national genius became impoverished and men had to be taught the difference between brake and accelerator.

When I first took the wheel the bulb horn and the Klaxon reigned—the magnificent Klaxon which, firmly struck, could stop the church clock at ten to three and lift the Oldest Inhabitant two feet into the air at thirty yards. Unlike pedestrians, horses had by then come to terms with the motor car and no longer had to be fed corn on the throbbing engine bonnet to show them that the monster was harmless.

There were as yet no traffic lights. When they came in, about 1930, people trooped up to town to stare at them. The police who had hitherto stood at crossroads delaying the traffic were now freed for other duties, like blowing their whistles at drivers who refused to take orders from "Robots", as the papers wittily called them.

There was much more to be seen in the countryside in those days. Every meadow had huge coloured pictures of pickle bottles and plates of beans, every gable-end showed a mother spooning radioactive goodness into her infant. This was known as the Art Gallery of the People. Every railway bridge carried Lord Northcliffe's favourite poem: "*Daily Mail* Million Sale." At night each bend in the road was marked by a silver-studded advertisement which lit up in the headlamps' glow to prevent the driver shooting into a cornfield, while reminding him which product built bonnie babies. Advertisers were convinced these signs were a major contribution to road safety, but the environmentalists of the day abolished them.

There were no boring motorways and very few by-passes. On the road from Glasgow to London—400 miles—you honked through every town and village, passing a hundred cinemas proclaiming "GARBO SPEAKS" and a thousand news-bills saying "HITLER SPEAKS." Traffic jams? We had absolutely magnificent ones in the Thirties.

We did not carry rear stickers saying "Club Sandwiches Not Seals", but some of us had warning red triangles with the

legend "Four-Wheel Brakes". This was a big mechanical advance and meant that a driver bound for Brighton no longer had to start braking at Horsham. My first motor vehicle, a 1925 Morgan three-wheeler, had one-wheel brakes; that is, it had two independent brakes, as the law required, but both operated on the single rear wheel. If both brakes were applied hard when that wheel was in a wet tram-line, the car spun and rolled over. I say car, but it was really a tricycle with an aero engine out at front. It just did not know its own strength. A chassis tie-bar kept breaking, which meant that the transmission would begin to sag, like the bowels of a shot stag.

A great plus feature of the Morgan was that there was no risk of backing into any-

thing, since it had no reverse gear.

In 1934 my Morgan proved immensely popular with Hitler's Brown Shirts, who crouched round admiring its all-chain drive, its visible oil drip-feed and its side-winding crank, exclaiming "*Wunderbar*" and "*Himmel!*" Don't blame me for World War Two—I did my best to show off our lead in technology.

Returning home I was held up at the Channel while a set of matched Buicks, or maybe Packards, was hoisted aboard the ship (no drive-on ferries then). I gathered that William Randolph Hearst had been touring Europe with a few friends, probably buying castles. If it had been a set of matched Bentleys they would have belonged to the Duke of Westminster, whose chauffeurs followed his yachts along the shores of France and Spain, ready to pick up his guests in port.

My own dreams of touring Europe as a one-man *concours d'élégance* never materialised. However, in 1936 (my bank account swollen by furious scribbling) I found myself briefly the owner of a Chrysler in Britain and a Chrysler in America. The home-based gangster-style sedan cost only £10, since nobody wanted what are now called gas-guzzlers. To me it seemed the smart thing to buy big cars cheap and lavish the money thus saved on petrol, often taking on board two or three gallons at a time. The rate of taxation was, of course, high; high enough to give one a fellow feeling for the Duke of Westminster.

I bought my other Chrysler for £15 on a

"Harvey has a theory linking premature ejaculation with the disappearance of the dinosaurs."

brief holiday in New York, driving it to Chicago and back in a week. The pound was worth five dollars then and petrol half the British price. A New York policeman gave me an eyesight test to make sure I could read signs saying "No Hospital Here", "Bums Keep Moving" and "All The Beer You Can Drink For $1." Along the road I stayed in dollar-a-night wooden cabins, the forerunners of motels, or in half-dollar rooms in sinister-looking tourist houses straight out of Charles Addams. It was still the Depression over there, but I was the one with the money, a two-Chrysler man on the loose. How could I not be happy?

Along the Lincoln Highway the Art Gallery of the People stretched for 900 miles. When the admen could find no more clients they ran general knowledge tests: Who invented the bicycle? What three coins make 76 cents? And there were peppy poems, mounted one line at a time, like: "To get away/From hairy apes/Ladies jump/From fire-escapes/Burma-Shave."

My car had been supplied with a certificate saying, "This automobile is sold as is, where is, and as shown. No guarantee whatsoever." Soon I was living off the land. When the radiator proved hopelessly incontinent I drove into a car graveyard in Indiana and bought a substitute from a cadaver, for ten dollars. I picked up a tyre or two in similar fashion, also a spare wheel, an absurd luxury. I was never reduced to the level of the "Ford families", who reputedly lived in their flivvers and were given just enough petrol to take them into the next state.

Dodging express trains at level crossings (as in the films), blasting through swarms of bees, picking up and setting down hoboes, running the gauntlet of plant quarantine stations, I reached New York again. It is a bracing city in which to drive and in those days it had a clever trap for British drivers. The rule was that if you saw a red traffic light several blocks ahead you had to stop at the first intersection, even though it had no light of its own. Could Britons at home have coped with such a system? I think not.

I gave my American Chrysler away and sailed back in the *Queen Mary*, arriving home with not quite enough money to buy a gallon of petrol for my other Chrysler, for which in due course I got £2. Somehow motoring has never seemed quite the same since.

Indeed, by that time decadence had set in on the roads of Britain. Women were refusing to ride in open cars; old folks objected to sitting in dickey-seats with their laps full of water; even the common people had demanded, and got, roofs on their charabancs. Nothing was what it was. Surly pedestrians had earned the right to hold up traffic at "Belisha crossings". There was some sort of Code which said you had to let drivers out of side roads. Worst of all, cars had all begun to look alike. But we still had some pride left: we didn't leave the dealers' stickers in our rear windows for years on end, as everyone does now. ✿

HOW ONE WILL DO
Married Queen

by OUR OWN REPORTER

Former Income	New Income	One Gets This Much More
£4,616,683	£4,833,900	£217,217

Beyond question, ROYAL FAMILIES did pretty badly out of the Budget, and they have not been slow to react. We asked one typical royal family (One, one's husband, one's four children aged 34, 32, 23, 19, including three unemployed) how they felt about being held to a pay rise of around 4%.

"Not to beat about the bush, Brian, one is sick as a parrot. One is hardly keeping pace with inflation, never mind a bit over for treats. One says to oneself: *Stone one, what does one have to do to make one's Chancellor see sense?* This was unquestionably a Budget for the small businessman, Brian, and one is seriously considering packing the whole thing up and going into video-hire or confectionery, possibly a little ironmongery on the side if the right premises come along.

"Look at one's water workers, practically twice the pay rise, one wonders whether one ought perhaps to have withheld one's labour, not that one wants to hold the country to ransom, Brian, but these are desperate times. One is a skilled worker, after all."

FALLING BEHIND

"And one would like to be brought into line with other skilled workers who have enjoyed pay rises averaging out at 6.2%?"

"Exactly one's point, Brian! One is definitely falling behind, no question, one is getting took advantage of, and for why? On account of one does not have big union backing, or is one wrong? One's is a small cottage industry, one breadwinner not counting son in Navy and bringing practically nothing in, one's husband is offered only casual work, e.g. driving a coach and four, which there is not a lot of call for, one does not have to draw pictures, and this can be very depressing for a grown man, while one oneself is rushed off one's feet making ends meet, is it any wonder there are rows, and on top of this one is asked to take what amounts to a pay cut, Brian, one feels it is nothing short of a diabolical bloody liberty, pardon one's French."

GINGER WIG

"What does one feel ought to be done about it?"

"One thinks it is time to get round a table, Brian, for frank and free discussions entered into in a spirit of meaningful negotiation. One is looking for a seven per cent minimum, definitely, also compensation for unsocial hours, e.g. up half the night with some daft American wally in a ginger wig, *and* for unpleasant working conditions, e.g. rain coming down stair-rods while one is riding side-saddle, etcetera, etcetera, they do not tolerate that up Arthur Scargill's premises, is one right? One is! One has had it up to here, Brian, one does not mind saying. Is it any wonder one's eldest has gone to Australia?"

HANDELSMAN

The Amorous Education of David

PART 1: INNOCENCE

IN THE SPRINGTIME OF HIS YOUTH, DAVID KNEW LITTLE OF WOMEN.

I am very fond of you too, Dave.

HAVING SPRUNG TO PROMINENCE THROUGH SLAYING GOLIATH — NEAR A SPRING — DAVID MET JONATHAN THE SON OF SAUL, AND THEIR HEARTS SPRANG TOWARDS ONE ANOTHER (AND THAT IS ENOUGH OF THAT).

*No, no, **no!** If you want to be my son-in-law, you have to marry my **daughter**.*

You know something, Michal? You are the first female I ever met who was not covered with wool.

No doubt this is the sort of conversation that caused Goliath to drop dead.

SAUL SENT DAVID AGAINST THE PHILISTINES, HOPING THAT HE WOULD BE KILLED — A TRICK THAT DAVID WOULD LATER TURN TO HIS OWN USE.

Well, here I am, sir, with the Philistine foreskins you ordered.

Damn.

May I ask what you plan to do with them? Just curious.

Here we are in bed, Michal! Is there an instruction manual?

Husband, much as I hate to lose the pleasure of your company, you had better hop it. My father intends to extirpate you during the night.

Oh, pooh! It seems I am doomed to remain a dunce, womenwise.

BETWEEN ELUDING SAUL AND SLAUGHTERING PHILISTINES, DAVID WAS KEPT SO BUSY THAT WOMEN PLAYED NO PART IN HIS LIFE UNTIL...

*Remember me? Abigail the wife of Nabal? I am grieved to say that I am now the **widow** of Nabal.*

What a pity! Condolences and so on.

I am prepared to wash your feet.

Really? The ovines never did that.

HE ALSO TOOK TO WIFE AHINOAM OF JEZREEL.

But why? You already have two wives.

Precisely! Bigamy is an abomination unto the Lord! But trigamy is acceptable.

David, two of your wives have been captured by the Amalekites!

*You mean I am down to **one** again? How time-consuming! Saddle my dromedary.*

DAVID SMOTE THE AMALEKITES UNTIL HE AGAIN HAD THREE SPOUSES.

SPRING FABLES

PART 2: EXPERIENCE

AFTER BECOMING KING, DAVID ACQUIRED MAACAH, AND HAGGITH, AND ABITAL, AND EGLAH.

How could I resist? They were on sale.

Are we all legally married, King Dave?

Are we all the queen?

Just bear sons and shut up.

THE DISPLEASURE OF MICHAL

Exposing yourself to the maidservants! If my father were here, he would throw a javelin at you.

Indeed! Has being dead improved his aim?

Come along, maidservants.

Are you going to marry us?

Sort of.

He has been **impossible** ever since someone told him about the erogenous zones.

Who is that person soaping herself so memorably?

Uriah's wife. She is called Bath-sheba.

Very logical.

Jabesh-gilead ladies sing this song, doo dah, doo dah... ♫

Uriah — or as I like to think of you, Mr Bath-sheba — I am going to give you a chance to do something patriotic.

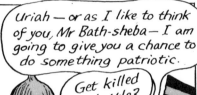 

Get killed in battle?

You guessed it.

My pleasure, sir.

I usually write to the bereaved, but as I was in the neighbourhood I decided to convey my sympathy personally.

How thoughtful.

What do you want to be when you grow up, Solomon?

A womaniser.

Heh heh heh! Chip off the old block.

I will have a thousand wives and concubines. Many of them will worship abominations.

WHEN KING DAVID WAS VERY OLD AND COLD, HIS SERVANTS BROUGHT HIM A YOUNG VIRGIN.

Climb in with him, Abishag. Lie in his bosom and keep him warm.

Brrr.

No kidding, kings have bosoms?

So, anyway, there was Goliath — big, but, you know, stupid. So he says... so I...

Yes, but what happens **now**?

How should I know? I forgot my carnal knowledge. So anyway...

MORAL: In the spring a young man's fancy, but an old man's even fancier.

Keith WATERHOUSE

Log: Jam

GOING by Pole Star, this should be mouth of Southampton Water. According to sextant readings, not to mention evidence of own bloody eyes, it is more like mouth of Bull Ring underpass. What took to be warning beacons on dredged channel off Gymp Foul Ground are in fact lights of Top Rank Suite. Suspect that Pole Star may turn out to be revolving neon sign of Pink Pussycat disco and steak bars. Upon Great Bear abruptly extinguishing itself shortly after commencement of middle watch, decided as emergency measure to substitute conventional navigation chart with two-colour map stapled into middle of "Let's Wine & Dine In Birmingham".

Making good speed, now two days out of harbour and approx 45 feet NW of Tesco's, where we took on supplies. If we can navigate our way back out of bloody car park, all should be plain sailing. Trouble is, take wrong exit and you pitch up aground outside Holiday Inn, where we had to lay up last night having caught our bulwarks in the revolving door.

We have lost our bearings. During first dog watch we passed International Trade Centre for third time, though this time on starboard side which makes nice change. We are also taking on loose chippings v. badly. The way we are going, nightfall will find us adrift on Spaghetti Junction. Have been dogged by ill-luck ever since we slid off fork-lift truck in Corporation Street and our historic voyage commenced. At three bells during last dog watch, Force Six headwinds blowing up from West Brom forced us to seek harbour at Little Chef. Will get caught by Neap Tides at this rate: either that or will run into road workings on motorway.

Britain's most land-locked city, Birmingham, is to sponsor a trimaran in this summer's Observer/Europe 1 Singlehanded Transatlantic Race.

Observer

Cones hoisted. They are all the way down bloody M5 – if it is M5. Motorway being reduced to single-channel narrows, and craft unable to sail with current owing to temporary road surface, we were forced to throw line to caravan "Doris" which v. kindly towed us clear of shallows. Unfortunately, when turning either NNE or SSW down slip-road to take on evening paper (compass not working, and cannot be sure that what looks like Dog Star is not Marilyn's Surf 'n' Turf Room, "where Brum's elite go to drink and eat") we sighted more "Men Working" signals and presently ran foul of a steam-roller, which despite our call of "Ahoy there! Sail before steam, you ignorant berk!" so damaged our larboard hull that we had to put into West Midlands 24-Hr Garages & Recovery Service for repairs. Took minicab "Re-Ly-Abel" ashore and relaxed to non-stop live music in friendly yet sophisticated atmosphere of one of Birmingham's swishest waterfront nightspots, previously thought to be Ursa Minor.

Woke at first light and persuaded skipper of French soft furniture tug "Henri Duval & Cie, Meubles Magnifiques" to take us aboard and drop us at West Midlands 24-Hr Garages & Recovery Service nor'-nor'-east or sou'-sou'-west of M5. No sign of craft in dry dock: thinking it to have gone adrift, called manager, who signalled M42 branch which confirmed that they had vessel safely under tarpaulin.

It's now very plain that as suspected we were never on M5 in first place and that

navigation chart in "Let's Wine & Dine In Birmingham" is stapled in upside-down. Thank God for collision with steam-roller, otherwise we should have continued on course up M42, turned to starboard in direction of North Sea and finished up scanning bloody Skagerrak for Statue of Liberty. Got lift on United Dairies milk tanker which was docking hard by municipal bus station. Took bearings and found that we wanted to be at Lat 15° Long D°, going by chart references employed in Greater Birmingham "A–Z Citimap" which we purchased at bus station chandler's. Engaged minicab "Re-Ly-Abel" to convey us to our berth.

It unbelievable. Minicab "Re-Ly-Abel", after having cheek to charge over pound per nautical mile for our voyage, dumped us not at West Midlands 24-Hr Garages & Recovery Service off M42, but at West Midlands 24-Hr Garages & Recovery Service off M6 half-way to bloody Coventry. Skipper carried no charts or navigational instruments and was so inept at reading our Greater Birmingham "A–Z Citimap" that we had to pilot him out of city centre, which took getting on for two hours as wind was against us. Intend to report him to harbourmaster when get back from crossing Atlantic. Meanwhile, was obliged to charter towing truck "West Midlands 24-Hr Garages & Recovery Service" to get us to our rightful mooring. So late by then that having checked our craft was seaworthy again, decided to put in for night at Lotus Blossom Dining Experience West and leave on first tide.

Cruising steadily down M6, hope to link up with M5 nor'-nor'-east of Smethwick by nightfall and thus be back on course. At least we do not have to steer through middle of Birmingham again—would sooner take a Cortina 2000 through bloody Needles than go through all that again.

Must have taken wrong slip-road—will write to council about this: road signs do not have flashing lights, sirens, bells or any indication whatsoever that middle shipping lane leads straight back to bloody Bull Ring. After taking on keg lager at Peter Dominic's, returned to our vessel to find traffic warden slapping ticket on hull for mooring on yellow line. Warned that next time she sighted craft we would find Denver boot clamped to rudder. Is it all worth it?

After laying up for night at Top O' The Tower prime meat carverie and licensed go-go bars, set sail at first light with aid of new simplified chart forming gatefold of "Where To Go—The Discriminating Nite-Life Guide to the West Midlands". Manoeuvring tricky Exit 7 which according to our readings should have carried us to M5, found ourselves carried instead to M6 and had to sail several miles off course before turning short round at Grotwood Services. Intend warning *Reed's Nautical Almanac* to accept no advertising from any firm purporting to supply pilot guides to Birmingham and environs. Managed by brilliant display of seamanship to find proper turn-off for M5 going south'ard, and so after five days before the mast are at last set on proper course.

Becalmed on hard shoulder. Mist came down and so it would have been hazardous to make attempt to get back on fast lane with our oars. Lit pipe and enjoyed mournful keening of gulls, or pigeons as they more probably are just off Smethwick, and rumble of passing juggernauts. Presently police car hove alongside and insisted on radioing towing truck "West Midlands 24-Hr Garages & Recovery Service" to take us in for barnacle scrape and MOT test, despite our protests that we were hardly likely to set off across Atlantic in unroadworthy vessel.

Luckily master of "West Midlands 24-Hr Garages & Recovery Service" was seasoned old hand who as soon as he saw colour of our money agreed to pilot us to Warwickshire border and set us on course for Southampton Water. Had mist not turned into fog and our pilot lost his bearings, we should have been just about off Lizard Point by now instead of hard by Ladbroke International.

Unhappily, we were just tying up when same police officers we had encountered out on open M5 came aboard and charged us with doing six knots in built-up area, cruising wrong way along one-way street and failing to heave-to at zebra crossing. As case does not come up until Thursday, this must end our present attempt to win Transatlantic Race. Nothing daunted, we shall set sail next week for Sheffield and get in training for Americas Cup.

"The usual? I serve six hundred drinks a day and I'm supposed to remember 'the usual'?"

"Funny, he managed to put Transubstantiation into a nutshell. With the bomb he's completely at sixes and sevens."

E.S.TURNER
ALBION AND ABITOFHELL

In pious times, ere Science was begot,
When hardware meant two kettles and a pot,
Ere hearts and lungs were ferried through the sky
From men just dead to men about to die,
Ere topping rogues gave way to topping charts,
And widows' rates were spent on ethnic arts,
Ere woman lusted after womankind,
And man to man was cruelly confined,
Ere fools hailed Dr Spock, or Dr Greer,
Ere every passing prig was made a peer,
Lived good John Dryden.
                              In the poet's day
The world seemed lost in godless disarray—
All plots and treasons, lechery and blood
Yet, from our times, who doubts that life was good?
Sweet, gentle dews instead of acid rain!
Unpoisoned fields by an untainted main!
A Europe not yet sunk in asses' milk—
A foe to conquer, not a friend to bilk.
In scrolls of fire the heav'nly message ran:
Subordination is the law of man.
The Little Woman, suitably repressed,
Knew better than to do what she thought best.
If doubts and hesitancies marred her sleep
She gave her conscience to a man to keep.
The peasants scratched their fields, or gathered kelp.
No need had they to utter Cries for Help,
Or call for Dialogues, or use their feet
To lug mock coffins up and down the street.
Too proud to butt, and too ashamed to spit,
The black-faced demons ne'er forsook their pit.
The world rolled on and they rolled on with it.

Now look on Albion, that contentious land,
Where mighty Juno rules her scarecrow band.
The storm cones rise; the crew prepare for squalls;
On each hard head an angry handbag falls.
"The Devil's fires," quoth she, "are fed with sneaks."

Then *exeunt omnes*, with the latest leaks.
The pecking Robins end as potted meat,
Who, then, shall topple Juno from her seat?
The freckled Taffy, pitilessly cuffed,
A farthing candle, lit but to be snuffed?
The Proust from Yorkshire, plosive with the strain
Of fifty essays dashed off in the train?
The bush-browed brute, that Rupert of offence,
Slow to instruct, but eager to incense?
The tea-pot slave, within whose moonstruck eye
Sweet reason and ethereal humbug vie?
Or that cold magister of discontents,
Who sits for Sidcup and two continents,
Incorporating in his heaving hulk
Conductor, sailor, scribbler and sulk?
Shall Ulster's lord be named our paladin?
Or shall we call the crazed Pretender in,
The Jack of Coals, Confusion's younger brother,
The Anarch ranting in the smoke and smother,
Who wags one hand six times, and then the other?

What hope for Albion, with this spavined crew?
How, in these swamps, shall sentient life renew?
In Parliament, that fount of classic wit,
The rafters ring with cries of "Four-eyed git!"
Before its screens a costive nation drools;
Communication is the feast of fools!
Pornography enlists her video slaves,
And Caxton's gift is in the hand of knaves.
What lowering creatures choke the rising gorge—
Archbishop Runcie, have you met Boy George?
Our singers drug to spark the empty brain;
Ophelia's stoned, like Shylock, on cocaine;
And, in a corner of the human zoo,
The holy innocents are sniffing glue.
From Albion's towers the bells of Hell now chime.
The Sons of Belial face a glorious time.
Dryden return, and finish off my rhyme.

BILL STOTT
Round Figures

"Tonight—thanks to a specially mounted remote control camera—you'll see darts as never before . . . !"

"And it's high drama here at the area finals as the defending champion tries desperately to make the weight."

"Yes!—I've definitely bust a lace."

"I'd rather you didn't mention this, out there."

"Quick—help me get him the right way up—they can die if they're left like this!"

MENAGE A TROIS

"We've both got headaches!"

"We think you're seeing someone else!"

"Neither of them understands me."

"It's not her birthday—it's my birthday!"

"OK, who's got the toupée?"

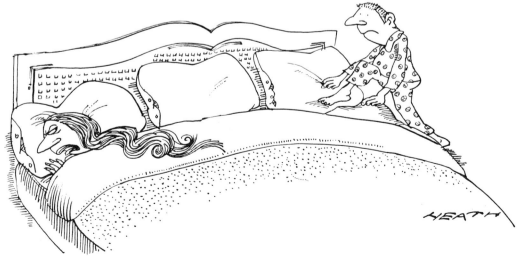

"It's Thursday, dummy! **She's** Thursday!"

David TAYLOR/CARS:

LOTUS TURBO ESPRIT

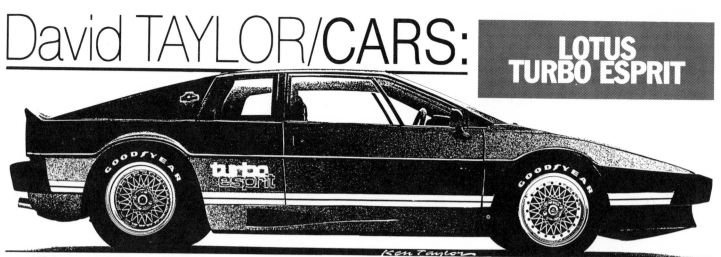

"A boost of adrenalin for two, if a dead loss at carrying loads larger than a well-stuffed wallet."

FOR every motor-mad Mitty, this is the Land of Cockaigne—but I'll be coming to John De Lorean in a bit. There can be few less leisurely performers than a blown Esprit and none that is fitter for the road, especially the kind of road where no-one's about or lurking at the kerbside with a radar gun. To sizzle to sixty from standstill takes under six seconds. Walloping on towards a maximum of more than 150mph, as it might be down some deserted stretch of Autobahn, you can never tell where supercar, tyre-scorching progress might not come in handy, the dynamic integrity of the Esprit's chassis and transmission would make even Enzo Ferrari whistle. It is unsurpassed at any price, never mind comfortably under £20,000—not counting insurance which, I'd imagine, could well work out about the same.

No question but that the Lotus range in general and this, Guigiaro's nonpareil for the Jehu, represent thoroughbred British sports car engineering at its world-beating best. No question either, alas, but that Group Lotus is in a lamentable mess.

As the latest damaging rumours and revelations continue to hit the fan, it begins to seem as if the late Colin Chapman's dream was for much of the time a nightmare. The buccaneering spirit of inspired commercial enterprise was apparently more than once blown by falling trade winds into murky waters, some of them well outside Britain's limits, and flamboyant, mercurial Chapman was perhaps not, it is now suggested, altogether in the *Boy's Own Paper* tradition.

Only a couple of years ago, things looked superficially good. James Bond was after the baddies with a Lotus Turbo Esprit in *For Your Eyes Only*—potent, but cheap, publicity. Mrs Thatcher was trekking out to Norfolk to congratulate the lads for their spirit and grit—more publicity, though possibly only cheap. But Chapman, meanwhile, must have already begun to realise that he was in up to his neck chasing another baddie, John De Lorean, in a hush-hush deal which was intended to remain very much For Their Eyes Only. Lotus, it was to turn out, had very sensibly determined to cash in on Chapman's legendary engineering know-how by developing the consultancy side of the business. Not so sensibly, it had picked the ill-fated DMC Northern Irish wonder-car as first big cus-

tomer. Millions were changing hands in, um, not altogether conventional fashion, much to the subsequent fascination of the Department of Trade and Belfast CID.

For quite independent reasons, I feel sure, Lotus's major financial backer, American Express, disclosed some months ago that the special relationship would not now do so nicely, yet Lotus continued to be in desperate need of funds to prepare in earnest for the new small sports car it intends to build in co-operation with Toyota at the rate of around 5,000 units a year—five times present output.

Then there were dark mutterings about some shareholders and moans from some shareholders, too, when trading losses for the first half of 1982 were published at £289,000. Just before Christmas, Colin Chapman, the man who almost single-handed had built up from making kit cars in a north London lock-up to one of the most illustrious names in racing and boss of Britain's No.1 independent maker of sporting supercars, died from a heart attack. Group Lotus began 1983 with spirits at their lowest-ever ebb.

Though I dare say still in Intensive Care, Group Lotus is still alive and kicked in only last week with a very stylish update of the Eclat Excel which now features, cynical Grundys please note, quite a number of Toyota components. If the Jap giant thinks there's life in the old firm yet, who are we to knock? They have teetered on the brink of collapse at Lotus many times. And still they turn out superlative cars.

Just as Concorde is a technical masterpiece, though not a lot of use commercially, the top-of-the-range Esprit Turbo seems to me to be in a class of its own for technical brilliance, even though it must appeal only to monied layabouts whose sole demand of a car is that it should be terrific fun. The Esprit is a boost of adrenalin for two and a dead loss for carrying loads larger than a well-stuffed wallet. The driver and, according to usual practice, driver's moll, sit or rather loll in the plushest of aromatic leathers at what feels

like about six inches above the deck. Stretch out the arms and everything falls immediately to hand whilst the feet enjoy a disposition of pedals second to none.

The immediate sensation of the Lotus is that all controls respond to the merest twitch. Everything is light, precise and just perfectly positioned, the sense of balance and poise continues through the car's every on-the-road function.

From a modest 2-litre, 4-cylinder engine, Lotus coax an astonishing 210bhp via a Garrett AiResearch T3 turbocharger and twin-choke Dellorto carbs. Unlike any other turbo I know, there are buckets of torque at low revs and response from the bottom is breathtaking both in its progressive smoothness and exhilarating push. In short, it goes like the wind. Twitchy as I tend to be over cars with firm suspension, I have no quarrel at all with the Esprit, its civility matched only by its tenacity round corners, streets ahead of most mid-engined sports cars. Steering is unassisted rack-and-pinion and a paragon of its kind, all-round discs have no trouble arresting the 2690 lbs of non-corroding GFRP on its steel backbone. The merest snitch of the fingers is sufficient to belt through the 5-speed box with unerring precision.

So is there anything wrong with it? It's bulky, I suppose, for some—a fact disguised by the aerodynamic rakishness, better, most would consider, than Ital's work on the Marina for BL, or indeed than the comparatively bulbous Ferrari. You can't really see out of the back, but then there's not usually much to see apart from fast-receding dots. It's a bit noisy, too, the way most owners are likely to want it to be.

Even without the added burden of successive oil crises, small-volume supercars are always vulnerable to the capricious market, but if any supercar deserves to succeed it is surely Lotus. Sad as it is to have seen the name muddied a bit of late, there is still no happier experience for the enthusiast than to take this most fling-able of expensive toys for a spin. 🌀

TechSpec:
Super-looking car which does: 0–30 in 2.05 secs, 0–40 in 2.85, 0–50 in 4.2, 0–60 in 5.55, 0–70 in 7.35 and, so I am told, 0–80 in 9.25, 0–90 in 11.85, 0–100 in 14.65—oh, all right, 19.7mpg urban, two seats, nicest in red, £18,406 plus £100s for air-conditioning, stereo, full leather etc.

Cyril RAY

Bars Sinister

BID time return, that I may mark with a black stone the day I wrote in this column that "I am off soon . . . to report on the bars to which Brighton beaux take their Brighton belles . . ."

It was wine bars I had in mind, and it would have been more profitable to follow a fish-and-chip trail in Frinton. Day after unfrabjous day I pounded the promenade and its purlieus from one self-styled wine bar to another—from the one that had to send to the next-door hamburger joint for a bottle of the Muscadet that it offered by the glass in its own misspelt list to another that advertised its eight-ounce glass of house wine—a glass that prompted my wondering, "Is that *really* eight ounces?" to elicit the answer, "Says so in the list, dunnit?"

"How many do you get from the bottle, then?"

"Six or so, guv'nor, give or take a bit."

The average wine bottle holds 25 ounces.

One wine bar announced itself as being "Closed for Lunch" but was open later—in a manner of speaking, that is, for the couple of young things sitting on bar stools and sip-

ping their drinks as I arrived nipped smartly to the other side of the counter to take my order, chosen from a list of some half-dozen, headed (as house wines) by Grierson-Blumenthal's famous Arc de Triomphe, red and white, familiar to all who patronise Trust House Forte establishments.

One half of this bar bore the notice, "Sea Food Service Counter" and I asked what they served there: "Well nothink, really," which was to do the establishment less than justice—there were sardine and tomato sandwiches, and a sardine is a seafood, or I am a merman. Another notice read, "If it's too loud, you're too old." This patently referred to the taped music, and was as patently addressed to me . . .

Certainly not to the young man whiling away his time at the Space Invader machine until "Happy Hour"—spirits half-price from 6 to 8, by which time I was gazing at the exterior of The Electric Grape, round the corner: three wines on offer—Riesling, Liebfraumilch and The Electric Grape House Wine; Live Band Every Night and the Sleaze (sic) Boys on Tuesdays.

No time, though, to indulge: I was agog to investigate the gentilities of Hove, so much more *comme il faut* than Brighton that it claims to have a much nicer class of hoolian at its Brighton and Hove Albion ground than Brighton gets at its racecourse. There may be others, but the only wine bar I could find in its decorous terraces, in spite of having its walls

decorated with blown-up labels of Latour 1929, Mouton 1952 and Lafite 1945 (Lafite 1945!) served its anonymous wines from optics along with its gins, and did not even bother to tell me that if it was too loud I was too old. Both.

A notice warned me: "No Drinks at Tables without Meals. Thank You." Thank you for nothing—not even their Cheeseburger and Chips.

So back to Brighton, where what used to be the Market Wine Bar (and very good, as I remember) is now The Market Wine House Restaurant and, as wine bars go, is a good restaurant.

The proprietor explained its transmogrification: all that Brighton had wanted was sweet white and Veuve du Vernay, and it was a pretty rum lot that wanted them, too. So he shortened his list, put up his prices, and went in for good grub instead.

I should be glad for my next wine-bar article to do what the TUC and the political parties have done in their time—forsake Brighton for Blackpool, which used to have the best wine bar in Britain. But it is closed, I am told, "for refurbishing". Oh, dear. 🖑

"What do you mean, there's no Father Christmas?"

Dame Edna
EVERAGE
Germane Gruyère

"I travel to Switzerland at least once a year to visit my money and, incidentally, to sneak a peak at my personal tax structure."

Hello Possums.

Statistics show that a percentage of *Punch* readers are hardened criminals. So because this exclusive contains a lot of never-before-published details of my personal wealth and jewelry holdings, I'm sure that "clean" and "straight" *Punch* readers will understand that I've had to change all names, addresses and Swiss bank account numbers in this composition to put mega-star-muggers off the scent.

When our Editor first asked me to pop a few thoughts on Switzerland through my miniaturised in-purse word-processor, both Interpol and my senior insurance advisers begged me not to divulge any unnecessary information which could precipitate the heist of the century.

Muggers be warned that all my jewelry is fake. The real rocks are safely locked away in a laser-protected Alpine nook, and that includes the worthless engagement ring my husband Norm slipped onto my digit at a matinee screening of *Mrs Miniver* at the Regal, Moonee Ponds.

The costly and glittering gems you see me wearing on the box, at first nights and at prestige court functions, are all clever replicas, hand-crafted in Taiwan, so mugging me would be a counter-productive waste of time. I'm sorry, but it really would.

I hope that hardened criminals reading this will now give my luxury penthouse a wide berth, and, incidentally, pass this info on to their colleagues who do not subscribe to *Punch* for reasons of illiteracy and/or an abnormally high laughter threshold.

The last thing I want, quite frankly, is to wake up in the middle of the night to find a hardened criminal at my bedside fumbling feloniously with my baubles. Let's face it, possums, even if he was only a *partially* hardened criminal, it would be pretty scary. "Thank heaven for Switzerland," I say, and thousands of ordinary megastars like me, as I hop on my regular B-Cal superstar shuttle to Geneva disguised as a commoner, in a discreet raincoat and anonymous rhinestone-encrusted "flyaway" sunglasses.

I can now reveal in this exclusive that I travel to Switzerland at least once a year to visit my money and, incidentally, to sneak a peek at my personal tax structure. Having a tax structure at all is sure sign of success in my industry. But although some of showbusiness's top earners have structures on *paper*, mine must be one of the few that is so big it has to be housed in a lakeside three-storey re-cycled cheese factory.

While I'm at it, I might as well reveal that it's going to appear in full colour, on the cover of a new Weidenfeld and Hudson coffee-table book: *Great Tax Structures of the World*. No prizes for guessing which film stars and so-called glamour pusses will be eating their hearts out when they see that.

I've always adored clean countries, and I tend to suspect that goes for most of my fellow Australians. Mexico, India, England and Egypt certainly have their charm, but I tend to prefer places where you don't have to wash the dishes in Perrier water.

Switzerland just has to be the most spotless spot I know, and last time I checked out my tiara and matching accessories, I couldn't help noticing that the vault was so clean and sparkling you could have eaten off the floor. In fact, I told my banker this (in halting schoolgirl Swiss) but those squeaky-clean gnomes take fiscal hygiene so much for granted that I'm afraid he missed my gist.

I fear the poor lamb thought I wanted to tuck into a three-course *fondue* there and then in the bowels of Basel.

Chances are the Swiss are inclined to take everything a bit literally, though I'm sure there are some excellent Swiss comedy shows which Channel 4 is bound to snap up sooner or later. Because Switzerland is terrifically *central* (you can hop on a plane and in half an hour you can be somewhere interesting) many of my very special showbusiness chums have taken up their abode there. Adorable fellow-Dame Joanie Sutherland finds the Alps an ideal jumping-off place for the opera facilities of Europe, and old buddies James and Clarissa Mason decided to live there ages ago so that they could be next door to their favourite patisserie.

It's an open secret in Swiss cake circles that snake-hips James loves to lubricate that famous voice of his with a daily gateau gargle. Although it's many moons now since Norm took me to the seventh veil, James Mason can smash my knuckles across a keyboard with his walking-stick any time he likes.

One of my companies very sweetly bought me a gorgeous little chalet in this neck of the woods where I adore to hibernate. As the cuckoo flies, it's just across the valley from Oona Chaplin and Mrs Nabokov, so there's never a problem if I need to borrow the odd cup of cooking-chocolate or condensed milk.

I don't ski—let's face it, no insurance company on the planet would dare insure my famous bones—but my bridesmaid Madge Allsop and I are heavily into some of the less dangerous après-ski activities. *Heidi* was one of my favourite books as a kiddie; in fact Heidi and I were always under the bedclothes together with a torch. Spookily enough, I suppose that's what first gave me a taste for the Swiss roll.

We take these scrummy cakes for granted in Australia and the UK, forgetting that they are one of Switzerland's most luscious legacies. A sponge in the form of a clock spring could only have been invented by the wonderful mountain race who gave us see-through cheese.

But what a wrist-conscious race the Swiss are.

You can't go anywhere without being forcibly reminded of the national timepiece industry. Just near my little haven there's Rolex Road, Longines Lane, Timex Terrace and Piaget Place. And yet—muggers once more note—I don't own an up-market watch.

I keep all my famous appointments, including lunches with the Queen and audiences with the Pope, by consulting the well-nigh valueless chronometer presented to my husband Norm when he was invalided out of a grateful Australian dried fruit industry.

Chances are, possums, I'm the only woman tourist in the world wearing her husband's watch while he's still alive. Incidentally, if you want to know anything more about Switzerland you'd have to be a hardened ratbag.

A joyous heart always,
Edna

*Dame Edna Everage is a division of the Barry Humphries Amusement Facility.

"Let me through—I'm an underwear salesman!"

"If you put your ear to them, you can hear Orson Welles, wheezing."

"Hello, it looks as if we're the first smokers here."

WINNERS

PERSONALLY, I THINK WE SHOULD MOVE DORIAN'S PICTURE UP INTO THE ATTIC.

B. Hall
of Lyme Regis, Dorset

NO, NO, OUR FRANCHISE IS SATELLITE, NOT CABLE!

M. Joyce
of Blackburn, Lancs.

1884 caption—"SIC TRANSIT GLORIA MUNDI!" "BY THE WAY, DUCHESS, SUPPOSING THAT WE *DO* SUCCEED IN GETTING THE HOUSE OF LORDS ABOLISHED THIS SESSION, WON'T IT BE A GREAT BLOW TO THE DUKE?" "YES, IF HE EVER HEARS OF IT; BUT I SHAN'T TELL HIM, YOU KNOW!"

1924 caption—*CONTRACTOR (MUCH AGITATED) TO FOREMAN.* "JOBSON, CALL THE MEN OFF AT ONCE. WE'VE DUG UP THE WRONG STREET!"

"I DIDN'T THINK LEGIONNAIRE'S DISEASE STRUCK THIS QUICKLY!"

D. Hinson
of London SW1

"WHAT WILL YOU DO WHEN THE AMERICANS LEAVE?"

M. Hosford-Tanner
of London EC4

1884 caption—THE FESTIVE SEASON. (MRS PONSONBY DE TOMKYNS AT HOME—"EARLY AND LATE.") *MR P DE T (TO THE WAITERS).* "*WOULD* YOU MIND, ONE OF YOU, BEING SO VERY KIND AS JUST TO GIVE ME THE LEG OF A FOWL, OR SOMETHING. I'M—I'M THE MASTER OF THE HOUSE."

1945 caption—"I'M LIKE YOU—NOW WE '*AVE* GOT PEACE I CAN'T REALISE IT!"